W9-CXM-162

THE RELIGIOUS EDUCATION OF ADULTS

THE
RELIGIOUS
EDUCATION
OF
ADULTS

Leon McKenzie AND *R. Michael Harton*

SMYTH&HELWYS
PUBLISHING, INCORPORATED   MACON, GEORGIA

BV
1488
.M35
2002

Smyth & Helwys Publishing, Inc.
6316 Peake Road
Macon, Georgia 31210-3960
1-800-747-3016
©2002 by Smyth & Helwys Publishing
All rights reserved.
Printed in the United States of America.

The paper used in this publication meets the minimum requirements of American National
Standard for Information Sciences—Permanence
of Paper for Printed Library Materials.
ANSI Z39.48–1984. (alk. paper)

Library of Congress Cataloging-in-Publication Data

McKenzie, Leon.
    The religious education of adults / Leon McKenzie, R. Michael
    Harton.— Rev. ed.
        p. cm.
    Includes bibliographical references and index.
      ISBN 1-57312-379-X
    1. Christian education of adults. I. Harton, R. Michael, 1946- II.
    Title.

    BV1488 .M35 2002
    268'.434—dc21

                                        2002011473
                                        CIP

TABLE OF CONTENTS

Foreword vi

Introduction: A Perspective on Adult Religious Education 1

Adult Religious Education: Historical Overview 29

Adult Religious Education: Problem Areas 45

The Post-Twentieth-Century Adult 73

Toward a Theory of Adult Religious Education: Part I 93

Toward a Theory of Adult Religious Education: Part II
    Theoretical Propositions to Guide Practice 113

Approaches to Program Development 133

Learning: Theoretical Considerations 159

Teaching: An Analysis 181

Evaluation in Adult Religious Education .213

The Intersection of Religious Education and Adult Life 243

FOREWORD

When I taught at what was once one of the premier theological schools, I spent a good bit of time working with "non-traditional" adult students. Mostly, I sought to build their confidence as returning students, helping them with study skills, suggesting ways to challenge the system in order to create a program that most fit their needs, and convincing them that they could not only survive, but they could thrive in classes filled with younger, "traditional" students.

Much of my motivation for working with these students stemmed from a combination of my own experience of returning to graduate work after ten years in the field, and from the inspiration of my mentor, Leon McKenzie.

My first introduction to Leon was his early book for Paulist Press, *Twentieth Century Adult Religious Education.* I was searching for a text for an introductory course in adult religious education and was delighted to discover that Leon was on the faculty of Indiana University. My predecessor and former seminary professor, Earnest Loessner, completed his doctoral studies at I. U. under Paul Bergevin and John McKinley (authors of the Indiana Plan used for decades by several denominations to plan adult education with adults). Leon had been one of their students, too (though much later than Earnest).

When the time arrived to explore seriously my own doctoral studies, it was natural to begin with I. U., only two hours from where I taught in Louisville, and the source of many classroom stories from Earnest. A call to the School of Education secured Leon's whereabouts (Indianapolis, where he served in the dual roles of Director of Human

Resource Development for I. U. Hospitals and as professor of adult education). Venturing a call to the professor's office with questions about where to begin my quest, I was surprised by an invitation for an extended conversation, not in his office, but at his home!

On the appointed day, I was both honored and humbled to spend several hours sitting at Leon's dining table, outlining a course of study and discussing issues in adult religious education, similarities in our experience in church-based education, and his latest research projects. I began my graduate students at Indiana-Perdue University Indianapolis precisely because that was where Leon lived and worked, and because I. U. offered the same graduate course work for first-year students on both the Bloomington and Indianapolis campuses (mostly because of the number of nursing educators attached to Indiana University Hospital).

Some might find it strange for a Catholic and a Baptist to work together so closely, but I found it fascinating and learned a great deal from Leon, not only about adult education, but about the similar issues in adult education that both traditions face. While I enjoyed course work with him, his mentoring through partnering on research and his guidance in researching and writing a dissertation were among my most valuable experiences in graduate work. Leon is an interesting combination of educator/theologian/philosopher. One thing I recall was his delight in making a good first impression on students, not to demonstrate his skill so much as to model regard for people. At the beginning of a new class he would call roll, then go around the room again calling each student by name without looking at his list. The interest and respect for people (for students as responsible adults) was genuine.

The first edition of *The Religious Education of Adults* was published by Religious Education Press in 1984 and found wide acceptance as a graduate text and as a reference for practitioners in the field. For many of the latter, the book provided the philosophical and theoretical background they needed as non-adult education majors. When James Michael Lee, R. E. P.'s owner/publisher asked Leon about a revision, Leon recommended me instead. Unfortunately, I was in the midst of a move to Virginia, so the project was delayed. Also, the delay affected not only the timing of the re-publication, but not long after handing the manuscript over to Lee, R. E. P. folded due to internal difficulties. Lee returned the manuscript with encouragement to seek another publisher, and Smyth & Helwys was gracious to pick it up.

Nearly every parish church faces the daunting challenge of improving adult participation in its educational activities. When adults fail to show up, or attend in small numbers, the assumption is voiced that "there's a commitment problem," or a failure to appreciate the effort invested on the part of the church and its staff. While these may be valid to a degree (a small one!), research clearly indicates another problem: adults do not see the church as a credible provider of quality education!

This work offers no easy answers, nor is its focus how to get adults to attend or be faithful to our educational offerings. What it does, however, is address the foundational issues of just what constitutes quality religious education for adults, how planners can determine and understand the needs of their constituents and involve them in the planning and execution of educational events, and how to determine if the goals and intentions of the planners and participants have been met. In the process, numerous tools and examples are offered that should be of practical value to the student of adult religious education, the professional educator, and the adult education practitioner. *The Religious Education of Adults* may once again become a primer for both professionals and practitioners now that few seminaries teach adult education. In that regard, Smyth & Helwys is helping to fill a void left by the demise of R. E. P., and for that all Christian educators should be grateful.

Mike Harton
Richmond, VA
July 2002

A PERSPECTIVE ON ADULT RELIGIOUS EDUCATION

Cassandra, the daughter of Priam, possessed the power of prophecy. Her gift, however, was not a source of joy for her. She was terribly fated. No one ever believed her. This was undoubtedly due to the fact that she was a bearer of bad news. No one likes to hear bad news. But we bear sad tidings: Adult religious education, as it is practiced in most local churches and parishes, is largely ineffectual. We make no claim to rare insight, nor do we claim to be endowed with the gift of prophecy. Our message is based not on vagrant intuitions but on a study and analysis of programs of adult religious education and on discussions with literally hundreds of religious educators of adults.

However negative our criticism of adult religious education may be, our intention in this book is to suggest ways of improving the practice of adult religious education. This means, of course, that there must be new ways of thinking about adult religious education. A mutuality exists between *thinking* and *doing*: thinking about doing can improve the doing of something; the doing of something can help in the development of new ways of thinking.[1] While the emphasis in the following pages is on thinking about adult religious education or theory, the doing of adult religious education is a major concern.

The central problem of contemporary adult religious education relates to the kind of thinking that controls the doing of adult religious education. Anyone who examines carefully adult religious education as it is practiced in most local churches and parishes will discover an underlying conventional wisdom, a network of interlocking beliefs. These beliefs shape the practice of adult religious education. It is the burden of this introductory chapter to identify and critique these beliefs. It seems only fair in this chapter to alert the reader that the perspective taken on adult religious education in the following pages is a viewpoint not commonly shared by religious educators. Indeed, the authors' perspectives will challenge values that are axiomatic to most religious educators. But axioms must be challenged to stimulate progress.

Conventional Wisdom

The beliefs that characterize the theory and practice of adult religious education may be stated as follows:

- *Belief 1*—The conceptual source for the development of adult religious education theory and practice is theology or the theological sciences. The Bible and/or ecclesiastical documents are source materials for the development of educational theory and practice.
- *Belief 2*—Those primarily responsible for preparing professional parish leaders (ministers of all capacities) need no preparation for their own teaching ministries. Rather, mastery of their own content specialty implicitly qualifies them to pass on that expertise to others from their seminary and college lecterns.
- *Belief 3*—There is no difference between religion and theology. The application of theology to life results in religious learning.
- *Belief 4*—Adult religious education must be exclusively concerned with subject matters that are biblical, theological, or ecclesiastical. Mundane issues may be treated only when the religious educator can bootleg pious language into a course of study that centers on a mundane issue.
- *Belief 5*—Belief 5 relates to Belief 4. The religious educator of adults should not be concerned with human development viewed as a whole but only with explicitly religious aspects of human development.
- *Belief 6*—There is little or no need to determine systematically what adults perceive to be their educational needs or interests. Church authorities, pastors, directors of religious education, and theologians already know what adults need and what their interests should be.
- *Belief 7*—Knowledge taken by adults on authority is education. Adult religious education is a process whereby adults are formed according to a given paradigm determined by church leaders and are told what they must believe and do.

- *Belief 8*—Religious knowledge is more important than religious learning. The transmission of ideas is at the core of adult religious education. Adult religious education is primarily an intellectual endeavor.
- *Belief 9*—Conclusion-oriented empirical research in adult religious education is unnecessary; a body of knowledge about adult religious education can be developed from a study of theology and ecclesiastical documentation. Practitioners of adult religious education in parishes and local churches need not be concerned with conducting decision-oriented research. Programs should be developed on the basis of theological propositions and ecclesiastical directives.[2] This belief is closely related to Belief 5.

These beliefs are foundations upon which theorizing about adult religious education occurs. Further, they are foundational beliefs for the development of educational programs and for the conduct of instruction. They are seldom articulated in so many words. Usually they take the form of hidden assumptions. While variant forms of these beliefs can be documented in the educational literature of different religious traditions, the beliefs are instantiated in actual programs of adult religious education. Analyses of these programs permit the observer to make inferences regarding the beliefs. The reader may dispute the logic of the constructions by which we inferred the foregoing beliefs, but only after undertaking similar analyses.

Belief I — Sources
It may be quite natural that even in seminaries and theological schools where religious education courses are offered, classical theological studies rule the day. However, the theological sciences (biblical and liturgical sciences included) are often the sources for the development and practice of adult education. Content specialists in theology write volumes about religious education, and renowned theologians and biblical scholars often dominate the programs of workshops and conferences on religious education.

Seminary and church-related college graduate programs in religious education are often controlled by theology departments and staffed by faculty whose academic preparation has been largely in the theological sciences. This may be due to the widespread belief among school administrators and faculties that the teaching of religion is largely a matter of telling theological/biblical/ecclesiastical things to people.

The dominant presence of content specialists in theology in the field of adult religious education does not appear strange at first glance, if adult religious education is conceived as the retelling of theological content to adults. One must question, however, what a biblical scholar or theologian actually knows about the body of research on adult development, adult psychology, or the principles of program and curriculum design in adult education. Are they trained to use the survey research methodologies necessary for conducting needs assessments, and the statistical techniques for testing educational hypotheses? What is their familiarity with instructional systems technology, the body of research regarding adult orientations toward participation in education, the design of evaluation research, and the application of various learning theories to specific instructional settings? They cannot be expected to be aware of the very purposes of adult religious education beyond evangelization, or many other topics that come to bear on the education of adults.

Of course, one need not necessarily be academically certified in the study of education in order to express an opinion about education. It would be expected, however, that one who has been a serious student of the field of education would have more credibility in their statements of opinion and judgment than content specialists in theology who do not hesitate to express authoritative views about education. The fallacy of misplaced authority is rampant in the field of religious education. This is not to say that the theological sciences have no place in adult religious education. James Michael Lee has shown that the theological sciences can contribute much, in a collaborative role, to religious education.[3] The issue is not whether theology actually has a place in adult religious education. The issue is defining that place.

Belief 2 — Preparation for Teaching

The source of Belief 1 may be explained in part by Belief 2. Most faculty in seminaries have no background in the field of education, nor are they given any orientation to teaching. There seems to be an implicit assumption that if you know your field, be it practical or classical theology, you automatically know how to teach the subject. A demonstrated mastery of content, by way of thesis, oratory, or application is all that is required. No knowledge of learning theory, teaching principles, mastery of teaching technologies or educational psychology applied to adults is needed. The underlying understanding of teaching therefore seems to be transference of knowledge from one head (the teacher's) to another (the student's). Thus the only technical skill required is logical ordering of the content for oral delivery (through lecture). The only skill required of students is good note-taking!

One proof of the assumption that content specialists can automatically teach their subject is the lack of interest in faculty development on the part of both seminary and college faculties and administrators. Thus, a new professor or instructor is given a teaching assignment with no orientation to the uniqueness of adult students, creating conducive learning climates, teaching techniques and technologies, or grading (which has changed little from grade school). A novice teacher can only hope that an experienced colleague will take pity and do some mentoring.

Belief 3 — Theology and Religion

Karl Rahner and Herbert Vorgrimler state that theology "is essentially the conscious effort of the Christian to hearken to the actual verbal revelation which God has promulgated in history, to acquire knowledge of it by the methods of scholarship and to reflect upon its implications."[4] The emphasis on verbal revelation in the definition may be questioned, but the definition rightly stresses the scholarly aspect of theology and its systematic approach. More recently, David Tracy wrote that a contemporary fundamental Christian theology "can best be described as philosophical reflection upon the meanings present in common human experience and language, and upon the meanings present in the Christian fact."[5] The two principal sources for such reflection, according to Tracy, are Christian texts and common human experience and language. Again, Tracy emphasizes theology as a disciplined, rigorous, and methodical intellectual pursuit. Is adult religious education supposed to make theologians of all adults? Or should we water down and otherwise dilute theological discourse, and feed this meager gruel to adults under the guise of adult religious education?

While there are many descriptive definitions of religion, it would not violate the general drift of these competing descriptions to say that religion is a mode of being-in-the-world defined by a person's comportment toward Ultimate Meaning. Religion is more than an intellectual pursuit; it is, in one sense, a deeply personal response of a limited creature to the Unlimited Absolute. This response is usually specified conceptually by the definite religious tradition affirmed by the individual believer, a tradition that comprises a system of values and principles. Religion is not a body of theological abstractions, nor does it involve, primarily and necessarily, an academic analysis of biblical texts or ecclesiastical documents. Religion is associated with the total experience of the believer. Adult religious education, then, must focus on the experiences of adults as these experiences are elucidated by the particular religious tradition, and must focus also on the particular religious tradition as this tradition is elucidated by adult life experiences. What is current in human experience—*total* human experience and not merely *pious* human experience—is no less revelatory than what is treasured of the religious past and formulated in doctrinal propositions, biblical texts, and/or theological discourse.

Belief 4 — Mundane Concerns

Most programs of adult religious education deal with themes that are explicitly and obviously sacred. A course of study on the book of Genesis is considered a legitimate educational activity. A course of study on how to be an effective parent is considered semi-legitimate. This is because sacred values or explicitly religious notions can be introduced by the instructor. But a course of study that aims at helping older adults live on a fixed income during inflationary times is rarely viewed as a religious education course. Even further removed from the spectrum of authentic religious education would be a course on home gardening or on automobile repair. Such topics as these are unworthy. They are secular or profane.

Ideally, religion is coextensive with life. The so-called secular experiences of adults are pregnant with the possibility of religious meaning. The fabric of any person's life experience is a continuous weave. Religious educators of adults may pay lip service to these hearty verities, but are either unwilling or unable to apply them to educational programming.

When adult religious education concentrates solely on topics perceived as sacred or holy, the implication is that a host of educational needs and interests arising out of daily life are trivial, a sort of second-class reality. What shapes a person's religious response, however, is the totality of his experience and not simply that part of life experience perceived as sacred. Likewise, a person's religious response influences the manner in which he experiences all of life and not just a segment of life designated as sacred.

In their disdain for the mundane, everyday educational needs and interests of adults, religious educators convey the impression that there are two orders of reality, the sacred and the profane, and that there are two corresponding categories of behavior. Attending church, reciting prayers, reading the Bible, and studying ecclesiastical documents are viewed as sacred behaviors. Completing tax forms, working in the garden, fixing an automobile, or studying emergency medical care for the home are irretrievably profane. Avoidance of mundane topics in church-based adult education affirms the dichotomies postulated by Platonic and neo-Platonic philosophies: the eternal versus the temporal, the soul versus the body, the other world versus this world, the sacred versus the profane. The message is clear: Religion is something to do in church on Sundays; religion has little to do with the way we experience our being-in-the-world on weekdays as we pursue mundane endeavors.

Alfred North Whitehead wrote that Western philosophy is little more than a footnote to Plato. This is obviously an overstatement, but not by much. And if Plato so profoundly influenced Western philosophical thinking, Western religious thought no less bears the stamp of his influence. This is nowhere more evident than in the generally accepted opinion that reality can somehow be neatly divided into sacred and secular spheres.[6]

Belief 5 — Religious Development

"Our goal is the religious development of adults, and therefore we concentrate on explicitly religious content and topics," religious educators may argue. "After all, that is our domain. And besides, we don't want to duplicate what is done in community education and other *secular* settings." This argument assumes that human development can be compartmentalized, that various aspects of life can be isolated from one another. Actually, this is an extension of the largely artificial separation of reality into the sacred and secular. It follows, according to the logic of some, that the human personality is fragmented into domains that are existentially separate and not merely logically distinct. Therefore, religious education programs are addressed only to the so-called "sacred parts" of personality.

Religious educators holding this view discount the context in which faith, the development of which most surely is their goal, is *lived*. Indeed, there is a considerable body of literature (including research reports) that links faith and experience inextricably. An accepted axiom of adult education is that life experience is an important resource in adult learning and provides the context in which they learn. When we broaden our view of the scope of content that religious education may encompass, we provide opportunity to address topics and issues adults face often on a daily basis. Life experience from the world context of adults may then be evaluated and examined, providing opportunity to explore the affect of experience on faith and of faith on experience.

Unfortunately, adults don't seem to expect to find help from religious institutions when in the midst of crisis. A Princeton study revealed that adults turned to other resources during life crises.[7] As one example, Search Institute found that "only seventeen percent of mainline churches emphasize the social and political dimensions of life in their Christian education programs."[8]

Perhaps religious educators are reluctant to move outside the realm of explicitly religious content because they know they cannot be content experts on every aspect of life. Nor is their parish likely to have vast resources to pull in recognized authorities on every subject of interest. What about the resources resident within the congregation? If the life experience of adults is indeed a valuable resource in the learning setting, surely among the collective experience of members of the congregation are people with knowledge and/or awareness of resources on many crucial areas of life.

Belief 6 — Determination of Educational Needs and Interests

Program topics in most parishes and local churches are determined unilaterally and assigned by authorities at the district or diocesan levels, by pastors, and/or by directors of religious education. Ordinarily, in the majority of places, no attempt is made to survey adults regarding their self-perceived educational needs or interests. What is at work here, in effect, is a well-meaning paternalism on the part of the providers of educational programs. Or, if paternalism is not responsible for such prescriptive approaches, the providers of adult education lack the technical skills required for survey research.

Program topics are based, by and large, on recent theological ideas or on available audiovisual packages or curriculum materials. The low rate of participation in these programs is attributed to adult apathy. The principal locus of the problem, however, is not adults who are apathetic (although this factor may come into play) but rather the providers of education who deal with adults as if they were children. Some adults are convinced that the pastor or director of religious education knows best; other adults are not so convinced.

Belief 7 — Formation or Critical Inquiry?

The belief that knowledge taken on authority constitutes education, as well as Belief 7 following, are noted by Nathaniel Cantor as the "assumptions of orthodox teaching." These assumptions represent commonly-held propositions that are, in Cantor's view, "false and unsupported by evidence."[9] Cantor's ideas have been adapted for use in the present context.

In the case of adult religious education the prevailing belief is that theological knowledge taken on authority constitutes religious education, and that the purpose of religious education is the formation or molding of adults according to an a priori paradigm. No doubt there are times and occasions when such an emphasis is legitimate, but formation or molding is only one purpose of education. There must be room for critical thinking, the expression of honest doubts, and the raising of discomfiting questions. In too many places, teaching is apprised as authoritative telling; learning is equated with listening and accepting. The faith-process becomes the receiving of a cultural hand-me-down and not the wrestling with Jacob's angel that leads to authentic commitment.

There may have been a time when the majority of adults submitted themselves docilely to teaching by edict, but too much water has passed under history's bridges for us to return to those days. Increasing numbers of adults today, particularly in industrialized democratic nations, tend to question what they are told. They do not permit themselves to be defined by others; they define themselves. They refuse to accept whatever does not mesh with the sense of the real they acquire from their life experiences. Adults may not openly dispute what they are told on every occasion, and they may live quietly keeping their own counsel, but they repudiate internally what appears unrealistic to them. Not all adults, to be sure, have acquired the habit of critical thinking, but most programs of adult religious education predicated on the assumption that teaching is authoritative telling are destined for failure. Religious educators will do well to heed the findings of Search Institute's research, which show that adults who exhibit mature faith report that their congregation promotes a "thinking climate" where critical reflection is encouraged.

Belief 8 — Knowledge Versus Learning

Because of the hegemony of theology in the theory and practice of adult religious education, there is a strong tendency for religious educators of adults to emphasize knowledge rather than learning. The educational process is overly cerebral. Educational activities are thought to be successful when adults have assimilated cognitive data. The experiences of the adult learners seldom become a part of the content of instruction. That is, the cognitive data presented by the teacher is seldom related to the experiences of the learners. Affective learning is hardly considered as a possible outcome of an educational activity.

Of course, the adult educator must deal with the expectations adults bring to the educational setting (usually born of previous schooling) that learning *is* essentially cognitive. To cite a disconcerting, but nonetheless real example, a board member of a prominent international missions agency was heard (and videotaped!) saying that she did not want her daughter to *experience* missions, but wanted her to be *taught* missions.

Victoria Marsick and Karen Watkins propose a concept they call critically reflective learning in which actual experience is "the center-piece of learning."[10] This is consistent with literature on adult learning that emphasizes the experience of adults as a valuable resource in the learning environment. Further, Brookfield points out that adults tend to report as their most significant learning those episodes in which they were challenged to connect content and experience.

> What is recalled with such satisfaction is the way in which the challenges were faced and dealt with so that the learners felt they had successfully survived a problematic situation. Such an experience is truly empowering. Areas which were previously viewed as being "out of bounds" to learners are reinterpreted as being within their purview. They come to see themselves as being potentially able to act upon such areas, rather than being closed off from them.[11]

The implication is that mastering a challenging situation, not the "banking" of knowledge, is the empowering factor. However, in most religious education programs for adults there is a teacher fixation on the manifest content of instruction, i.e., a fixation on what must be imparted to the adults. This fixation on the manifest content predisposes the teacher to a role as content disseminator, which largely limits the active involvement of the learner (that is, the learner's role is limited to being "active listener"). This also limits the likelihood of critically reflective learning, which requires "challenging assumptions, challenging the importance of context, imagining and exploring alternatives, and reflective skepticism."[12]

Preoccupation with the manifest content of instruction also disposes the teacher to overlook the latent content of instruction. There is much to be learned from the *context* as well as content of the instructional episode. Simply stated, learners take away from an instructional setting far more than knowledge of a particular topic of instruction. What the learners take away from instruction transcends the cognitive aspects of learning or the simple mastery of knowledge. Affective gains or deficits—changes in the emotional life of the learners—are also outcomes of instruction. How the learner feels about himself, about others, about the manifest content of instruction, and about the learning process itself are crucially important issues that are seldom considered.

When the teacher of adults is fixated on the manifest content of instruction (on *what* must be imparted) the focus becomes the *product* of the educational activity, considered principally from the standpoint of the topic of instruction. The product of the educational activity considered as affective outcome for the learner is correspondingly neglected. This same fixation with the manifest content of instruction also contributes to a neglect of focus on the learning process. "It is the process of learning," states Cantor, "and not answers to questions which constitutes the core of education."[13]

The matter may be stated in another way. Teacher fixation on the manifest content of instruction disposes the teacher to overlook the latent content of instruction. When a person participates in an instructional activity revolving around a particular topic, the person can learn much more than the topic itself. She can learn something from the total instructional context; she can appropriate to herself the mood of the instructional context. If a teacher encourages critical inquiry, the adult can learn that critical inquiry is valuable. If the adults in a learning situation work collaboratively on a project, the individual can learn that participative problem solving is sometimes the most effective way of dealing with a problem situation. If an individual's views and opinions are seriously considered by the teacher and by fellow learners, the individual can grow in terms of self-esteem. The teacher who does not provide easy answers, but structures learning so that adults may develop their own approaches to puzzling questions, may help adult learners gain greater analytic competence.

These are but a few examples of the latent contents of instruction. The list could be multiplied a hundredfold. To summarize, learners take away from an instructional activity far more than knowledge of a particular topic of instruction. What the learners take away from instruction transcends the cognitive aspects of learning or the simple mastery of knowledge. Affective gains or deficits—changes in the emotional life of the learners—are also outcomes of instruction. How the learner feels about himself, about others, about the manifest content of instruction, and about the learning process itself are crucially important issues that are seldom considered.

Belief 9 — Empirical Research

Research traditionally has been classified as either basic or applied. Basic research is concerned with generating a body of conclusions that are relevant to a specific field of endeavor. Applied research is concerned with generating knowledge that is pertinent for decision-making in a particular place. Knowledge that derives from basic research in the field of adult religious education is useful for most religious educators of adults; knowledge that derives from applied research in the field of adult religious education is useful principally for a particular religious educator in a particular parish or local church. The distinction between basic and applied research is by no means a settled issue among research theoreticians. For present purposes let us stipulate that basic research yields conclusion-oriented findings that may be extrapolated to different settings, while applied research yields decision-oriented findings that are relevant for a particular setting.

With the exception of limited inquiry in the area of adult faith development, the situation regarding research in the field of adult religious education has changed little since the first edition of this book. Theoreticians of adult religious education apparently remain minimally interested in generating empirically-based, conclusion-oriented findings. The body of knowledge relevant to the field of adult religious education is essentially a collection of deductively reasoned "thought pieces." Such speculations are necessary but not sufficient for the development of a body of knowledge that refers to a social-practice field. Adult religious education is a social-practice field. There is a need, therefore, for the generation of a body of knowledge about those served by educational programs, about the effectiveness of various instructional strategies, about the settings most conducive to learning, and about a host of other concerns.

Practitioners of adult religious education at the level of the parish or local church are not ordinarily equipped to conduct sound decision-oriented empirical research. Neither are they generally able to comprehend reports of conclusion-oriented research conducted by others. This means religious educators in parishes and local churches should be able to understand statistical analyses of data. Unfortunately, there is little in the academic preparation of religious educators at the graduate level that prepares them for understanding or conducting empirical research. A check with the Association of Theological Schools, the accrediting agency for seminaries in the United States, reveals no seminaries with required courses or seminars in research at the masters level.

A Different Perspective

Adherence to the foregoing beliefs no doubt will result in unattended educational programs, instructional processes of questionable value, and continued frustration of those responsible for the religious education of adults in parishes and local churches. In contrast, the following beliefs may serve as bases for invigorating adult religious education.

1. Educators must take a more substantive role in developing the theory and practice of adult religious education. The development of theoretical foundations for adult religious education and guidelines for the practice of adult religious education is properly the work of professionals thoroughly grounded in the systematic study of adult education. Content specialists in the theological sciences, all things being equal, are not usually qualified by competence in the theological sciences to address complex issues relating to adult education as a field of practice. This is another way of saying that they are not equipped by the study of theology, the Bible, or ecclesiastical documents to render professional assistance in the areas of program development or instructional practice.

On the other hand, adult religious educators and theological content specialists can work together to determine the shape of the global goals and general directions of their particular religious traditions. While in many areas substantial differences exist between traditions, there are worthy examples of cooperation between educators and theologians. One such example is the development of a definition of faith and its dimensions that provided the basis for the Search Institute project titled "Effective Christian Education: A National Study of Protestant

Congregations," published in 1990.[14] At the outset of the project, theologians and religious educators collaborated to arrive at eight core dimensions of mature faith. Ensuing research that measured these dimensions among adults not only revealed data on the effectiveness of participating congregations, but also implications for needed programs and development of curricula. (This research is discussed in chapter three).

Theological specialists and religious educators must engage in closer dialogue, complimenting one another's efforts rather than competing to prove their superiority. Religious educators need to recognize, however, that theological content specialists help to describe a normative state of affairs that should occur as a consequence of adult religious education. They enunciate the major values of the religious tradition. They may contribute to the development of religious educational theory and practice in their own way. Theological specialists must recognize that religious educators are theological educators who fulfill no secondary role. And it is the adult religious educator who must attend principally to the development of educational theory and practice.

Church leaders and content specialists in the theological sciences fulfill an important role when they delineate the global goals and general directions of their particular religious traditions. That is, church leaders and theologians should be concerned with the development of what would be called in another context the "organizational goals" of the religious tradition. The religious educator of adults takes these goals as normative parameters for the practice of adult religious education, reconciles these goals with the empirically identified educational needs and interests of adults in a given population, designs programs or curricula, supervises the instructional process, and evaluates systematically the educational programs and instruction.

Church leaders and content specialists in the theological sciences may be called upon on occasion to serve as resource people for a group of adult learners. As resource people, they function to explain the core meanings of the religious tradition and to explicate the values peculiar to the particular religious tradition. The resource person, of course, is not a preacher but an expert in a specific area of human knowledge who places himself at the disposal of a group of learners.

Is the role of the theological specialist as outlined here a secondary role? By no means. Church leaders and theological specialists actually operate at a higher level than the adult educator in the religious tradition. They define the general parameters within which adult religious education takes place. They describe a normative state of affairs that should occur as a consequence of adult religious education. They enunciate the major values of the religious tradition. They contribute to the development of religious educational theory and practice in their own way; it is the adult religious educator, however, who attends principally to the development of educational theory and practice.

2. Mastery of theological content is not essential to religious development. There is a difference between the systematic study of theological topics selected by pastors or religious educators and personal reflection on one's life experience in terms of the central values of a religious tradition. The former approach may increase an adult's knowledge store, but the latter approach is gauged to invigorate the adults' religious response to reality.

Research among mainline denominations indicates that effective religious education programs that contribute to faith focus on issues faced by adults in their daily lives. The content of those programs includes biblical understanding and awareness, focus on social issues and the moral questions adults face, and commitment to helping adults develop greater global understanding and awareness. According to the Search report, effective content "blends biblical knowledge and insight with significant engagement in the major life issues each age group faces. To a certain extent, these life issues have a value component in which one is called upon to make decisions.... For adults, they include global, political, and social issues, and issues related to cultural diversity."[15]

While mastery of theological content is not crucial, there is relevance in helping adults learn to think theologically about their world. A significant contribution religious educators can make to adults' spiritual development is helping to them to "examine every situation to see how God is revealed or concealed in it and what truths from biblical revelation apply to that circumstance."[16] Researchers in the area of adult faith development contend that faith develops at the intersection of life experience and biblical revelation.

Hunger in the horn of Africa? Think theologically about it. Random or deliberate violence in America's cities? Think theologically. Health care reform a matter of public debate? Think theologically . . . . Thinking theologically is never a process reserved for seminarians, professional theologians or trained clergy. It is one of the disciplines that should characterize our lives as redeemed and growing believers.[17]

By attending to the experience of the adult learners in reference to the core values of a religious tradition, educators allow the cognitive aspects of the learning process to take on a personal salience for the learners. Further, the affective or attitudinal aspects of the learning process come fully into play. The growth of religious commitment depends not on the mastery of abstract theological subject matter but on the authentication of personal experience under the central values of a religious tradition; the authentication of a particular religious tradition is accomplished in an ongoing manner when the tradition is scrutinized in the light of the collective experience of believers. This position underscores the fact that the religious commitment of many adults is rooted primarily not in rational analysis of theological propositions or biblical interpretations, but in affective orientations toward religious symbols, ritual, and in social participation in communities of shared belief.

Does this position represent an anti-intellectualist approach to adult religious education? We think not. It merely recognizes that the systematic study of theological topics, unrelated to learner experience, is not necessarily associated with religious development. It is not our position that adults need not exert themselves intellectually, but that little is gained when they address themselves to topics foreign to their serious life concerns. This position also underscores the fact that the religious commitment of many adults is rooted primarily not in rational analyses of theological propositions or biblical interpretations, but in affective orientations toward religious symbols, rituals, and social participation in communities of shared belief.

3. Religious learning can occur in educational activities that do not revolve around the study of explicitly religious themes. Adult religious education, it is offered, may be religious: 1) by virtue of the explicit or manifest content of the educational activity, 2) by virtue of the cultural/psychosocial context in which the activity occurs, 3) by virtue of the intentionality of the learner, and/or 4) by virtue of the intentionality of the teacher. Failure to define religious education according to these multiple criteria is equivalently a failure to come to terms with the full scope of religious education. To define religious education solely in terms of the manifest content of instruction bespeaks a simplistic view of both religion and education. Religious education programs for adults that take their shape from such a simplistic definition reinforce the notion that religion is not coterminous with life, that the secular interests and experiences of adults are divorced from the religious experience of adults, and that life must be separated into two compartments. In a word, such programs are one-dimensional.

Ontologically there is a single order of reality. Reality may be perceived to be bifurcated into the realms of the sacred and profane by those who look at reality from behind Platonic spectacles, but such a dichotomy of being, ontologically, is unintelligible. Issues of ultimate concern in human consciousness are inextricably yoked to issues of immediate mundane concerns. Religion, ideally, permeates life. From this it may be inferred that a program of adult religious education may justifiably embrace topics that are labeled as secular.

Whether the course offerings that comprise an educational program are religious in an explicit sense or not, course offerings can be veritably religious by virtue of teacher intentionality, learner intentionality, and/or by virtue of the cultural/ psychosocial context of learning. This latter criterion is of crucial importance. Adults learn far more in an instructional situation than the manifest content of the course; they learn the entire instructional situation. As Edward T. Hall has pointed out, the spoken and written language of any culture (or specific setting within a culture) is but a single message system within that culture.[18] The external behaviors that characterize interpersonal interactions, for example, communicate powerful meanings.

One of the most substantial flaws of most adult religious education programs is the flaw of constricted focus. Educational activities exclusively revolve around topics that are religious in the most obvious sense. Course offerings designed to serve the everyday needs and interests of adults are almost totally disregarded. For example, in the Search Institute project, research showed that only 44 percent of the congregations surveyed addressed the issues of moral decision-making in their adult education programs.[19] By contrast, Roehlkepartain points out that "the church may be one of the few places where adults can feel safe enough to ask aloud the moral and ethical questions that arise out of their daily lives at home, at work, at play, and in the community. What do I do when an employer asks me to compromise my integrity? How can I treat my employees justly? What is my responsibility as a Christian in my neighborhood, community, nation, and world?"[20]

The contention here is that the parish and local church may legitimately be within the scope of religious education by offering a course in English as a second language for immigrants if the *intent* is help these people live fully functioning, productive, and meaningful lives in the community. A Texas church offered as a course "An Orientation for New Teachers in the Dallas School System" to help new teachers get off to a good start in their new work setting. The course drew some fifty participants (with the blessing of the local school board!). By the same token, courses that focus on multicultural awareness through study of art, traditions, and customs of various cultures, or that raise adults' ecological consciousness, or that explore topics such as those raised by the National Issues Forum's efforts fulfill the aforementioned broader scope of religious education by virtue of the cultural/psychosocial context, the intentionality of the learner, or the teacher. [21]

4. The religious development of a person may be distinguished logically from the total human development of the person, but logically distinct developmental processes are not existentially separate; all logically distinct developmental processes are coextensive and ineluctably linked. It is quite possible for a person to achieve developmental gains in one area of personality while remaining arrested in another area. Some people, for example, have highly developed quantitative-computational skills while others remain slow in verbal capacities. Why is it not possible, then, for religious educators to concentrate their efforts helping adults develop religiously while allowing the so-called secular providers of education to help adults develop in other areas?

The argument has some merit, but only under the assumption that religion is one subject matter among others. As noted previously, the issues and values associated with a person's religious response ideally permeate all of life's endeavors. One's religious stance toward reality is really a meta-stance that influences and governs the stances a person takes toward all of life's experiences. One's commitment to religious values provides one with a meta-meaning that helps one interpret all of the meanings in one's life.

But let us grant, for the sake of argument, that the religious component of one's developing personality is one component among others, and let us move the level of discourse about religious-human development to another plane. A way of approaching this question is through the avenue of what has been called systems thinking.[22] The systems approach views any whole as a totality in terms of the inter-relatedness of its parts. There are mechanical systems, social systems, biomedical systems, communications systems, and so forth. Let us look, by way of analogy, at the adult as a system. The systems chart on page 22 is basic and incomplete, but it does exhibit five components of the adult system. Note that each component of the system exists in a relationship of mutuality with every other component.

The social component of the system represents the capacity to relate productively to others, including family members. The psychological component represents the capacity to deal productively with one's feelings and emotions. The intellectual component represents the capacity for recognizing and solving complex problems. The moral component represents the capacity of distinguishing between good and evil. The religious capacity represents the capacity of orienting oneself more perfectly toward God. These definitions of the components are, of course, neither exhaustive nor highly sophisticated. But our major business here is the explanation of the adult as a system.

The introduction of any change into one of the components introduces a corresponding change in each of the remaining components and, therefore, into the system as a whole. Suppose you gain a penetrating religious insight, a revelation of sorts. This change in the religious component of your system will guide you in the interpretation of your feelings (psychological component), affect your relationships with others (social component), stimulate your thinking (intellectual component), and increase your grasp of moral issues (moral component).

On the other hand, suppose you learn experientially something that increases your capacity for relating productively with others. This outcome will have impact on you psychologically, intellectually, morally, and religiously. Or suppose you develop psychologically in some way. This will affect the developmental processes in each of the remaining components, and will affect the development of your whole personality.

The matter that religious educators must face is this: There are times when they have access to one component of the adult system but not to other components. An adult may not wish to study religion, to engage in an intellectual pursuit, to discuss moral issues, or to develop insight into self. But the same adult may wish to engage in some kind of educational activity for the purpose of meeting other people. This component in the system, then, is the point of access. (It should be pointed out that many adults participate in educational activities simply to make social contacts.) A course on English as a second language or "Managing Your Family Finances" could very well offer access to the total adult system, including the religious component.

Reduced to its most simple elements, our contention is that religious educators must be concerned with the development of the total adult, and with the manifold educational needs and interests experienced by adults. To concentrate exclusively on the explicitly religious development of adults is to fall victim to the fallacy of constricted focus as applied to the question of adult development.

5. *Data yielded by decision-oriented research in a particular parish or local church must be considered in the design of religious education programs for adults.* The topics of educational programs must be related to the felt needs and interests of adults. The determination of these needs and interests requires empirical research at the level of the parish or local church. Knowledge of the target audience of any adult education program is at least as important as knowledge of a particular program topic. Paternalism in educational programming, or the assignment of particular topics simply because an audiovisual package is available, is self-defeating.

Maurice Monette has challenged the traditional "service orientation" typical of the adult education movement in the United States. He suggests that the real starting point for educational planning should not be needs assessment data but "an effort on the part of the educators, together with the community to be served, to establish a direction for inquiry through a commitment to chosen values within a given sociocultural context."[23] He approvingly cites the work of Paulo Freire in developing educational programs for South American peasants. Freire, Monette claims, did not cater to the felt needs of adults but rather explored with them the causal factors underlying their felt needs to the end that these adults become more autonomous and free to transform reality. Freire, of course, accused the oppressors of the peasants of cognitive imperialism. One wonders if Freire's approach does not involve a more subtle form of cognitive imperialism, namely, the substitution of one political approach (Freire's) for the solution of social problems for the political approach of the oppressors. Monette is correct, then, in stating that neither the felt needs of adult learners nor the values of the educator be absolutized.

However, two observations must be made in response to Monette's philosophical analysis: (1) The status of the cognitive development of the peasants served by Freire is quite different from the status of the cognitive development of most literate adults in Western industrialized societies, and (2) it is useless to talk about a dialogue between teacher and adult learners relative to the felt needs of adult learners if they do not initially attend an educational activity.

As we shall see in chapter 4, the abilities of illiterate peasants for critical reflection are seriously impaired. They need much help in formulating issues for critical inquiry. This is not the case of most adults served by religious educators in relatively advanced societies. These adults may also need some help in clarifying their felt needs and interests, but dialogues around these issues could quickly degenerate into *pop psych* sessions with the religious educator playing the role of Messiah. Educational counseling is necessary for all adult learners, but the counseling strategies will differ with respect to the client population being served and the individual differences within these populations.

Pragmatically, it is virtually impossible to attract most adults to educational programs without designing programs that are responsive to their felt needs and interests. Opportunities for dialogue are possible only when adults are present for the dialogue. In any event, the researcher-program developer should follow conventional research methodologies in determining program topics. The researcher-program developer does not simply make decisions on the basis of empirical raw data. The raw data are analyzed and findings are generated from the data. The findings are weighed in terms of numerous related situational variables. That is, the findings of needs assessment research are interpreted and programs are constructed on the basis of these interpretations.

Monette's challenge of "service oriented" adult education programs based on identified felt needs and interests of adults is essentially not a call to disregard needs assessment data but to utilize these data in a more sophisticated manner. Unfortunately, human nature being what it is, some religious educators may "interpret" needs assessment data to correspond with their preconceived notions and with agendas that may even be hidden from them.

The Adult as a System

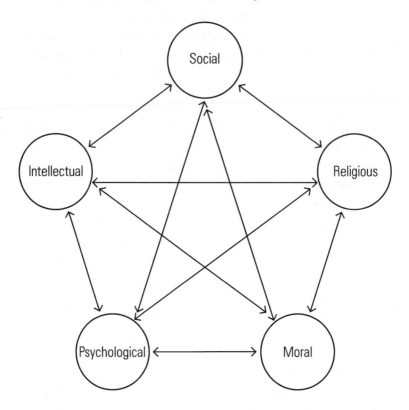

There are many aspects to the adult's personality. Each of these aspects is interrelated. A few of the aspects or components of personality are shown above. Counseling strategies will differ with respect to the client population being served and with respect to individual differences within these populations.

6. *While the formation of adults according to the values of a particular religious tradition is legitimate, such formation must respect the critical thinking of adults. Adult learners must be encouraged to voice their honest differences with the teacher and with one another.* The "National Study of Protestant Congregations" conducted by Search Institute measured "mature faith" according to the integration of two dimensions, the *vertical* ("having a deep, personal relationship with a loving God"), and the *horizontal* ("translating this personal affirmation into acts of love, mercy, and justice").[24] The study found that in most adults the vertical dimension is out of balance with the horizontal, indicating in part that adults have difficulty translating personal piety into concern for fellow

humankind. This is understandable if adults lack opportunity to explore through dialogue and critical reflection the implications and potential applications of the formative faith principles being "taught." It may be asserted that content, even that intended as formative, will not be "owned" by the learner until he or she thinks critically about the subject matter at hand. Some religious educators may view this as risky since, as Brookfield observes, "Being critical thinkers entails a continual questioning of assumptions."[25] Questioning assumptions can be threatening, not only to the teacher (the one "in charge" of the learning activity), but to the whole sponsoring establishment. Nonetheless, such challenge is essential to critical thinking. In fact, Brookfield lays down four components of critical thinking.[26]

(1) Identifying and challenging assumptions that underlie beliefs, values, and actions.
(2) Challenging the importance of the context in which the content was formed, in which it is studied, and in which it is applied.
(3) Imagining and exploring alternatives to existing ways of thinking and behaving.
(4) Developing reflective skepticism of claims to universal truth through imagining and exploring alternatives.

Reuel Howe points out that the church, in carrying out its teaching function, "has put too much faith in the use of words and used too little the language of relationship. The result is that people have not been helped to understand the meaning of their own experiences or to bring these meanings into relationship with the meaning of the words used in preaching or formal teaching."[27] Howe insists on the necessity of dialogical teaching as contrasted with the kind of teaching that is simply a shared monologue. He stresses that learning can occur as a consequence of the relationship formed between teacher and learners, and between learners themselves.

A prerequisite to effective dialogical teaching is a sufficient level of *trust* between learners and between learners and teacher. Why? There is a sense in which our ability to learn in a given situation is limited to the extent to which we enter emotionally into the learning transaction. In order to share of one's self in ways that enhance appropriation of the content under study, we must trust members of the group and the teacher to handle with respect what we contribute to the dialogue.

Trust is inevitably bound to relationship and is therefore foundational to effective dialogical teaching.

In the dialogical teaching situation there is a climate of openness that invites learners to raise questions and doubts, to register their misgivings and reservations, and to evaluate what is taught in the light of their own experiences. The dialogical teacher, according to Howe, is open to communication, alert to the meanings brought by the learners to the instructional situation, ready to help learners formulate questions, willing to help learners correlate what is taught with their own experiences by encouraging them to reflection, intent on helping learners dialogue with one another, ready to tolerate disagreement, accepting of the independent otherness of the learners, and dedicated to a fundamental trust of the learners.

There is little potential for conflict when education is equated with accepting knowledge on the authority of the teacher. Conversely, the dialogical teaching-learning situation may occasion conflict. But conflict, as Donald Bossart[28] has shown, can be creative and can stimulate the growth of both teachers and learners.

7. *The concepts that constitute the manifest content of education* (what *is learned) are sometimes not as important as the appreciations that constitute the latent content of education* (how *something is learned in a definite kind of learning context).* Learning involves the heart as well as the mind, and often cognitive learning is secondary to affective learning. Cognitive learning is related to the affective state of the learner. J. R. Kidd asserts that it has long been recognized "that there may not be much learning of consequence unless a marked interest is present."[29] This view of the cognitive affective relationship places the heart at the service of the head. An adult will not get something into his head unless his heart is set on it.

A different approach suggests that feelings and emotions regarding a particular person, thing, or value will change when the learner gains more facts and information about the person, thing, or value. No doubt both of these approaches are correct. Changes that occur in the cognitive dimension of personality are associated with changes in the affective dimension, and vice versa. The two dimensions of personality are but two aspects of the same reality.

Thomas Ringness states that affective learning "deals with the emotional aspects of one's behavior—the influences on our choice of goals, and the means we choose for attaining them. These aspects include our emotions themselves, our tastes and preferences, attitudes and values, morals and character, and our philosophies of life or guiding principles."[30] Affective learning, it would seem, should be a supereminent concern of religious educators of adults.

Affective changes—the more or less permanent directional shifts in emotional orientation or changes in the intensity of emotional orientation—can occur as a result of many factors: the totality of a person's previous life experiences, changes in life situations, neurophysiological variations, and so forth. In fact, there are probably so many factors associated with affective change that no one has yet identified them. This is why it is exceedingly difficult to speak about affective change in respect to education. Educational theorists have only begun to uncover the complexity of affective education. Be that as it may, some general observations can be made.

When we address affective learning in educational terms we must turn our attention to: (1) the structure of the instructional process for adult learners and (2) the personal interactions that occur within that structure. It is possible, of course, that a learner will become effectively oriented positively toward a religious value, or experience a greater intensity of positive affective orientation toward the value, as a result of a cognitive mastery of the value through reasoned discourse. But it is equally true, and more probably true, that a learner will become effectively oriented in a desired way because the teacher has structured a supportive, open, friendly, accepting, and sociable instructional process within which the learners can communicate with the teacher and with each other in meaningful ways. In effect, we emphasize again the effectiveness of what Reuel Howe calls the dialogical teaching-learning situation.

8. *Conclusion-oriented empirical research is necessary if a more adequate body of knowledge is to be developed for the field of adult religious education. Decision-oriented empirical research is necessary to improve the quality of decision-making by religious educators of adults in particular settings.* Loren Eiseley, in his brief but powerful book on Francis Bacon, explained that to the theologically inclined scholar of the Middle Ages, truth was founded on ideas largely independent of direct observation.[31] Knowledge was established on the basis of a priori assumptions and logical arguments unrelated to systematically collected empirical evidence.

A review of literature in the field of adult religious education suggests that data from social science research, gathered by religious educators of adults, are almost nonexistent. The body of knowledge relevant to the field of adult religious education consists mostly of speculation deduced from theological principles or from the empirical research conducted by those in other fields of social practice. This is one of the most serious problems confronting adult religious education as a field of study.

A Preview

The themes addressed in the foregoing pages come into closer focus in the remainder of this book. Occasionally these themes are confronted separately. More often than not they are intertwined and discussed in terms of a broad theory of adult religious education.

Chapter 2 offers a brief historical overview of adult religious education in order to provide the reader with important background information. Chapter 3 identifies some specific problems facing adult religious education both as a field of study and as a social practice, and expands on some of the notions presented in this introductory chapter. In chapter 4 an attempt is made to identify the contemporary adult. Knowledge of the contemporary adult, at least in broad terms, is a *sine qua non* for the adult educator.

Chapter 5 outlines a theory of adult religious education and indicates the implications of this theory for the practice of adult religious education in the parish and local church. In chapter 6 several program development approaches are developed and analyzed. The emphasis of chapter 7 is learning; teaching is the concern of chapter 8. Chapter 9 addresses one of the greatest needs in church education generally and adult religious education specifically: evaluation. Types, techniques, and tools for evaluating educational offering and programs are included. Finally, chapter 10 deals with practical ways adult religious education may intervene positively in the lives of the adults with whom we work and among whom we minister. Though certainly not exhaustive, examples are drawn not only from the experience and observation of the writers, but from actual parish ministries with adults.

Notes

[1] For a brief but highly useful clarification of the relationship between thinking and doing see Kenneth Benne, "Some Philosophic Issues in Adult Education," *Adult Education* 7, no.2 (1957): 74-75.

[2] The distinction between applied and basic research is often blurred. Fred Kerlinger's definitions are helpful: "Basic research is research done to test theory, to study relations among phenomena in order to understand the phenomena, with little or no thought of applications of the results of the research to practical problems. Applied research is directed toward the solution of specified practical problems . . . " (See Kerlinger's *Behavioral Research: A Conceptual Approach* (New York: Holt, Rinehart & Winston, 1979), 283. Lee Cronbach and Patrick Suppes refer to decision-oriented and conclusion-oriented research. Decision-oriented research serves pragmatic needs; conclusion-oriented research is more free-wheeling and exploratory. See Lee Cronbach and Patrick Suppes, eds., *Research for Tomorrow's Schools* (Toronto: Macmillan, 1969), 19-27.

[3] James Michael Lee, *The Shape of Religious Instruction* (Birmingham: Religious Education Press, 1971), 225-57.

[4] Karl Rahner and Herbert Vorgrimler, *Theological Dictionary*, trans. C. Ernst (New York: Herder & Herder, 1968), 456-59.

[5] David Tracy, *Blessed Rage for Order* (New York: Seabury, 1975), 43.

[6] Years ago, when I first studied Plato in a college philosophy course, I was amazed that this pagan philosopher had anticipated (on the basis of reason alone) so many ideas of Christian theologians. Later I realized that many Christian apologists and theologians simply "baptized" Platonic philosophy. Unfortunately, many Christians today have embraced Platonic ideas thinking these ideas are integral parts of Christian doctrine.

[7] Eugene Roehlkepartain, *The Teaching Church* (Nashville: Abingdon Press, 1993), 149.

[8] Ibid., 151.

[9] Nathaniel Cantor, *The Teaching-Learning Process* (New York: Dryden, 1955), 58.

[10] Victoria J. Marsick and Karen E. Watkins, "Paradigms for Critically Reflective Teaching and Learning," in *Facilitating Adult Learning*, ed. Michael Galbraith (Marabar FL: Krieger, 1991), 85.

[11] Steven Brookfield, "Grounding Teaching in Learning," in *Facilitating Adult Learning*, 43.

[12] Marsick and Watkins, 85.

[13] Ibid., 70.

[14] This project is detailed in a report by the same name, published by Search Institute, Minneapolis, 1990.

[15] Search Institute report, 54.

[16] Michael Clingenpeel, "Think Theologically," in *Religious Herald* (13 January 1993), 4.

[17] Ibid.

[18] Edward R. Hall, *The Silent Language* (New York: Doubleday Anchor, 1959), 42-62.

[19] Roehlkepartain, 130.

[20] Ibid.

[21] National Issues Forums are supported by the Kettering Foundation. NIF groups organize in communities to study issues facing the nation and world. Many churches have begun such groups, adding to their discussions a consideration of a Christian response to the issues.

[22] For a good introduction to the systems approach of analyzing any phenomenon see Ervin Laszlo, ed., *The Relevance of General Systems Theory* (New York: George Braziller, 1972).

[23] Maurice Monette, "Needs Assessment: A Critique of Philosophical Assumptions," in *Adult Education* 29, no.2 (1979): 83 ff.

[24] Search Institute report, 13.

[25] Steven Brookfield, *Developing Critical Thinkers* (San Francisco: Jossey-Bass, 1987), 6.

[26] Ibid., 7-9.

[27] Reuel Howe, *The Miracle of Dialogue* (New York: Seabury, 1963), 136-37.

[28] Donald E. Bossart, *Creative Conflict in Religious Education and Church Administration* (Birmingham: Religious Education Press, 1980). See especially chapter 7, "The Uses of Conflict," 147-75.

[29] J. R. Kidd, *How Adults Learn* (New York: Association, 1977), 112.

[30] Thomas A. Ringness, *The Affective Domain in Education* (New York: Little, Brown, 1975), 3.

[31] Loren Eiseley, *The Man Who Saw Through Time* (New York: Charles Scribner's Sons, 1973), 53.

ADULT RELIGIOUS EDUCATION
HISTORICAL OVERVIEW

Prior to any historical review of adult religious education, it is necessary to distinguish the various meanings of learning. It is also necessary to draw a distinction between learning and education. This distinction will be explained more fully in a later chapter. These distinctions are unavoidable. Unless we have some relatively clear idea of what learning and education are, we cannot speak historically about adult religious education.

Here is a preliminary stipulative definition of learning: Learning is any change in a person's cognition, affect, and/or external behavior or lifestyle. A fuller examination of learning will be offered in a subsequent chapter. It suffices here to view learning in a general way. There are four general strategic modes of learning. Adults may learn: (1) as a result of a random experiential process, (2) incidentally as a result of participation in activities in a formal setting whose main purpose is not instructional, (3) as a result of self-planned activities or individual learning projects, and (4) through involvement in instructional activities.

All learning is experiential in some way. In random experiential learning the learning experiences are not planned at all. The learning experiences in incidental learning occur as a side effect of a planned activity whose major purpose is other than instructional. The experiences in an adult learning project are planned, to some extent, by the individual adult working alone. Finally, some learning experiences are planned systematically with instruction as the primary intent of the activity.

Random Learning

Random learning is simply the result of moving through life with a minimal level of advertence to what is happening in one's environment. Involvement in life's activities, interpersonal transactions, interactions with life situations, and daily problem-solving lead ordinarily to changes in a person's cognition or knowledge, feeling states, and/or external behavior. An adult learns merely by attending to the "contents" of each day, by organizing life into a coherent whole, and by integrating daily life experiences with previous experience. We learn particularly in the great events of life: assuming adult responsibilities, choosing a mate, selecting a career, love, marriage, the birth of a child, the death of a friend, crises in work, relationships, health, and so forth. These have been called in adult education jargon "trigger events" that create teachable moments, heightening our readiness to learn. (These will be discussed at more length in the last chapter on interventions.) Random experiential learning is akin to what anthropologists call enculturation: the appropriation of the mental, spiritual, and moral "furniture" that occupies space in our native culture. In the event we appropriate the "furniture" of a culture different from our own, the process is called acculturation.

Quite often random experiential learning occurs at the threshold of conscious advertence. When we learn to speak as children we are not reflexively aware that we are learning a new language. Yet learning occurs. We are immersed in a particular culture the way a fish is immersed in the water of his pond. This culture speaks to us, shapes our attitudes, affects our orientation to life, and provides us with the means of identifying ourselves socially, psychologically, religiously, and in a host of other ways.

Incidental Learning

Incidental learning occurs as a side effect of another process. Later we will refer to this kind of learning as other-managed experiential learning. An initiation ceremony illustrates this kind of learning. When a person is initiated into an organization, the primary purpose of the ceremony is the ratification of a formal social relationship. As a side effect of the initiation process (a planned effect!), a person may learn something about the norms of the organization and what is expected of its members. The initiation ritual is systematized and ordinated to the formal reception of the new member into the organization. At a different level the initiation ritual is directed toward the facilitation of learning in the new member.

Learning Projects

In self-planned learning an individual adult attends consciously to the attainment of a learning goal in a more or less systematic manner. The learning project terminates ideally in the acquisition of new knowledge, a new way of feeling about something, and/or the acquisition of a skill of some kind such as being able to replace spark plugs in an automobile. The learner plans a strategy for learning, marshals material resources for learning such as printed materials, and sometimes consults a resource person—someone who has already achieved the goal sought by the learner. Self-planned, self-implemented learning involves a purposeful organization of experience on the part of the learner.

Most adults design learning projects for themselves. Quite frequently they set about learning something that will help them in their daily living. Research studies suggest that adults pursue learning projects but often fail to remember these pursuits, or fail to define the projects as activities by means of which they purposively learned something. This is perhaps due to the fact that many adults think of learning only in terms of attending school. When a researcher asks someone, "Have you been involved in any learning projects in the past six months?" the respondent may say, "No." If the researcher continues to ask probing questions, the respondent may say, "Well, now that you jarred my memory, I did spend several hours last month learning how to prune my trees. I read two books and talked to my next-door neighbor. Yes, I learned how to prune the trees in my backyard." When we embark on a learning project, we seldom bestow the label "learning project" on the activity.[1]

Instruction

Learning occurs as a result of participation in an instructional situation. This is teacher-facilitated learning or learning that is related to what I define stipulatively as education. Education is a process that occurs in an intentionally structured environment and involves the activity of a teacher, a learner or learners, and definite objectives that specify the manifest content of what is to be learned and the means by which learning is to take place. Anyone who has studied the logic of educational discourse knows that definitions of education vary considerably from one theorist to another. We shall return to this issue in chapter 7. It does not serve the plan of this book to pursue the matter fully here. Later we will discuss the reasons why we are inclined to speak of education in terms of teacher-facilitated learning. At this point, however, we should return to the discussion of learning.

Learning occurs ideally as at least a partial result of teaching. Teaching is understood broadly as the systematic facilitation of learning. This facilitative activity may emphasize overt action on the part of the teacher (lecturing, for example) or overt action on the part of the learners (group discussion, for example). In all cases, teaching attempts to stimulate an internal activity in the learners that leads to cognitive, affective, lifestyle (external behavior), and/or volitional change in the learners. Education is, by dint of the stipulative definition, programmatic.

The educational activity may aim principally at the formation of the learners or may be organized in such a way as to maximize evaluative thinking on the part of the learners. This distinction between formative and critical education can be viewed best in terms of the types of cognitive learning outlined by Benjamin Bloom and his colleagues.[2]

As a consequence of formative education the learner (1) *knows* or is able to repeat what was taught in precisely the same manner in which it was conveyed; (2) *comprehends* or is able to repeat something back in his own words; (3) *applies* or is able to relate that which was taught to his daily life. Bloom and his associates do not specifically state that these three types of cognitive learning constitute a formative process or shaping of the learner, but the concept of formation is obviously pertinent.

The contrast between these first three types of cognitive learning and the latter three types that constitute critical learning is striking. As a result of critical education, the learner (1) *analyzes* that which is taught or takes it apart conceptually; (2) *synthesizes* or assembles conceptually that which is taught after analyzing it; (3) *evaluates* or critically assesses that which is taught in the light of her own experiences. Critical education is ordinated toward the *examination* of educational "givens." Formative education is ordinated toward the *reception* of educational "givens."

Religious Institutions and Adult Learning

The church's encouragement of lifelong learning is evidenced in the model for learning called the catechumenate. Very early in Christian history an initiatory process for converts to Christianity was assimilated from the pagan mystery religions and Essenian practices.[3] Those who wished to enter the Christian community were required to live in the community for an extended period of time. During this time the catechumen was to learn the ways of the community. At the end of a prescribed time period, a decision was made by leaders of the community (on the basis of the catechumen's acceptance of Christian ways) to permit or forbid further entrance into fellowship. In carefully graded steps the catechumen became incorporated into the community. Biblical knowledge was revealed to the catechumen; he was instructed in moral, social, and liturgical practices. Even after he was admitted into full fellowship through baptism, the new Christian was expected to continue his study of the Scriptures and commentaries on the Scriptures.

In the catechumenate process, the aspiring member of the Christian community was bonded to the community. The Christian community provided a social milieu that influenced the catechumen and by means of which he could become socially affiliated. Random experiential learning occurred simply by dint of the catechumen's presence in a particular community. The individual continued to learn Christianity merely by attending to the structured context of the Christian community. The Christian community was, in effect, an environment that embodied values, standards, and norms that could be appropriated by the catechumen.

The impact of liturgical observances was especially conducive to learning of a formative nature. While the primary purpose of liturgical celebrations was the worship of God, incidental learning also occurred as a side effect. The catechumen experienced a continuing change of heart or turning toward the message of Jesus. Participation in liturgical functions served to deepen the faith commitment of those who sincerely endeavored to worship God according to the prescribed ways. Learning that occurred through random experiential processes, and incidentally through participation in liturgical activities, was supported by the learning that took place as a result of individual, self-planned efforts to gain greater enlightenment through the study of the Bible.

The model of the catechumenate was, in fact, the primary model for adult learning during the major part of Christian history. That is to say, adult learning was advanced largely outside of education or formal instructional settings. Indeed, most Christian adults today learn Christian ways not so much by taking part in educational activities (instructional activities in formal settings) but by experiencing reality according to the value system they have appropriated from a specific Christian community, by participating in liturgical activities, and through self-planned learning projects. This fits appropriately into the ancient principle that truth is something that is *done* and not simply the object of speculation. Biblically, truth is a quality that belongs properly to God. Applied to people it means the ability to perform what is required; truth characterizes a particular activity when that activity corresponds to one's role. (Role is all too pallid a word, but it conveys a sense of what is meant by truth as that which is done). Knowledge, likewise, does not mean, in the Bible, primarily to grasp cognitively an abstract principle but rather to experience someone or something.[4] The word *know* in reference to sexual intercourse in the Bible is not a meaningless euphemism. To know one's spouse resulted in an intimate experience of the spouse, and this knowledge was the consequence of *doing* one's truth as a spouse. Orthopraxis (doing what is right) was not separated from orthodoxis (thinking right).

We hesitate to use the next example of truth as that-which-is-done, and of learning by doing, because one of the most prominent philosophers to grasp the ancient principle of truth as deed was Karl Marx: "It is not the consciousness of men that determines their being, but, on the contrary, their social being determines their consciousness."[5] We hasten to add that truth-as-deed, as important as this principle is, is only one side of the coin. The principle of truth-as-thought is the other side of the coin. One learns by doing; one learns by thinking; one also learns by integrating doing and thinking. There is a reciprocal relationship between consciousness and social being. One's consciousness influences one's social being; social being influences consciousness. For all of his profoundness (except in certain crucial areas), Marx missed the subtlety involved in relational reciprocity.

In any event, the religious learning that took place for most Christian adults for most of Christian history was learning by *doing* religion. This approach is still valid and important. But adult religious education or religious learning in formal instructional settings is also important. We can and should go beyond random learning, incidental learning, and self-planned learning.

The church's support of education (systematic instruction) cannot be understood without coming to terms with the Jewish and Greco-Roman matrices in which Christianity took shape. Coming into contact with both the Jewish and Greco-Roman cultures, Christianity could not help but borrow from these cultures.

This is particularly true regarding cultural values affecting education. The family was the principal focus in Judaism. The transmission of the knowledge and the inculcation of the spirit of the Torah constituted the all-surpassing cultural and religious norm. Children were instructed in the Torah through participation in family religious observances and ceremonies. Adult learning was encouraged and advanced by means of adult participation in family religious rituals. After the spread of local synagogues in the postexilic period, religious instruction was provided for adults in the synagogues. During the week, while adults were working, the synagogue attendant instructed the children.[6]

In the post-Alexandrine Jewish world, the Greek classical school became the model for the education of boys and young men. Schools were associated with the synagogues. By 75 BC, schooling for boys and young men was compulsory. Literary studies in the Greek schools were based on Homeric texts; in Jewish schools literary studies were undertaken in terms of the written Torah.[7] Adult "higher" education—rabbinical schools—eventually evolved out of major synagogue schools.

In the Greco-Roman world the so-called classical schools were organized systematically and featured regular curricula. "Elementary" schools (for boys seven to fourteen) emphasized the study of language. The "secondary" curriculum included vigorous physical training and often military training for boys aged fifteen to seventeen. From ages eighteen to twenty, young men pursued advanced studies. Formal schooling was the norm for children of freemen; participation in "higher" education was usually reserved for those who wished to become career intellectuals.

Early Christian thought on education was strongly affected by the cultural assumptions of the Jewish and Greco-Roman worlds; these worlds were not always in concordance. Jewish education was thoroughly religious in the explicit sense of the term. Scribes learned to read and write in order to prepare themselves for lifetimes of serious study of the Torah, Mishnah, and Talmud. All education was ordinated directly to theological and explicitly religious themes. Greco-Roman education, on the other hand, was broadly humanistic and explicitly religious values were not taught. Mythology was not studied as religious doctrine but for literary purposes. The study of act, rhetoric, music, philosophy, and literature was an end in itself. This difference in orientation toward education was argued thoroughly by the fathers of the early church.[8]

There is no intention here to leave the reader with the notion that unanimity of purpose regarding the scope of Jewish religious education was ultimately realized and that Jewish adult religious education is today restricted to theological or explicitly religious topics. Alexander Schindler writes that no effort is made to ". . . compartmentalize education into well-defined, only thinly related segments labeled 'secular' and 'sacred.' Tradition did not conceive 'religious' education to be a discipline apart; *all* education was held sacred and seen to serve religious ends."[9]

Historically the argument as to whether adult religious education was to be conceived as including only theological/explicitly religious topics or was to embrace all kinds of learning was an argument between two theoretical camps that cut across the boundaries of denominationalism. Those who insisted that adult religious education should concern only theological or explicitly religious topics, it seems to me, conceptualized religion in a narrow sense; the opposite camp tended to identify religion with life.

The tendency of Christian educators to concern themselves exclusively with theology or explicitly religious topics in adult religious education has a long history. Many of the fathers of the church and early Christian apologists taught that Christians should not devote time and energy to pagan learning. Tertullian was most vehement in his denunciation of the classical Greek system of education and pagan learning. He viewed philosophy as nothing more than a network of contradictions. His hostility toward human reason is well-known (*Credo quia absurdum*—"I believe because it is absurd"). Tertullian's anti-intellectualism was, in the minds of many, virtuous.

Basil wrote a treatise concerning the reading of profane authors and warned advanced students to be aware of possible dangers to their faith. That Basil even countenanced the reading of pagan literature was considered by some to be liberally permissive. Hippolytus cautioned that Christians should not be teachers of the sciences of this world, unless they had no other means of economic subsistence.

The scholar Jerome told of a vision in which God accused him of being a Ciceronian and not a Christian. (This did not dissuade Jerome from leading, in a most fruitful manner, the life of a scholar.) At the request of friends, Jerome drew up a curriculum for the education of two girls in the family. The curriculum revolved entirely around the study of the Bible. On the other hand, his curriculum for boys included the study of grammar, Virgil, and the Greek poets and historians. Jerome's attitude toward so-called secular learning was ambivalent.

Augustine followed the lead of Ambrose and worked for an integration of what was known as profane and sacred learning. This accommodation is evident in his writings, chiefly *On Christian Doctrine* and *The City of God.* Later in his life Augustine expressed misgivings about his attempt to assimilate pagan learning to the cause of Christianity.

Gregory the Great, in the sixth century, considered secular learning to be unnecessary for the Christian. As late as the twelfth century, priests were forbidden to read pagan books and were permitted to study the works of heretics only out of necessity.

Other leading writers took a different tack. Justin Martyr used the categories of Greek philosophy to defend Christianity from its antagonists. Clement of Alexandria was a strong supporter of education and saw utility of all kinds of learning for the Christian. All learning, according to Clement, should be ordinated to man's final end, but the scope of learning should include both temporal as well as eternal verities. Origen, a student of Clement, was also attracted to secular learning. He sought to integrate the sacred and profane spheres, and to use secular learning as an instrument for the conversion of non-Christians.

It must be noted that many of the fathers of the church and apologists opposed the learning of secular topics because Greco-Roman curricula were thoroughly saturated with the pagan ideologies that challenged Christianity. Given the benefit of historical hindsight, it is not difficult to understand the siege mentality of early Christian leaders that urged them to view secular education as a threat or as a work of the devil. Nor is it difficult to admire those who wished to meet the challenge of secular education in direct fashion and forge an integration of so-called secular and sacred knowledge so that nothing human would be alien to Christianity.

Adult Education as Higher Education

Christian schools evolved in generally the same manner as early Jewish schools. Generally the curricula stressed the learning of Bible and doctrine. Christian education—the phrase was first used in AD 96—meant the systematic study of biblical/doctrinal topics. Initially Christian education referred to the development of a Christian consciousness in children. Children would learn the basics of Christian teaching in their homes. At an appropriate age they would advance to more structured and programmatic learning experiences provided in the context of specific Christian communities, but these "schools" were not widespread.

Following the pattern of the rabbinical schools in Judaism, centers for advanced learning began as early as the second century under Christian auspices. These early forms of "higher" education (schooling for career intellectuals) concentrated on theology but began to decline shortly after the time of Constantine. While Christian schools were initially established for the purpose of instructing or forming children, the need to develop teachers and apologists was also felt. Adult education, therefore, was restricted to advanced studies that we would identify today as institutions of higher learning.

This pattern continued during the Dark Ages in the monastic schools. By and large, adult education was restricted to members of monastic communities and to adults who constituted the leadership castes of feudal society. This trend continued in force into the Medieval period. Whether we speak of the "cathedral schools" or the universities that evolved from these schools, educational opportunities were not universally extended to adults. In the Britain of 1530, for example, enrollments in "elementary" schools did not exceed 26,000 out of a population of 5 million. Enrollments in institutions of higher learning were considerably less.[10]

The observation that adults were not served educationally in any large number is not made by way of criticism. It does absolutely no good to judge the past in terms of contemporary contexts and standards. It should be remembered that the democratization of knowledge is a phenomenon of the past few centuries, that adult learning was encouraged and facilitated outside of formal instructional settings (e.g., participation in liturgy), that the socio-economic context was structured in such a way as to require many workers at the base of the social pyramid (mainly to provide food and other essential goods), that there was little leisure time for adult participation in educational activities, and that the resources for reaching out educationally to adults were not available.

When many religious education programs were eventually established for adults on a widespread basis, it is easy to see why theology (watered-down suitably to meet the intellectual levels of ordinary adults) was so strongly emphasized. These religious education programs for adults were patterned after the biblical/theological studies addressed in institutions of higher education. Many adult religious education practices of the twentieth century were rooted firmly in the models for theological education taken from centuries ago.

Indicated above were some of the reasons why large numbers of adults were not afforded the opportunity of participating in programs of adult religious education, and why adult religious education as we know it today did not exist until relatively recent times. There is one more reason for this phenomenon, a reason that looms larger than all the rest: adulthood was not "discovered" by society at large until the twentieth century.

The Discovery of Adulthood

The differentiation of adulthood as a distinct period of life is related to the "discovery" of childhood and adolescence. Childhood was not delineated as a special period of life (except in global poetic metaphor) until the seventeenth–eighteenth centuries. The term "child" was ordinarily used to denote a status of subservience and not a commonly accepted life period. Childhood and adolescence, of course, were not discovered.[11] The delineation of these age periods was a social invention. Prior to this social invention (in the latter part of the nineteenth century), children were perceived as miniature adults; most adults (especially those at the base of the social pyramid) were perceived as grown-up children. Reduced to its barest expression, childhood was not carefully differentiated from adulthood because of a cultural-perceptual bias that allowed people to see only "human beings." This bias was fostered by the philosophical assumption that adults and children were essentially the same since they shared the same human nature.

Adulthood was "discovered" implicitly in the discovery of childhood. While many prominent people in the history of philosophical thought wrote about children in broad terms, child psychology as a scientific specialization is less than a century old.[12] Correlative to the attention given to childhood in the latter part of the nineteenth century, the interest in adulthood, from a scientific standpoint and as an issue for systematic inquiry, began with Adolph Quetelet in the middle of the nineteenth century. Quetelet's attempts to measure development through the adult life span, however, were not pursued with any ardor by nineteenth-century psychologists.[13]

The advent of Charlotte Buhler's landmark studies in adult developmental psychology in 1933 ushered in a new perspective on adult life, namely, that adult life was highly variegated during the life span, that adult life was not all of one piece.[14] A new focus of consciousness, beginning slowly in the seventeenth–eighteenth centuries and gathering clarity in the nineteenth century, was responsible both for the initiation of scientific studies of adulthood and for the adult education movement. A number of writers in previous periods had noted changes during the life span (one thinks of Shakespeare's seven ages of man in *As You Like It*), but these changes were investigated neither systematically nor inductively. Nor were they conceived as grounds for the differentiation between childhood and adulthood. The growth of adult developmental psychology was accompanied by what has come to be known as the adult education movement.

The Adult Education Movement

"It is time that we had uncommon schools, that we did not leave off our education when we begin to be men and women. It is time that villages were universities, and their elder inhabitants the fellows of universities with leisure—if they are indeed so well off—to pursue liberal studies the rest of their lives."[15] Thoreau was not alone in the nineteenth century in professing the importance of adult education, but the voices that proposed this innovation were in the minority. Adult education programs, other than university courses, were available to some adults but only on an occasional or sporadic basis. These programs were exceptions to the general rule that education was a preparation for life and, therefore, suitable mostly for children.

In Great Britain, the Society for Promoting Christian Knowledge (SPCK) was founded in 1698. Samuel Wesley, John Wesley's father, organized a religious association along similar lines in 1702. The primary aim of the association was "to set Schools for the Poor, wherein Children (or if need be, Adult Persons) may be instructed in the Fundamentals of Christianity by men of known and approved piety."[16] In its earliest modern beginnings, the adult education movement was inspired out of religious motives. John Wesley was the moving force in furthering the basic education of British workers in the eighteenth century. His main effort, however, was directed not to the founding of schools but to the distribution of reading materials. This was a general trend in Great Britain at the time. To this day the Society for Promoting Christian Knowledge is active in the publication of religious materials.

The first school exclusively for adults was established by Thomas Charles, a minister, in 1811 in Wales. Emphasis was placed on literacy and the reading of the Bible. C. H. Grattan, a historian of adult education, points to the foundation of this school as a landmark in the history of adult education.[17] These early plans for adult education, however, did not meet with success. Until the middle of the nineteenth century, the British schools for adults did not enroll more than 50,000 in their best single year. By 1851, however, over 120,000 adults participated in educational activities and the adult education movement gained momentum.

One of the most prominent organizations providing educational services was the Mechanic's Institute, founded in the latter part of the nineteenth century for teaching workers reading, writing, arithmetic, drawing, geography, history, and morals. These efforts in behalf of workers were motivated in part, to be sure, to prepare skilled personnel for the work force. The industrial revolution was in full bloom. The teaching of morality arose, in part, out of the need to "domesticate" workers and inculcate in them the values of their employers. Undeniably, though, many of those who supported worker education were motivated by altruistic ideals. Institute programs spread rapidly beyond the British Isles and were established in the United States. Other adult education associations in Great Britain included the Chartists (1840), the Quaker Adult Schools (1852), and the Workers' Educational Association (1903).

In America, Benjamin Franklin was instrumental in organizing discussion groups known as the Junto. The intellectual and social climate in the United States, however, was not favorable to the growth of the ideals of the French Enlightenment supported by Franklin and other Americans at the top of the socio-political pyramid. The American Bible Society (1816) and the American Tract Society (1842) were concerned with adult literacy education. Illiterate adults, it was recognized, could not read the Bible. Malcolm Knowles states that the earliest form of discreet nineteenth-century adult educational activity operated by Catholics was the reading circles frequently associated with parish libraries (1854).[18] Knowles may be too generous in claiming such an early beginning for Roman Catholic adult religious education. Most religious learning by Catholics was incidental and related to their participation in parish liturgies. In 1934, the Confraternity of Christian Doctrine was founded for the purpose of providing religious education for children not attending parochial schools. Gradually the Confraternity moved in the direction of setting up discussion groups for adults. The key date for the beginning of Roman Catholic adult religious education would more likely be 1934. As Sebastian Miklas wrote in 1959, "as far as Catholics are concerned, adult education is in its infancy."[19] As for Jewish adult religious education, David Zlatin suggests that 1914 is a benchmark date; it was at this time that synagogues began sponsoring public forums. A period of rapid growth in synagogue adult religious education continued after 1921.[20]

The Lyceum movement was launched in 1826. Lyceums were concerned with the dissemination of useful knowledge and were community-based. The movement peaked in 1835 with the registration of over 3,500 local Lyceums. Other early adult education associations in America were the Cooper Union (1859), the Peoples' Institute (1897), and the Chautauqua movement. The Chautauqua movement began in 1874 and was an outgrowth of educational activities sponsored by the Methodist Episcopal Church. Eventually other Protestant bodies collaborated in providing a type of adult education that evolved out of camp meetings. Chautauqua meetings, however, were much more sedate than the enthusiastic camp meetings of early America. Programs were initially concerned with organizing, administering, and teaching in the Sunday school context.

John H. Vincent, a Methodist clergyman, published *The Chautauqua Movement* in 1886. He noted that while religion is the basis of all education, all knowledge (sacred and secular) is sacred to the religious person. Eventually the Chautauqua movement stressed liberal education for adults and programs embraced a wide variety of topics. The movement was popular in small towns, and by 1894 over 10,000 study circles had been formed.

Without diminishing the importance of the adult education enterprises of the nineteenth century, it should be emphasized that the adult education movement in the United States did not begin in earnest until well into the twentieth century. In 1926, the American Association of Adult Education was founded. The organization was absorbed in 1951 by a new national organization, the Adult Education Association of the United States of America. In the same time period (1926) Eduard Lindeman produced *The Meaning of Adult Education,* a work that must be classified as a watershed in the history of American adult education.[21]

Adult education in North America, as a major movement affecting the socio-cultural system, is yet in a gestatory period, notwithstanding the fact that there are nearly two score university graduate programs that prepare adult educators professionally.[22] It could be stated that the adult education movement had its earliest roots in Jewish rabbinical schools and in Christian academies of higher learning, but this would be claiming too much. Neither the rabbinical schools nor the early Christian academies attempted to reach adults on the grand scale. The main purpose of these schools was the continuance of the scribal culture through the education of adults who were to assume leadership positions in religious institutions. The historical antecedents of the adult education movement as we know it today, a movement that aims at the provision of educational opportunities for all adults, must be located in the ideals of the French and German Enlightenment. This is not to disparage the contributions of religious people to the development of the modern adult education movement. If anything, religious people must be congratulated for assimilating Enlightenment values that led to the democratization of knowledge.

Conclusion

Two general inferences may be made from this brief historical overview. The tendency among religious educators of adults to deal only with theological ideas and explicitly religious themes may be traced to a historical emphasis on childhood religious education, an emphasis that valued the transmission of doctrinal/biblical subjects to children. Second, the tendency of many religious educators of adults to form adults (indoctrinate?) rather than provide programs of religious education that stimulate critical inquiry is rooted in the same historical matrix.

The conventional wisdom of modern adult religious education did not appear suddenly without historical antecedents. The beliefs about adult religious education that constitute the conventional wisdom can be understood adequately only in the light of history.

Notes

[1] For a fuller treatment of adult learning projects see Allen Tough's *The Adult's Learning Projects* (Toronto: Ontario Institute for Studies in Education, 1971). See also Patrick Penland's "Self-Initiated Learning," in *Adult Education* 29, no.3 (1979): 170-79.

[2] Benjamin Bloom et al., *Taxonomy of Educational Objectives: Cognitive Domain* (New York: David Mackay, 1956).

[3] For a summary of the Essene "catechumenate," refer to Flavius Josephus, *Josephus: Complete Works*, trans. W. Whiston (Grand Rapids: Kregel, 1960), 476-78.

[4] Cf. Alan Richardson, *A Theological Word Book of the Bible* (New York: Macmillan, 1967), 269f and 121.

[5] Quoted in Erich Fromm, *Marx's Concept of Man* (New York: Frederick Ungar, 1961), 19.

[6] Simon S. Laurie, *Historical Survey of Pre-Christian Education* (London: Longmans, Green, 1907), 78-100.

[7] Martin Hengel, *Judaism and Hellenism*, trans. John Bowden, (Philadelphia: Fortress, 1974), 66ff.

[8] For the information contained in this section of the chapter we acknowledge our indebtedness to E. Power's *Main Currents in the History of Education* (New York: McGraw-Hill, 1962) and to H. I. Marrou's celebrated *A History of Education In Antiquity*, trans. George Lamb (New York: New American Library, 1956).

[9] Cf. Alexander M. Schindler's "Jewish Religious Education," in *An Introduction to Christian Education,* ed. M. J. Taylor (Nashville: Abingdon, 1966), 375.

[10] G. G. Coulton, *Medieval Panorama* (London: Cambridge University Press, 1944), 388.

[11] Cf. Philippe Aries, *Centuries of Childhood*, trans. R. Baldick (New York: Vintage, 1962), and John Harold Plumb's *In the Light of History* (New York: Dell, 1972) 153ff.

[12] Paul N. Mussen, *The Psychological Development of the Child* (Englewood Cliffs: Prentice-Hall, 1965), 2.

[13] Merrill F. Elias et al., *Basic Processes in Adult Developmental Psychology* (St. Louis: C. V. Mosby, 1977) 4-6.

[14] Charlotte Buhler, *Der menschliche Lebenslauf als psychologisches Problem* (Leipzig: S. Mirzel, 1933). An updated report of Buhler's research may be found in her article, "The Course of Human Life as a Psychological Problem," in *Human Development II* (1968), 184-200.

[15] Henry David Thoreau, *Walden and Civil Disobedience* (Boston: Houghton Mifflin, 1960), 75.

[16] Quoted in Thomas Kelly, *A History of Adult Education in Great Britain* (Liverpool: Liverpool University Press, 1970), 64.

[17] C. H. Grattan, *In Quest of Knowledge: A Historical Perspective on Adult Education* (New York: Arno, 1971), 72.

[18] Malcolm Knowles, ed., *Handbook for Adult Education in the United States* (New York: Association, 1960), 23.

[19] Sebastian Miklas, *Principles and Problems of Catholic Adult Education* (Washington, D.C.: Catholic University of America Press, 1959), 3.

[20] David Zlatin, "Synagogue Adult Education," in *Lifelong Learning: The Adult Years* 3, no.1 (1979): 14.

[21] Eduard Lindeman, *The Meaning of Adult Education* (New York: Harvest House, 1926).

[22] Gabriel Moran sees the professional field of adult education as possessing doubtful value. See his book *Education Toward Adulthood: Religion and Lifelong* (New York: Paulist, 1979) 3-15. This may represent a specious reaction of a theologian whose grasp of adult education is, to put it kindly, minimal. For a systematic analysis of the conceptual foundations of adult education, see Robert D. Boyd and Jerold Apps, *Redefining the Discipline of Adult Education* (San Francisco: Jossey-Bass, 1980).

ADULT RELIGIOUS EDUCATION
PROBLEM AREAS

For decades adult educators have gloried in reports that indeed a majority of adults are "lifelong learners." Tough reported that nearly all the subjects of his study were engaged in a variety of learning projects in a year's time. Actually, however, the assumption that adults can and do learn has been accepted since Thorndike offered "proof" through his landmark research in the 1920s. In fact, we now know that even Thorndike was a pessimist in the sense that the ability to learn declines much later and at a slower rate than even he believed. Research since that time has explained the ways adults learn, their orientation to learning, and factors that affect their rate of learning—motivation and conditions for learning. At least one element that most studies have in common is the assertion that adults want to learn, and specifically with regard to voluntary learning programs, they will participate to the extent that they perceive needs to be met or problems to be solved through their involvement.

In light of the evidence that most adults can learn, that they want to and will learn, and that they actively seek learning opportunities, it is cause for concern that religious education programs planned for adults often suffer from low participation. Statistically, fewer than fifty percent of adult church members take advantage of educational programs planned by their church. Even when programs are planned in light of the literature describing adults' needs and life tasks, religious educators are frequently disappointed that adults do not attend in greater numbers. Adults seem not to be actively seeking the kinds of learning activities their churches sponsor. In short, many do not see the church as a viable provider of quality adult education.

Religious educators have used a variety of convenient excuses to rationalize the low attendance rates in their adult program offerings. "Just not dedicated enough" may top the list, but it is not uncommon to hear rationalizations for low attendance that border on the pseudo-mystical. "It doesn't matter how many adults attend our programs. God judges our efforts, not our accomplishments in term of numbers. Let's not play the numbers game. The Holy Spirit is in charge and all is well." Lest we be considered infidels, let us acknowledge that yes, God does judge our efforts, and yes, the Holy Spirit is in charge. Let us also acknowledge that this argument represents a not too artful dodge of personal accountability on our part while seeking to shift the blame for low attendance elsewhere.

Indeed large enrollments in themselves do not signify that an educational program is successful. But attendance rates do provide information for an analysis of the relative impact of educational programs and can be measures for the assessment of program appeal. In places where attendance rates are low, and fiscal and human resources limited, it may be advisable to close down the adult religious education program and pool resources with neighboring churches.

The Interest in Participation/Nonparticipation

A myriad of studies have explored reasons why adults do and do not participate in adult education. The wave of interest in why they participate was intense in the 1960s and early '70s. Population samples were fairly easy to identify; just find a group of adults actively participating in an educational activity and ask them why they are there! In the '70s and '80s interest turned to the motivational orientations of adults, and to explorations of reasons why they *do not* choose to participate. Merriam and Caffarella offer a brief but adequate overview of the past thirty years of research into participation.[1]

A number of studies conducted to date would no doubt reveal telling data if applied to adult participation in religious education. For example, to address the issue of participation, Hayes and Darkenwald used an instrument titled "Adult Attitudes Toward Continuing Education Scale." They identified three conceptual dimensions of attitudes they named Enjoyment of Learning, Importance of Adult Education, and Intrinsic Value of Adult Education.[2] It is no stretch to observe that adults who encompass all three attitudes (they enjoy learning and understand both the importance and intrinsic value of adult education) may still not only fail to participate, but may actively *avoid* adult programs offered by parishes and churches!

McKenzie and Shipp were perhaps the first to study seriously reasons for participation of adults in adult *religious* education. In the 1980s, their factor analytic study among Roman Catholics was replicated numerous times with similar findings in a variety of faith traditions by their students at Indiana University. As an example, one such study conducted among Protestants is profiled below.[3] The factors, named according to a salient theme arising from the pattern of reasons given for nonparticipation, were:

- *Secular Orientation*: Reasons clustered in this factor seem to indicate a profile of people who no longer consider the church a viable alternative for investment of their time and attention.
- *Resistance to Education*: People who were not oriented to education in general were described as "resistant to education." They seem almost to be overwhelmed and intimidated in the educational setting.
- *Estrangement*: This factor was so named because the reasons included in the cluster give a profile of adults who are estranged, or feel excluded from relationship within the congregation.
- *Aversion to Church-based Education*: Some people who are interested in learning do not believe the church-sponsored educational programs have anything to offer them.
- *Marginality*: There are those adults "on the fringe," who are not included in activities because of their own inaction rather than by active choice.
- *Activity*: Adults described by this factor gave reasons for nonparticipation that centered around time or activity, such as being too busy with work and family.

Not all of the adults in the study gave all of these reasons. What all of these studies uncovered were general patterns of nonparticipation that exist in the population of nonparticipants as a whole.

It may be instructive to note that all the reasons contained in the six factors of the above research example fall into the three categories of "barriers to participation" identified by Cross.[4] *Situational* barriers were represented by the "Activity" factor, which contained the work and family-related reasons for nonparticipation. The fact that for some the scheduling of activities is inconvenient presents an *institutional* barrier.

It appears that many more of the reasons, spread among the other factors, are *dispositional* barriers. These are in a sense related to a "state of mind" but also encompass attitudes and values. These ill-defined dispositions seem to pervade nonparticipation studies as adults exhibited some degree of aversion to the program offerings of their churches and parishes.

Reasons for not participating given by adults, when factor analyzed, suggest an attitude of expectation (negative) toward not only the educational activities of the church but also toward the church or parish that offers them. Many adults seem to assume that their needs or interests are outside the scope of what their churches can or are willing to address. Stated differently, the "anticipated benefits" of participation were not sufficient to entice adults to attend.

At this point we can take one of two tacks: (1) We can interpret the findings of the study by blaming adults for nonparticipation (we can say, for example, that they are just not sufficiently committed), or (2) we can search for problems in the ways adult religious education programs are developed. The latter route seems more productive for present purposes. Analysis of the data developed in this and similar studies points to several problem areas in the theory and practice of adult religious education. We will return to the six factors of nonparticipation later in this chapter, but first let us delineate some key problems in the current theory and practice of adult religious education.

Problem Areas

With no intention to appear cynical, it seems clear that many local churches and parishes are: (1) dominated by a scribal caste vis-à-vis the determination of program content, (2) ordinated out of all proportion toward formative rather than critical education, (3) fixated on theological content and explicitly religious content to the exclusion of all other adult concerns, (4) conducted by religious educators who are prepared academically in theology and only minimally in the study of education as a social practice, and (5) conceived in a research vacuum.

Determination of Program Content

In the middle of the fifth century BC, during the reign of Josiah in Judea, the learned priest Esdra called the people together for a solemn reading of the "newly discovered" Book of Moses. This occasion is often cited as the event that marked the inauguration of a new institution among the Jews: the establishment of a new social class, the *sopherim* or scribes.[5] The scribe was adept at reading and writing, and also functioned in the role of expounder or teacher.

The introduction of written materials into preliterate cultures, or largely preliterate cultures, produced profound changes in those cultures. The introductory phrase "It is written" became a signal that the message to be delivered by the expounder was authentic, authoritative, and vested in power and mystery. Use of the written word, of course, required people who were trained in writing (coding) and reading (decoding). These skills were not easy to come by. For the majority of adults living at the time of transition from an aural-oral culture to a visual culture, the written word was fraught with an almost divine character.

The emergence of a literate class alongside an unlettered majority was associated with a new social division or stratification. One became a member of a higher social class (and sometimes a higher socio-political class) by being able to read and write. Those chosen in childhood for scribal roles were recruited from the upper echelons of society. However one interprets the social processes and dynamics involved, literacy influenced social stratification immensely. Class boundaries, if not already established, became more pronounced: those who could read and write became leaders and teachers; those who lacked literacy skills became followers and listeners. A scribal culture was set over against the vulgar culture.

Literacy suited a person for membership in the scribal culture; it also bestowed the power that comes from being recognized as an expert. The scribe was looked to for decisions, interpretations, and directions. The scribe was not only the possessor of a mysterious skill (in the minds of the vulgar); he was also the possessor of wisdom. He controlled the most valuable of human resources: knowledge. In so doing he controlled, to a large degree, the society in which he lived.

The division of society into two major classes in terms of literacy also obtained in early Christianity. The church as a community of believers was not unaffected by the trends that influenced the development of other communities and societies. There arose a special class, almost a separate caste.

The account of the emergence of two classes within the church is not presented in an effort to condemn. The advance of civilization depended on those who mastered the techniques of literacy. The ability to read and write, as we shall see later, is related to the very development of human consciousness. Lacking the sophisticated form of consciousness associated with literacy, the human race would have stagnated. Christianity proposed that an equal valuation be placed on all individuals, that while there were many works there was but one spirit, that in the church there was neither Greek nor Jew, freeman nor slave, male nor female. But these normative ideals did not inhibit stratification. There would be, inevitably, the scribes who wielded power and the majority who were subject to this power; there would be those who determined what would be learned and, ineluctably, those who learned what was determined for them to learn.

To express the matter in a different way: It was not the fault of Christianity that individual Christians often did not learn how to deal with one another as brothers and sisters within a system of socio-political stratification. Even at this point in the development of the human race we have not learned how to be unified with one another in a truly caring way within the structures imposed by socio-political stratification. We hardly see the person who collects our garbage; we pay great deference to someone who is wealthy or in a position of power.

Social stratification can be examined in terms of the differentiation of social roles and the division of labor.[6] When a person moved into a role that required special competencies, the person also came to be defined in terms of the role. Responsibilities were associated with the role of scribe, and so also was a degree of social power. It is doubtful that any society ever existed without some degree of stratification. The vision of a classless society is perhaps unrealizable; the vision of a perfectly attenuated and homogenous society—a society without a variable division of social power—is chimeric. Individuals may be equal in the eyes of God and under the law, but, de facto, people are not equal in regard to the richness of their experiences, their acquired competencies, and their social roles. All previous societies in recorded history were in some way hierarchically structured; people attached a variable significance to these roles in proportion to the manner these roles were perceived as contributing to the survival and development of society.

That a scribal class came into being in the church, that certain individuals were vested with expert power, and that these individuals used this power for purposes of social control are facts of life. Without this control the church would have perished long ago in a twilight scripted by anarchy. What is recounted here, then, is simply that a scribal class came into being and that this scribal class was set over against a vulgar class.

The person who advanced into the scribal class and fulfilled the role of expounder was in a position to exercise expert power. But expert power is but one type of power. French and Raven developed a typology of the bases of social power that is germane to the present discussion.[7] Five types of power are delineated in regard to the relationship between the possessor of power and those who are influenced by the power:

(1) Expert power is based on the perception of those who are influenced that someone has special knowledge or expertise.
(2) Legitimate power is based on the perception of those who are influenced that someone has a legal right to prescribe behavior for others.
(3) Coercive power is based on the perception of those who are influenced that someone has the ability to mediate punishments.
(4) Reward power is based on the perception of those who are influenced that someone has the ability to mediate rewards.
(5) Referent power is based on the-identification of those who are influenced with an individual or group, e.g., I behave in a certain way because I refer to a group for behavioral norms.

The scribe possessed expert power. When the scribe became an official in the institutional church, i.e., a cleric, legitimate power was added to expert power. Once the church gained political ascendancy in the aftermath of Constantine, the scribe-cleric became also a possessor of reward and coercive power. Those who have been in power historically in the church have been ecclesiastics, clerics, theologians, and pastors. They have been accustomed to using power in a highly directive way; governance by way of *ipse dixit* has been the historical pattern. "You are to do this because I am the legitimate expert in religious matters and the holder of divine rewards and punishments which are mediated through me." In all fairness it must be mentioned that highly directive ways of using power are not characteristic in all Christian traditions, but these highly directive, and sometimes autocratic, orientations toward the use of power are predominative.

We can no more run away from the history of Christianity than we can run away from our individual histories. It is not difficult to see, then, how past uses of power in the church, uses of power based on the monarchical political model, have produced a residual effect in our own times regarding the determination of the content of parish adult education. The subject matters and topics treated in most parish adult education programs are determined by pastors and directors of religious education without regard for the self-perceived needs and interests of the adults who are to be served by the educational programs. The content of programs is determined unilaterally by those in positions of authority in local churches and parishes sometimes on the assumption that the pastor/religious educator knows best what adults need to know. In most instances, this assumption is both invalid and paternalistic.

Does this mean, then, that educational programs should be determined exclusively by adults and that religious educators may not contribute to the selection of topics that comprise the total educational program? Certainly not. There are occasions when the needs of the parish community must be served, occasions when adults should be put into contact with the norms and values of their particular religious traditions, occasions when (for the sake of the entire local church or parish) continuity with the traditions of a religious body must be emphasized. But adults must come to see these needs "on their own terms" which presents a unique challenge to the adult religious educator. The mere offering of prescribed programs with the enjoinder "You must attend" will be effective only in those places where adults are thoroughly dominated by pastoral power.

It must be heavily underscored that when we speak of adult education in local churches and parishes we are talking about *voluntary* adult education. Prescribed programs in business and industry attract employees because the programs are essentially nonvoluntary. Employees show up for presentations on company policy and procedures because they fear losing their jobs. (Whether they actually learn anything about company policies and procedures is a different question, and a complex question at that. But that is another issue).

Pastors and religious educators no longer possess coercive-reward power in most places. The faithful, then, must be consulted. Adults must have a strong part in determining what takes place in the adult education program. Religious educators must attempt to determine the educational needs and interests of adults. This does not mean that religious educators should refrain from proposing educational topics, from providing direction and guidance, or from reconciling the educational needs of adults with the educational needs of the parish or church as a community. We must, however, become more alert to adult concerns than to "subject matters" thought important by religious educators. For one thing, when the latter occurs it is easy for institutional concerns to override concern for the welfare and discipleship of adult members. When analyzed, both program and promotion may reveal (often subtly, sometimes subversively) emphases on institutional needs. This is particularly true of "leader training" where the subtle message is "Come to this training so you will be a better leader and so the organization will run better." Institutional needs are real and significant. However, the challenge is to meet the needs of the individual and group *while* meeting organizational needs. Perhaps a better approach might be focusing on the personal development of those called to be leaders, broadening the content to enable adults to generalize the skills developed to other arenas of life.

Formative and Critical Education

As we have seen, adult education may be formative or critical. Formative education emphasizes the reception on the part of the learners of "givens"; critical education stresses the evaluative examination of "givens." Formation is conceived as a process by which a learner is shaped by a teacher according to some a priori ideal or model. Critical education is conceived as a process by which teacher and learner engage in a systematic inquiry relating to the issue at hand.

Now that the distinction between formative and critical education has been made, it needs to be qualified. All critical education is somewhat formative: The adult who examines an issue critically cannot escape being influenced by the values that surround the issue. Likewise, all formation is somewhat critical: The adult who is subjected to formative education in twenty-first-century, post-industrialized societies is likely to examine critically that which is handed on. It is unlikely that adults who are accustomed to question most things evaluatively will merely accept information passively.

Nevertheless, a distinction between formative and critical education must be made as an expository device or methodological postulate. That is, the two types of education are contrasted as dichotomous, whereas they are really points on a continuum. The contrast is made to throw light on the approaches of religious educators to adult education. The point made here is that many religious education programs for adults stress formative education and neglect critical education. Both formative and critical educational processes are important. Indeed, they are complementary.

We have seen that formation is similar to what anthropologists call enculturation. Enculturation is a process by which a child assimilates the mental, cultural, and moral "furniture" that is in place in a given culture. The person who is enculturated assimilates, acquires, acquiesces; he accepts and receives that which is handed over. Enculturation aims at the development of a homogeneous group; convergent thinking and uniformity are encouraged. Acculturation is similar to enculturation. Acculturation refers to the assimilation of a culture other than the culture into which a person is born. While acculturation is not defined with any degree of consensus among anthropologists, it may be stated that acculturation stresses the accepting of that which is taught.[8]

Quite often the enculturative/acculturative processes occur informally. It is simply through living in a culture that a person learns the culture randomly and experientially. At times these processes are systematized, e.g., norms, mores, and folkways are transmitted via structured ceremonies; these processes may be systematized as formative education, instruction in a formal setting. Enculturation and formative education are culture's way of preserving itself. In the context of religious education, formative education assures the preservation of that which was handed on. The challenge to adults and their religious educators is to manage the tension as culture, tradition, and accepted ways of thinking are dissected for examination.

Critical education is culture's way of assuring its growth and development. Divergent thinking is permitted and even fostered; individual insight is prized over collective vision; the cultural "furniture" is taken apart and reassembled in new ways. In the context of religious education, critical education contributes to the growth and development of that which is handed on.

Let us suppose that someone wishes to join a particular fraternal organization. The person submits to a formative process. During the formative process he learns he must subscribe to the organization's meaning system or nomological network. There is no question of challenging that which is handed on. If the person does not accept that which is handed on, he merely disassociates himself from the organization. Or, if the person does not master that which has been handed on, the organization (through its officials) tells him that he is unacceptable for membership.

Critical education is best exemplified in the Socratic dialogue. It was Socrates' critical examination of the reigning meaning system of Athens that cost him his life. In the dialogue *Euthyphro,* Socrates encounters the priest, Euthyphro.[9] Euthyphro learns that Socrates has been brought before the authorities for introducing novelties in religious belief and for questioning the conventional wisdom. As a representative of the conventional wisdom, Euthyphro was certain he knew the meaning of piety. Through a series of incisive questions, Socrates leaves Euthyphro in a condition of angered perplexity. Euthyphro breaks off the dialogue when it becomes evident he is unable to define piety in absolute terms.

One of the foremost strategies for the facilitation of adult learning in the early church was based on the formative model. Faced with early challenges to Christian unity, the Christian community did not encourage critical examination of its tenets. Critical examination took place willy-nilly among many adults. There were always those who expressed heterodox or heretical teachings. The tendency to shy away from critical education today has its historical roots in early Christianity. In many local churches and parishes, and in some conservative religious traditions, the formative mode of adult religious education is very strong in order to preserve doctrine in its pristine condition. There is nothing wrong with formative education per se. But formative education that excludes critical education is little more than indoctrination. And indoctrination will not "work" for multitudes of adults today who are wont to use their critical powers. No doubt there will always be adults who want someone else to think for them. These adults are numerous, but as the level of education rises in the adult population, their numbers will be reduced substantially.

The problem of the exclusion of the critical mode of education in adult religious education is not due to willful attempts on the part of pastors and religious educators to practice cognitive imperialism and manipulation. Their motives are not in question. What is at work are those subtle and often unrecognized habits of mind that constitute a heritage received from previous centuries.

The Theological Fixation

In many, if not most, parishes and local churches, adults may learn about the Bible, ecclesiology, eschatology, liturgy, and a host of other theological or explicitly religious topics. They are unable to find help regarding income tax preparation, literacy, health practices, financial planning, and so forth. Secular learning for adults, it seems, is out of place in the church. The tendency of religious educators to disdain the everyday, mundane educational needs of adults has a long history. We have seen that most of the fathers of the church and the early Christian apologists taught that so-called sacred learning was alone important.

The sharp division between sacred and secular learning was a consequence of the dichotomization of reality advanced by the Platonic and neo-Platonic philosophies that dominated patterns of thought in the early Christian centuries. These patterns prevail today. That Christian thinking was thoroughly Hellenized cannot be disputed.

Plato described reality as consisting of the world of ideas set over against the world of everyday experience. The world of ideas was the locus of eternal and divine permanence. The world of historical experience, on the other hand, was a world of change, decay, and tenuous reality—a world that only dimly and imperfectly reflected the values of the world of ideas. Mircea Eliade has averred that Plato was the outstanding philosopher of the primitive mentality; Plato attempted to justify theoretically the vision of archaic humanity.[10]

Archaic peoples, and perhaps Plato himself, were aware of two kinds of experience: (1) consciousness of everyday reality and (2) consciousness, in moments of "peak" experiences, of the "totally other." Plato and his followers assumed that these experiences pointed out, as it were, two orders of reality. The Platonic dichotomization of reality, which served as a basis for Platonic epistemology, was recruited early on to serve as a schema for interpreting the religious presence in the world. The religious order (the element of the sacred) was set over against the merely human order (the secular element). Sacred learning (divine revelation) was opposed to secular learning (at worst a futile concern for the fleeting things of this world, at best "natural" revelation). The City of God, represented by the church, was preeminent; the City of Man was passing and not worthy of regard.

The political ramifications of this dichotomy were evidenced in the notion of the Two Realms, the temporal and the spiritual. It was claimed that the institutional church held jurisdiction over the sacred order of things—all those things ordinated to the supernatural end of man— while the duly constituted secular government held jurisdiction over the secular order of things—all those things related to the natural end of man. Attempts were made by some in the church to establish hegemony over secular jurisdictions on the basis of the superior value of the sacred order. This was carried to its logical conclusion in the middle ages when Boniface VIII declared in 1302 that for every human creature it is absolutely necessary for salvation to be subject to the Roman pontiff.

Just as the church qua institution experienced a stormy and adversarial relationship with secular political institutions, an adversarial stance by some Christian scholars was adopted in reference to secular sciences. The sacred sciences, it was claimed, must reign supreme. Theology must be the queen of the sciences and all other scholarly pursuits were to be subordinated to theology. If the knowledge generated in the "merely" secular sciences contradicted the knowledge produced by those in the sacred sciences, so much the worse for secular scholarship.

Parish programs of adult education that provide explicitly religious offerings and neglect secular learning are carrying on in the best tradition of Platonism. Further, these programs convey to many adults (some of whom do not divide reality into two neat categories) that the church is greatly concerned about ideas affecting its institutional welfare, but not about the welfare of people who struggle in the workaday world. Further, adult religious education programs that deal solely with theological subject matters and exclude so-called secular learning actually promote the fallacious notion that religion is something one does in church, and that religion is not coextensive with life.

Thus far we have reviewed three problem areas. Religious educators determine the content of educational programs unilaterally without reference to adult needs and interests; what happens in adult religious education is mostly formative and minimally (if at all) critical education; the content of most educational programs is exclusively theological in orientation. These three problem areas are interrelated. Taken together they are related even more directly to the academic preparation of those who fulfill the duties of religious educator in parishes and local churches.

The Preparation of Adult Religious Educators

A certain irony should strike any reader of this book (assuming an interest in the subject) that in a day when adult and continuing education is the "growing edge" of education and when university graduate programs in the field are proliferating, such emphases in seminaries, divinity schools, and even religious education programs are still difficult to find. A perusal of academic catalogs in the latter cases will reveal few if any courses in adult education, much less the possibility of a major emphasis. Granted, resources are too scarce in most settings for a broad array of offerings. There are two further ironies. By far, the people ministers will be preaching to, teaching, counseling and ministering with will be adults (this includes those who may serve as children's or youth ministers). Shouldn't we take time to understand them, to discover their developmental issues and how they learn so we can teach them effectively? The attitude of both academic administrators and ministers may be akin to that encountered by a DRE in enlisting adult church school teachers for training focused on effective ways to lead adults. The response of one woman, a public school elementary teacher and the teacher of a young adult class at church: "I just assumed that a person with a masters degree in elementary education did not need that training." The subtle assumption in religious academia seems to be that *being* an adult is sufficient to qualify one to teach or lead adults. Or, if one had a course in child psychology somewhere along the way, that is enough.

The other irony is that the smattering of courses that do address adult religious education as a field of study are ordinarily (though not always) taught by those who have advanced degrees in theological sciences, who have never attempted educational research, and who possess no credibility in the professional field of adult education. This issue of credibility deserves fuller treatment even if it is tangential to the central concern of the preparation of adult religious educators.

It seems that religious educators of adults possess little credibility as *real* adult educators for at least four reasons: (1) they are perceived as theologians who just happen to be interested in adult education; (2) they tend to isolate themselves from the general field of adult education; (3) they often employ language that is ambiguous (from the standpoint of education), archaic, and generally uncommunicative; and (4) they often do not *practice* sound adult education in their programming and teaching.

Item 1: Only a few hundred religious educators are listed among the several thousand members of the primary professional organization for adult educators, the American Association of Adult and Continuing Education. AAACE's annual meeting, its publications, and its special study sections are primary sources of research, information, and dialogue on adult education issues. Religious educators of adults tend to associate with one another while avoiding association with professional adult educators through AAACE. Indeed, many are not even aware of its existence! Credibility is related to visibility.

Item 2: Since the first edition of this book, the situation with regard to religious educators' written contributions to the broader field has changed little. A review of *Adult Education Quarterly*, the journal of research and theory in adult education, reveals few articles by adult religious educators, including practitioners *and* professors of religious education.

Item 3: Certain terminology in continued use by religious educators seems increasingly archaic and fails to communicate with contemporary adults. For example, Scott points out that "catechesis" and "catechetics" have no currency outside ecclesiastical circles.[11] The ability of the linguistic world of catechetics "to probe the religious and educational questions of our time is severely curtailed by a parochial and introverted self interest."[12]

Drop Scott's reference to catechetics and his criticism applies equally to much of Protestant religious education's language as "parochial and introverted self interest." For example, few would argue that the term "Sunday school" is both archaic *and* fails to describe the educational activities provided for adults under this rubric. It also carries substantial "baggage." For many adults, the term Sunday school denotes activities for children, and they have no interest in anything under that heading. It has come to imply anything simple and irrelevant, as in "Ah, that's Sunday-school stuff." Many churches and parishes have begun to use more descriptive titles like Adult Bible Study (the primary use of the time and focus of the program) to avoid these problems.

Item 4: While extolling the uniqueness of adult concerns and learning processes, religious educators of adults continue to violate even the most basic principles of teaching adults. For example, while proclaiming that "teaching is not telling," many religious educators concentrate on information dissemination to the neglect of reflection, interaction, and encouragement of serious study. If any reflection or interaction occurs, often it must be outside the classroom or apart from the learning activity itself. Apparently they fail to realize the importance of modeling the best in adult education practice.

Rather than outline an academic program for adult religious educators, let it suffice to list the subject matter religious educators should master in order to be effective in programming for and leading adults.

Theoretical foundations. As a basis for sound practice, religious educators who would claim professional identity as "experts" in distinctly *adult* religious education must have a grasp of the various philosophical positions set forth historically in the field. A good survey of the broader field may be found in Merriam and Elias's *Foundations of Adult Education*. More recent contributions include McKenzie's *Adult Education and Worldview Construction* and numerous perspectives shared over the past ten years in *Adult Education Quarterly* (a subscription that comes with membership in AAACE).[13] Theological foundations may be added by consulting Elias, *Studies in Theology and Education* (of primary interest to Catholic educators), and Nelson, *How Faith Matures* (of more interest to Protestant educators). Chapter two of Wickett's *Models of Religious Education Practice* is useful to all traditions.

Developmental characteristics. There is a plethora of literature on the changing views of adult development, and though early contributions of those like Havighurst ("Developmental tasks") and Erikson ("Eight psychosocial stages of man") are still worthy of note, the field has generally moved beyond stage theories to consideration of life span studies and a reflection of the dynamic nature of adulthood. A thorough familiarity with the literature is essential to program planning that meets the needs of adults along their developmental journey.

Characteristics of adults as a learners. It is one thing to proclaim that adults do not learn in the same ways as children, but quite another to articulate exactly *how* they learn differently. In fact, it has been argued that adults and children do not learn differently at all. They *do*, however, approach learning differently. In what unique ways, then, do adults approach a learning task, and what are the determining factors for how adults learn? What is the role of experience in learning? What affects adults' motivation to participate in a learning activity?

An understanding of adults as learners is foundational to facilitating their learning. Approaches that match the content and goals of learning must be selected. Thus, religious educators must also give attention to the teaching-learning processes in adult education. We will address these subjects in subsequent chapters. However, Brookfield, Galbraith, and Merriam and Caffarella are but a few excellent sources published in the past decade to consult for a thorough understanding of adults as learners, as well as approaches to effect facilitation of learning. Joyce and Weld offer a compendium of models of teaching.[14]

An understanding of adult learners and processes that facilitate their learning has implications for provision of a conductive learning climate. Knowles claimed that creating such a climate was the single most important thing he did as an adult educator. Physical comfort and a healthy psychological environment are but two of the factors that contribute to such a climate.

Research and statistics in adult education. At this point the reader may be tempted to close the book and say to the writers, "Get real." However, if the religious educator is to read *Adult Education Quarterly* with understanding, and if he or she is to conduct decision-oriented research (as in conducting an *adequate* needs assessment), there must be an ability to understand research design, including sampling techniques and at least descriptive statistical applications. Religious educators *can* conduct a self-directed study of research approaches, though the study of statistics may require a tutor in addition to reading. The best avenue may be an introductory course at a nearby college or university.

Program-planning approaches with adults. Effective programs for adults, adult educators as well as most adults will agree, are based on an assessment of needs and interests. Program-planning models abound (we will offer our own later), and the setting and audience often dictate the approach used. The point to be made here is that with a variety of models available in the expanding literature on program planning for adults, there is little justification for unilateral decision-making and program planning by religious educators. In addition, a familiarity with an array of models for religious education programming is essential. Wickett provides a somewhat comprehensive overview of models for adult religious education practice.

This list is by no means exhaustive and many specific issues could be added. These are seen as basic to effective practice *and* to identification as a professional adult religious educator.

The Research Vacuum

In the first edition of this book the assertion was made that lack of research in the field of adult religious education constituted a major block to any substantive progress in the field. In nearly twenty years the situation has changed little. While the literature base in the field certainly has increased, not much of what has been published contributes to theory building, an essential foundation of any serious educational enterprise. Thus, the same conclusion stands, namely that lacking sound research data any number of claims can be made as to what "works" in adult religious education. Perhaps religious educators with adults should not be faulted severely, since theory building in the larger field of adult education is not well developed. This is because research in adult education may be said to have barely passed its infancy!

Some may question whether we should bother with research in a field where we are concerned with the "spiritual" welfare of adults. But the position of this work is that to be concerned with the spiritual welfare of adults is to be concerned about their functioning in the "temporal" world in which the Divine has placed them, presumably, in part, to care for one another. If we are to assist in improving their functioning, in helping them reach their potential as divinely endowed, they must be involved in learning. Ah! And how does learning occur? In what settings and under what circumstances does it occur best? In what ways can we plan and administer programs to enhance the effectiveness of their learning? There is no end to the questions that may follow logically upon these examples.

How are questions such as these to be answered? Long suggests at least four sources of information to guide us: authority, experience, intuition, and science.[17] Unfortunately, religious educators with adults are likely to rely on the first three almost exclusively. It is easy (perhaps in some traditions mandatory) to defer to an authority figure or bureaucracy to hand down the principles and "answers" upon which programs are to be built (indeed, even the programs themselves "come from above"). Never mind that these authorities are largely trained theologians with little or no knowledge or experience in education. It is also easy to rely on our own experience, generalizing it to our constituency, assuming our experience is normative. Intuition is often the source of approaches to problem-solving, ascription of needs, and assumptions regarding appropriate approaches. While there is nothing inherently *wrong* with intuition, at least as a starting point, it is rarely sufficient or entirely accurate.

Scientific approaches, hereafter referred to as research, are preferred by serious adult educators. Whereas intuition may be a source of what might be termed "soft" data, research provides "hard" data upon which more confidence may be placed as a foundation for decision-making and problem-solving (although wise researchers avoid claiming data derived from such approaches *prove* a conclusion and choose to speak instead of "confidence levels"). It may be argued that only scientific research adequately answers the crucial questions that build sound theory and improve practice. For example, two foci of research in adult education over the past twenty years, adult learning theory and motivation for participation (and reasons for nonparticipation), have contributed significantly both to the theory base and to more effective practice.

It seems that the situation in adult religious education with regard to research trails by roughly twenty years the serious pursuit of research in the broader field. It may be argued that the most serious and most scientific research in adult religious education is done by graduate students at major universities such as the University of Georgia and Indiana University. Seminarians educated in the classical model follow the approach of most Ph.D. studies in theology and thus do library-based historical and/or philosophical research. Few include field research.

At this point clarity requires a definition of research before reviewing the two major types of inquiry available to religious educators who refuse to rely solely upon authority, experience, or intuition. Long posits an adequate definition of research as "systematic observation and interpretation of data associated with the process of problem definition, observation, data collection, interpretation, and conclusion."[18] A review of research reports in *Adult Education Quarterly* over the past ten to fifteen years reveals that data generated for such observation, collection, and interpretation has been primarily through empirical approaches. Such "quantitative" approaches seek to quantify everything for "number crunching" for application of simple descriptive statistics (i.e., frequency tables) or more sophisticated treatment as through factor or regression analyses. Computers and the availability of statistical software packages enable researchers to analyze data at home or in their offices without mainframes or punch cards. The participation studies previously described are examples of such quantitative or empirical research and were analyzed by such means.

The Search Institute Report

A notable exception to the dearth of field-based or empirical research in adult religious education is Search Institute's "Effective Christian Education: a National Study of Protestant Congregation." In 1989, with the help of a Lilly Endowment grant, Search Institute in Minneapolis undertook a research project among six major Protestant denominations to determine factors that contribute to the development of mature

FAITH TYPES AMONG MAINLINE ADULTS: AGE BY GENDER

Age	Gender	FAITH TYPES			
		Undeveloped Faith (%)	Vertical Faith (%)	Horizontal Faith (%)	Integrated Faith (%)
20–39	Males	54	5	29	13
	Females	43	14	21	23
40–59	Males	50	6	29	15
	Females	30	12	17	40
60 or older	Males	32	6	27	35
	Females	20	13	13	49

Peter L. Benson, Carolyn H. Elkin, *Effective Christian Education: A National Study of Protestant Congregations* (Search Institute, March 1990) 18.

or "integrated" faith.[19] Search Institute surveyed eleven thousand people from a stratified random sample of 561 congregations in six Protestant denominations. The focus of attention was formal Christian education programs designed to teach the faith. Both the research and the conclusions of the researchers are noteworthy and are summarized below. The source of the summary is the official report[20] and a follow-up book titled *The Teaching Church: Moving Christian Education to Center Stage*[21] by Eugene Roehlkepartain, one of the research associates.

With the help of leaders and adults from the six participating denominations, as well as through literature review, Search identified eight "core dimensions" of faith that became the basis for their research. Thus, a person with mature faith:

(1) Trusts in God's saving grace and believes firmly in the humanity and divinity of Jesus.
(2) Experiences a sense of personal well-being, security, and peace.
(3) Integrates faith and life, seeing work, family, social relationships, and political choices as part of one's religious life.
(4) Seeks spiritual growth through study, reflection, prayer, and discussion with others.
(5) Seeks to be part of a community of believers in which people give witness to their faith and support and nourish one another.
(6) Holds life-affirming values, including commitment to racial and gender equality, affirmation of cultural and religious diversity, and a personal sense of responsibility for the welfare of others.

FAITH MATURITY

	Low	Moderate	High
1	2 3	4 5	6 7

All Adults	4.63
20-29	4.40
30-39	4.45
40-49	4.53
50-59	4.66
60-69	4.78
70 or older	4.96
Males	4.51
Females	4.71

Peter L. Benson, Carolyn H. Elkin, *Effective Christian Education: A National Study of Protestant Congregations* (Search Institute, March 1990) 12.

(7) Advocates social and global change to bring about greater social justice.
(8) Serves humanity, consistently and passionately, through acts of love and justice.[22]

From these eight dimensions, thirty-eight "indicators" were derived and developed into survey items. For the most part the researchers used simple descriptive statistics to report their findings as indicated in the accompanying tables provided as examples.

To summarize their findings, Search discovered that thirty-two percent of all adults have integrated faith (integrating the vertical and horizontal dimensions). Thirty-six percent are in the undeveloped faith category. They also discovered major gender differences, with thirty-eight percent of women having integrated faith compared with twenty-one percent of men in the survey. As might be expected, faith maturity increases with age. Also of interest is their finding that "denomination is not nearly as important as the dynamics of congregational life for explaining faith maturity."[23]

Search actually discovered six factors related to congregational life that were important in faith formation. In order of importance they were: quality of formal Christian education, a thinking climate, a climate of warms, the quality of worship, a caring fellowship, and service to others.[24] Roehlkepartain reports, "Churches with thinking climates expect people to devote time to thought and study. They expect members to grow and learn and think for themselves. They encourage people to ask tough questions about themselves, their world, and God."[25]

One further significant finding of the Search project, though not surprising, is that the way Christian education is done in a congregation is as important as any single area of the church's life together. Specifically with regard to educational process and content, they found the following characteristics in the churches where adults scored high on the faith maturity index:

Teachers
Are high in mature faith
Know educational theory and methods for adults

Pastor
Has high commitment to educational program for adults
Devotes significant hours to adult Christian education program
Knows educational theory and practice of Christian education
for adults

Educational Process
Emphasizes building understanding of faith applied to political
and social issues and understanding of oppression and
injustice
Emphasizes life experiences as occasion for spiritual insight
Creates sense of community in which people help each other
develop faith and values
Emphasizes the natural unfolding of faith and recognizes each
person's faith journey as unique
Strongly encourages independent thinking and questioning

Peer Involvement
Has high percentage of adults active in Christian education

Goals
Has clear mission statement for adult education
Has clear learning objectives

These are stated as the ideal, with acknowledgement that most are not well-developed in the congregations surveyed.

An Alternative to Quantitative Approaches

More recently qualitative research, an old but previously disdained approach, has gained respect. Unfortunately, competition between dedicated empirical researchers and those who prefer other approaches is sharp and has prevented needed dialogue. Some journals have in the past refused to publish qualitative research. In fact, as Kidder and Fine point out, "Quantitative researchers who value numerical precision over 'navel gazing' and qualitative researchers who prefer rich details to 'number crunching' betrays not only a preference for one but also a distrust of the other."[27] Cook and Reichardt claim that at the heart of the conflict are philosophical differences between the schools of realism and idealism, and therefore the two approaches should be seen as separate paradigms. In their apologetic for qualitative methods, they observe:

> It is the clash with respect to these basic philosophical stances toward the nature of the social order which distinguishes quantitative and qualitative paradigms. The quantitative paradigm's approach to social life employs the mechanistic and static assumptions of the natural science positivism model . . . . On the other hand, the qualitative paradigm has the decidedly humanistic cast to understanding social reality of the idealist position which stresses an evolving, negotiated view of the social order. The qualitative paradigm perceives social life as the shared creativity of individuals. It is this sharedness which produces a reality perceived to be objective, extant, and knowable to all participants in social interaction.[28]

Is qualitative research credible? Merriam cites Piaget's work on stages of cognitive development; Kubler-Ross's work on death and dying; Levinson's study of male development; Gilligan's work on moral development; and more recently Belenky and associates' well-known research reported in *Women's Ways of Knowing* as examples of qualitative research.[29]

The foregoing discussion is provided as mere introduction for religious educators who may find qualitative research more applicable to their needs for gathering information about their adult parishioners. They seem particularly well-suited to inquiry into faith development, attitudes, past religious experiences, personal goals, and life issues that religious educators can address. In qualitative research there are no predetermined hypotheses to be proved or disproved, no need for experimental and control groups, and no need to quantify data (though this is not precluded). A key strength is that phenomena are reported from the perspective of the subject. This does not mean the research can take less care to maintain objectivity, reliability, and validity. One of the major criticisms of qualitative research historically has been the lack of safeguards that prevent manipulation of the subjects and the data, and the subjectivity of the conclusions drawn. Such were the criticisms of Allan Tough's early research that sought to query adults about their learning project.

The uniqueness of qualitative approaches lies largely in their data gathering techniques. Wolcott groups all such techniques into three categories he commonly calls watching (or experiencing), asking (inquiring), and reviewing (examining).[30] In the research literature these would be labeled with more sophistication as observing, interviewing, and archival research, but Wolcott's terms are more descriptive. When engaged in watching, the researcher is concerned with gathering sensory data; asking involves probing for feelings, perceptions, and opinions through conversation or interviews; when reviewing, the source of data is likely materials prepared by others (as in library research). The focus is most often upon experience and the meaning adults derive from their experience. Merriam observes that "qualitative researchers are interested in *meaning*—how people make sense of their lives, what they experience, how they interpret these experiences, how they structure their social worlds. It is assumed that meaning is embedded in people's experiences and mediated through the investigator's own perceptions."[31]

Through watching, asking, and reviewing, adult religious educators may glean valuable data about people's understandings of not only explicitly religious themes (as in doctrines of their religious tradition), but also life issues and their interpretations of experiences. Whether the researcher is concerned with gathering data about parishers' "stages of faith," the factors that influence faith formation, or specific life needs (all of which are difficult to quantify), qualitative approaches may be appropriate. However, there are many examples of research that mix both qualitative and quantitative approaches for data gathering and analysis.

As previously stated, this somewhat lengthy treatment of qualitative research is provided as an introduction for religious educators. The intent is to encourage cessation of reliance upon outside authority, intuition, or our own experience in order to *guess* what people want and need, what their perceptions are, and what faith and life issues they have. Merriam makes the case well when she says, "The potentional for discovery, a researcher's sensitivity and analytic abilities, and increasing resources for help in the technical aspects of data collection and analysis form a mixture ripe for new significant additions to be made to the knowledge base of adult education."[32] The same may be said of the potential contribution of such approaches to adult religious education. Religious educators are referred to Harry F. Wolcott's *The Basic Technique in Qualitative Inquiry* for a fuller treatment of qualitative research.

Conclusion

Some who read this chapter will give serious thought to the problems identified. It would be frivolous to think that others would not become defensive and even angered. The purpose of the chapter, however, is not to hurt feelings or to attack the intentions of religious educators of adults. What is surely under attack is the "system" that emerged out of habitual mindsets shaped by centuries of practice. The system exalts the transmission of theological concepts and neglects to stress the necessity of effective sensitivity to the life situations of adults. What is implied by this system is a fixation on subject matters and a turning away from the real world of adults' everyday lives. As a result, this question is never really asked: "Who is today's adult?" The question is asked in the next chapter, and some responses to the question are outlined.

Notes

[1] Sharon Merriam and Rosemary Caffarella, *Learning in Adulthood* (San Francisco: Jossey-Bass, 1991), 79-95.

[2] Elizabeth R. Hayes and Gordon Gerald Darkenwald, "Attitudes Toward Adult Education: an Empirically-based Conceptualization," *Adult Education Quarterly* 40, no. 3 (Spring 1990): 158-68

[3] R. Michael Harton, "A Factor Analytic Study of Reasons for Nonparticipation in Church-based education among Southern Baptist Adults" (dissertation, Indiana University, 1984). A similar study was conducted with similar results by Kale Rufner among a population of United Church of Christ adults.

[4] Patricia Cross, *Adults as Learners: Increasing Participation and Facilitating Learning* (San Francisco: Jossey-Bass, 1981), 108.

[5] Daniel J. Silver and Bernard Martin, *A History of Judaism* (New York: Basic Books, 1974), 163.

[6] For a discussion of role concept in sociology see Paul Sites, *Control: The Basis of Social Order* (New York: Dunellen, 1973), 62ff.

[7] The work of J. French and B. Raven is a classic in the study of social power. Cf. "The Bases of Social Power," *Studies in Social Power,* ed. Dorwin Cartwright (Ann Arbor: University of Michigan Press, 1956). For a somewhat different look at social power see Kenneth Boulding's *Ecodynamics: A New Theory of Social Evolution* (Beverly Hills: Sage, 1978), 233-52.

[8] Cf. R. Beal, "Acculturation," *Anthropology Today*, ed. Sol Tax (Chicago: University of Chicago Press, 1965), 375-95.

[9] Plato, "Euthyphro," *Readings In Philosophy*, ed. John Hermon Randall, Justus Buchler, and Evelyn Urban Shirk (New York: Barnes and Noble, 1970), 3-17. See also Romano Guardini's *The Death of Socrates* (Cleveland: World, 1962).

[10] Mircea Eliade, *Cosmos and History* (New York: Harper Torchbooks, 1959), 34.

[11] Kiernan Scott, "Communicative Competence and Religious Education," *Lumen Vitae* (published in Belgium) 35, no. 1 (1980): 82.

[12] Ibid., 82.

[13] A number of studies have been undertaken to discover adult reasons for participation in education. A review of these studies may be found in Roger Boshier's "Factor Analysts at Large: A Critical Review of the Motivational orientation Literature," *Adult Education* 27, no. 1 (1976): 24-47.

[14] Bruce R. Joyce and Marsha Weil, *Models of Teaching*, 3rd ed. (Englewood Cliffs: Prentice-Hall, 1986); see also Steven Brookfield, *Understanding and Facilitating Adult Learning* (San Francisco: Jossey-Bass, 1986); Michael W. Galbraith, ed., *Facilitating Adult Learning* (Malabar FL: Krieger, 1991); and Sharon Merriam and Rosemary Caffarella, *Learning in Adulthood* (San Francisco: Jossey-Bass, 1991).

[15] Malcolm Knowles, *The Modern Practice of Adult Education*, 2d ed. (Chicago: Follett, 1980), 224.

[16] R.E.Y. Wickett, *Models of Adult Religious Education Practice* (Birmingham: Religious Education Press, 1991).

[17] Huey Long, *Adult Learning: Research and Practice* (New York: Cambridge, 1983), 18.

[18] Ibid., 24.

[19] Search Institute defined integrated faith as the balance of vertical faith (one's relationship with God) and horizontal faith (one's relationships with others), specifically how vertical faith is translated into concern or ministry on behalf of others.

[20] *Effective Christian Education: a National Study of Protestant Congregations—A Summary Report on Faith, Loyalty, and Congregational Life* (Minneapolis: Search Institute, 1990). This summary and a report of each participating denomination may be ordered from Search Institute at 122 West Franklin Ave., Minneapolis, MN 55404.

[21] Eugene Roehlkepartain, *The Teaching Church: Moving Christian Education to Center Stage* (Nashville: Abingdon Press, 1993).

[22] Search Institute, 10.

[23] Ibid., 16.

[24] Ibid., 45

[25] Roehlkepartain, 61.

[26] Search Institute, 55.

[27] Louise H. Kidder and Michelle Fine, "Qualitative and Quantitative Methods: When Stories Converge," ed., Melvin Mark, *Multiple Methods in Program Evaluation* (San Francisco: Jossey-Bass, 1987), 57.

[28] William J. Filstead, "Qualitative Methods: A Needed Perspective in Evaluation Research," eds. Thomas Cook and Charles S. Reichardt , *Qualitative and Quantitative Methods in Evaluation Research* (Beverly Hills: Sage Publications, 1979), 34.

[29] Sharan Merriam, "Contributions of Qualitative Research to Adult Education," *Adult Education Quarterly* 39, no. 3 (Spring 1989): 166.

[30] Harry F. Wolcott, *The Basic Techniques in Qualitative Inquiry* (San Diego: Academic Press, 1992), 19.

[31] Sharan Merriam, *Case Study Research: A Qualitative Approach* (San Francisco: Jossey-Bass, 1988), 19.

[32] Merriam, "Contributions of Qualitative Research," 167.

THE POST-TWENTIETH-CENTURY ADULT

The focal point of the problems identified in the previous chapter revolve around the widespread failure of religious educators to adequately take into account the adults they seek to serve through their programs. Seldom do adults have opportunity to participate in determination of program content; they are formed or molded according to the predilections of the pastor or religious educator. Even when religious educators wish to involve adults in the decision-making process, their input is limited to decisions about logistics and seldom about content. Whatever needs assessment is conducted is seldom done by the principles of social science research, but rather by simple survey or checklist, the content of which is limited to the ideas or guesses of the religious educators as to what adults might be responsive. Unfortunately, too, many religious educators of adults are more concerned about what *they* need to teach, i.e., theology, that they are oblivious to the needs of adult learners. The life situations and issues faced by adults, their changing worldviews, and their questions about meaning are largely ignored. The "unchanging truths" from the particular religious tradition are "laid on" adults who are assumed to be static, unchanging, unthinking recipients of the religious educator's predetermined content. Many adult religious educators have failed to come to terms with what may be called "the post-twentieth-century adult."

Who is the Post-Twentieth-Century Adult?
At least the last third of the twentieth century saw in this culture radical shifts in thinking and significant changes in worldview, precipitated in

part by our entry into the "information age." This period also has seen, however, the maturing of the most educated generation in history with its multicultural awareness and global consciousness. Prophetically, a song in the 1960s that heralded the advent of a new era was Bob Dylan's "The Times, They Are A-Changin'." Thirty years later, Schaller identified the effect of those changes as he spoke to pastors about why it is so much harder to "do church" now than it was as late as the 1950s. His aptly titled book of the late 1980s was right, indeed *It's a Different World!* While vestiges of the industrial era remain, so many of the "givens" of the first two-thirds of the last century no longer apply.

Anyone who speaks of adults in twenty-first-century industrialized societies must do so guardedly. We must admit, first of all, that heterogeneity is the foremost characteristic of the adult population. To speak of the typical adult in any exact sense violates logical standards as well as the critical use of language. The typical adult exists only as a statistical abstraction. If anything, the typical adult is protean. A generation ago Gordon Allport stated that people grow idiomatically; they are individuals.[1] This must be accented today in the light of many so-called stage theories of the life span that offer neat patterns of adult development, and in the light of many simplistic applications of these stage theories of adult development to the practice of religious education.[2] Bernice Neugarten avers that we are not likely soon to have a Dr. Spock of adulthood, "for the course of adult change is too complex and the individual differences are too great for any how-to-do-it book."[3] She is correct.

We are compelled, nevertheless, to seek formulas and to fashion propositions that bestow some kind of order on the heterogeneity of the adult population. We seek to formulate general postulates about adult development and adults that serve as guidelines for program development in adult education and as signposts for the conduct of the instructional process. While adults are of variable ages, educational levels, levels of cognitive competence, socioeconomic strata, perceptual and motivational sets, and so forth, we are constrained by some passion for intelligibility to generalize. So be it. But our generalizations must always be anchored in the realization that adults are individuals and that the adult population is vastly more heterogeneous than the childhood population.

There is a segment of the adult population, represented in several factors of the nonparticipation studies, for whom church-based education is not a serious option. This segment of adults, characterized in this chapter as the post-twentieth-century adult, has been largely bypassed by most religious educators as they develop educational programs. These adults are not attuned to the "churchy" culture that exists in every local church or parish. Programs developed for this culture cater to those who are attracted by and who speak "the language of Zion."

Many religious educators, it often seems, are hermetically encapsulated in a "churchy" bubble. Their concerns are limited to theological/liturgical/scriptural matters; the scope of their vision of reality is narrow and restricted to those dimensions of reality that are explicitly religious. Their conversation is directed almost entirely to intramural church affairs, to ecclesiastical policies and politics, and to happenings that are reported in the religion sections of *Time* or *Newsweek* magazines. Quite often religious educators have a perception of reality that excludes purely mundane matters; they possess a perceptual screen that filters reality in a peculiar manner. All discourse and every exchange of ideas eventually is directed to turn around some form of God-talk or church-talk.

Several years ago one of the writers described some technical procedures for the development of adult education programs at a gathering of religious educators. In the evaluation session following the presentation, one religious educator expressed the thought that the presentation was totally devoid of religious considerations and lacked any sense of spirituality. In essence the presentation was faulted because it was not "churchy." Perhaps it is not overly optimistic, however, to believe that most religious educators of adults, usually those in the vanguard of the adult religious education movement, must attempt to see the world through the eyes of the post-twentieth-century adult.

Educational programs for adults that are "churchy," developed by educators who are possessed of a thoroughly "churchy" consciousness, will appeal mainly to adults who are inclined to be "churchy" in their outlook. If religious educators wish to broaden the appeal of their programs, they must come to terms with the values and orientations of those adults we categorize as post-twentieth-century adults.

The post-twentieth-century adult is differentiated from previous adult generations in terms of a transformation of consciousness that has been taking place slowly since the eighteenth-century period of philosophy known as the Enlightenment.[4] The post-twentieth-century adult segment of the total adult population is probably only a strong and growing minority, but the values of post-twentieth-century adult consciousness touch all adults in industrialized societies to some degree. Whether the transformation of consciousness evidenced in the behavior of the post-twentieth-century adult is for good or for ill is not our present concern. We are concerned simply with a descriptive analysis of post-twentieth-century adult consciousness. Furthermore, the designation "post-twentieth-century" should be understood in the special sense outlined in this chapter. All adults presently alive may be said to be cohorts in that they share the same time frame, but not all adults have a post-twentieth-century mindset from the standpoint of their perceptions of reality and/or conceptions of the world. Intellectually, many adults maintain a sense of being in the world that is more congenial with the assumptions of archaic humanity or medieval values. They have been bypassed, or have bypassed, the great efflorescence of values and ideals that has taken place during the past few centuries of Western civilization. By way of stipulative definition, then, these adults are excluded from the designation "post-twentieth-century." The post-twentieth-century adult, as understood in this chapter, is the person whose consciousness and sense of being in the world has developed along the lines marked out by many of the central values that flourished in the eighteenth-century philosophical Enlightenment, values that were subsequently developed and refined in the twentieth century.

Transformation of Consciousness

Some would maintain that human consciousness has not changed in any significant way since Adam.[5] Underlying such a contention is a static view of reality that derives from the assumption that human nature is impermeable to change, crystalline, and unalterably fixed in the scheme of things. Such a position, of course, is itself rooted in pre-Enlightenment values. The position offered here is that a transformation of consciousness has occurred, and that this transformation involves both a new focus of consciousness and a new structuring of consciousness.

There has been a new centering of consciousness on aspects of reality that were previously unattended by adults on the large scale. This shift in the focus of consciousness has produced a new kind of experience for post-twentieth-century adults and a new orientation toward reality. It must also be noted that this redirection of consciousness has been associated with a major alteration of worldview. There is abroad in the world a new way of "minding" reality.

Alexander Luria's research among adults provides an analogue for understanding the qualitative development of human consciousness that has taken place over the past few hundred years.[6] In comparing illiterate adult peasants with adults who were exposed minimally to education, Luria discovered that those in the latter group possessed enhanced perceptual powers; greater abilities for deduction, inference, and reasoning; keener imaginations; and more pronounced competencies for the analysis of their own inner lives. He concluded that the most important forms of cognitive processes vary in relation to changing conditions of social life. It is maintained here that the social, economic, political, and cultural changes that have occurred over the past few hundred years have altered human consciousness significantly and that religious educators of adults have not seriously considered the implications of this shift in consciousness for the practice of adult education.

There are, no doubt, major continuities in human consciousness over the past several thousand years. But there are also discontinuities of immense importance that are often overlooked. The post-twentieth-century adult is attuned to new conditions of social life, interprets self-in-the-world differently than, say, the peasant of four hundred years ago, acts with a different kind of intentionality, and lives in a field of perceived relationships that is relatively novel. While the seeds of the development of consciousness have been planted in every century since the advent of human life on this planet, the seventeenth and eighteenth centuries can be identified as the historical time frame in which a mega-leap in the development of consciousness occurred.

The Heritage of the Enlightenment

Consciousness, in the post-twentieth-century adult, has undergone secularization, sophistication, individualization, and liberalization. The post-twentieth-century adult is more interested in this world than the world beyond, for various historical reasons. Thanks to the information explosion since the Enlightenment, the post-twentieth-century adult has at his disposal a host of resources for learning and, in many cases, is better educated than the clergy and/or religious educators. While the post-twentieth-century adult's social milieu contributes to his sense of self-identity, he is more an individual person and less likely to take his psychosocial definition from membership in a tribe, a village, or a parish community. Because of individualization of consciousness, the post-twentieth-century adult population is vastly heterogeneous; -

post-twentieth-century adults have broad, diverse, and complex interests. The post-twentieth-century adult apprises herself as relatively
autonomous and not as under the tutelage of others. She no longer
fears civil reprisals, except under totalitarian regimes, when she fails to
subscribe to prescribed beliefs. She lives in a pluralistic society and is
exposed every day to values that contradict or conflict with her own
values. The post-twentieth-century adult is secular, sophisticated, individual, and free. Each of these qualities deserves a more detailed
examination.

Secularization

A major problem in speaking about secularization is the lack of consensus about the meaning of this process. Secularization can be
interpreted in meliorative or pejorative senses. At least four major
denotative senses of secularization can be delineated. Secularization
can mean: (1) an all-surpassing preoccupation with the world and a corresponding absence of reflection about ultimate meanings, (2) a
heightened interest in the world of historical experience coupled with
an inability to interpret the world in terms of traditional religious symbols and concepts, (3) a fascination with the world of historical
experience as it adumbrates religious meanings, and (4) a turning away
from ecclesiastic-clerical culture, a rejection of conventional forms of
traditional piety, devotion, and theological formulations.

The Absence of Reflection. Martin Heidegger remarked that thoughtlessness is an uncanny guest who comes and goes everywhere in today's
world.[7] Many people live on the surface of existence. They have been
seduced by immediate concerns and are almost unable to seek transcendent meaning. These people, Heidegger noted, have fallen from
human authenticity. Life is characterized by idle talk, by a passionate
curiosity about novelties, and by ambiguity—the appearance that
everything is genuinely understood, though ultimately nothing is understood.[8] Among those who fall into this kind of secularism there is a
deficit of ontological awe and, subsequently, a neglect of issues of ultimate concern. There is no carefulness about uncovering the visage of
reality, no quest of ultimate truth.

Often the refusal to ask ultimate questions—questions about the
destiny and meaning of the cosmos and one's place in the cosmos—is
linked with a passionate concern for technique. There is an avoidance
of questions that lead to wisdom or what the classical Greek

philosophers called *sophia*, and an exclusive concentration on practical information regarding the operation of things, what the Greeks called *techne*. Some people avidly seek to know how something works or how something can be manipulated expeditiously, but fail to ask *why* something exists at all or what a technique does (or should do) in respect to the development of people.

This is not an attack on technology. Technology in itself is neither an enemy of reflection nor the nemesis of humankind. What is stressed here is that some people can become involved in technological concerns to such an extent that their access to the mystery of being is blocked. Their sense of ontological awe is dulled. In turn, they become mere technicians instead of human beings who have mastered a particular set of techniques. One can become immersed in the world either through habitual thoughtlessness or by an excessive concern for technology, which leads to thoughtlessness.

A Lack of Vision. The second type of secularist seeks ultimate meaning, but hesitatingly and with great difficulty. This person lives a life of quiet desperation; the world is too much with him. He turns to reflective moments, usually in times of minor and major tribulations, but is unable to sustain a long-term pursuit of meaning. It is not a matter of denying the possibility of the ultimate meaning of the world and self-in-the-world; nor is it a matter of refusing to seek meaning. It is largely a matter of being unable to deal with the world interpretatively, given the conceptual and symbolic tools of conventional religion. Vision is not lacking because of ill will on the part of this type of secularist; vision is lacking because conventional religion has obscured the sun.

The interpretative schemes provided by conventional religion are not attractive for some people. These schemes strike no responsive chords. The interpretations of the world offered by conventional religion are mysterious in the sense that these interpretations tend to mystify or befuddle. The words and symbols furnished by conventional religion are powerless since they belong to another epoch. As evidence, consider Gallup's findings that a majority of today's adults do not understand the terminology and theological "lingo" of the church. Must a believer accept the conventional three-tiered universe (heaven, earth, hell), an image of God that was derived from Hellenic philosophy (and that reflected the Zeus of Hellenic myth), doctrinal formulations couched in a language that is out of joint with the believer's experience? Very often, it is submitted, conventional religion drives people into thoughtlessness. It is much easier to stop thinking about the ultimate meaning of the world and self-in-the-world than to reconcile one's experience of it with the interpretation offered by conventional religion. And once someone has welcomed thoughtlessness as a guest, immersion in the concrete world is not far removed.

Religious Secularism. John Macquarrie pointed out the fallacy of placing the secular over against the religious, as if the two concepts existed in a relationship of antinomy.[9] The genuinely religious person is concerned about the world, but the world is not the be-all and end-all of his existence. The religious person faced with a choice between a thoroughgoing secularism and a false religiosity need not be forced to make a choice. Both extremes must be rejected in favor of caring for the secular in the light of authentic religious faith.

There are those adults who do not dichotomize the sacred and the secular. They seek transcendent values at the core of immediate secular affairs; they find that the so-called secular sphere of things is filled potentially with the sacred; they see secular being-in-the-world as pregnant with the possibility of the sacred; they view ultimate concern as wrapped in issues of proximate concerns. This type of post-twentieth-century adult is not seduced by "this world." She believes that seduction to the wiles of the "world beyond" is no less a problem than being seduced by "this world." This adult has her own path; she walks to the beat of a drummer never heard by those who are conventionally religious. In her own way she is religious, but her faith is not so much a profession of traditional formulas as it is a consuming search for ultimate meaning (God) within the sociocultural context that conditions her consciousness. And yet, this post-twentieth-century adult is often classified as a secularist, at least by those who are conventionally-religious.

Pseudo-secularism. The religious secularist described above is a pseudo-secularist. So also is the person who rejects the "churchy" culture and is thereby viewed as a pariah by those who are conventionally religious. There are many adults who find the concerns of the "churchy" culture to be incongruent with their experience, their aspirations, and their sense of reality. These adults may be profoundly religious, but they have learned to define themselves as religiously lukewarm because they do not seem to fit the devotional mold prescribed by those who thrive in the rarefied atmosphere of the ecclesiastical culture. Many post-twentieth-century adults have mistakenly defined themselves as not very religious because they have accepted the definition of "religious" developed by those who hold membership in the ecclesiastical culture. On the other hand, Gallup claims that what it means to be religious is being re-defined by an increasing number of adults who claim to have a deep, personal faith quite apart from participation in an organized church.

Those who are at home in the "churchy" culture are usually interested in news about the bureaucratic structures of the religious organization. They are interested in latest theological trends and frequently discuss the sayings and doings of prominent clerics. They share similar devotional values and a language that sets them apart. There is nothing wrong, of course, with entertaining such interests, conducting such discussions, or sharing particular values. But quite often those who are at home in the churchy culture appear to be unable to discuss nonchurchy issues; they seem to be sealed off from the concerns of the workaday world; they seem to be contained within a separate reality. Adults who are not concerned exclusively, or even to a high degree, with churchy issues feel themselves more at home in a weekday world than the world of Sunday devotions and sermons. They apprise themselves as secularists when they are simply not "professional" religionists.

That there is an overlap of some forms of secularism is obvious. True forms of secularism blend with pseudo-secularism. Instead of neatly marked boundaries we have points on a continuum. The post-twentieth-century adult may vacillate from one point to another. Indeed, the post-twentieth-century adult may even find comfort in the "churchy" culture, but the comfort does not last. This vacillation may be attributed to a certain instability on the part of the post-twentieth-century adult. More often than not it reflects the fact that the post-twentieth-century adult lives in a world of conflicting values and perspectives, a pluralistic world where competition among values is the standard operating procedure.

Sophistication

Over the past four centuries, adult consciousness has become more sophisticated. The typical adult of seventeenth-century Europe—and his predecessors—was far less sophisticated than the typical adult of the twentieth century who lives in an industrialized society. The foregoing observation must be qualified, of course. The sophistication of the post-twentieth-century adult is relative and not absolute. Nor is it claimed that post-twentieth-century adults are universally and uniformly more sophisticated; many adults today are intellectually naive and emotionally underdeveloped. The point made here is that a larger proportion of today's adults are more sophisticated than their forebears, and that by and large the typical twentieth-century adult who lives in a developed society is intellectually better prepared to address religious issues.

There was a time when the majority of chronological adults were intellectual children. They lived in a world of concrete realities and were hardly able to classify these realities in terms of abstract categories. They could not make inferences that went beyond immediate experiences. Problem-solving was largely a matter of trial and error; systematic thinking among the masses of chronological adults was uncommon. Creative imagination was the exception rather than the rule among these peoples.

These adults were docile, malleable, and easy to manipulate by those who dwelt in the higher niches of rigidly stratified societies. The image of the sheep herd readily comes to mind in thinking about such people. They were easily led and unable to do more than accept unreflectively what they were told to accept. They lived a hand-to-mouth existence, a day-to-day existence at a subsistence level. They had little information about the world outside their immediate vicinities or villages or serf quarters.

Those who maintained power, in feudal society for example, did so largely because they controlled access to knowledge. Those who lacked power also lacked economic advantage, technology, and military force, but their largest deficit—in terms of the means of attaining power—was the knowledge deficit. To what extent the peasants were purposely kept in ignorance by the power elite cannot be known. That this control tactic has been used is evidenced in American history: the laws in antebellum slave states that prohibited the teaching of literacy skills to slaves. One must believe that the tactic has had a long history in human affairs.

How did this situation change to the degree it did during the Enlightenment? While many factors contributed to the sophistication of human consciousness, no factor looms larger than the invention of moveable type. The advent of printing prior to the Enlightenment introduced a sociocultural revolution of immense impact on subsequent centuries and, pari passu, a major development in consciousness vis-à-vis the masses of adults. According to Will Durant, printing made manuals in religion, literature, history, and science available to the masses of adults. Printing paved the way for the philosophical Enlightenment; without printing there would have been no Rousseau, Voltaire, Bayle, Diderot, and no trend in philosophical thinking known as skepticism. Printing prepared the way for Luther, permitted rationalism to challenge the gospels, ended the clerical monopoly of learning and control of education, encouraged the vernacular languages, and facilitated widespread communication.[10] In effect, the dissemination of printed materials slowly but inexorably set the stage for a transformation of consciousness in untold millions of adults.

The post-twentieth-century adult, as defined above, bears little resemblance to his medieval and ancient ancestors. He has access to information transmitted via printed materials. And even if he is illiterate, he has access to information transmitted via the electronic media. Further, he has access to education. Never before in the history of the world have more people participated in more educational activities conducted in such a splendid variety of institutional settings.

Laypeople in many congregations are better educated than the clergy in such fields as literature, economics, finance, science, history, social sciences, languages, mathematics, fine arts, administration, and a host of other specialized branches of human knowledge. Indeed, it is possible to find laypeople who are extremely well-read and well-informed in matters relating to religious issues. Should we doubt that some laypeople, in some churches, are not better informed in religious matters than their pastors?

Another contributing factor to the sophistication of consciousness is the availability of transportation. Adults have come into contact with a variety of cultures. The norms of their culture of origin are measured against the norms of a variety of cultures. The initial contact between European "Christian" culture and foreign cultures in the fifteenth–sixteenth centuries raised questions in the minds of those who assumed that European "Christian" culture was superior. For the first time adults on a large scale began to see the extent to which their beliefs and practices were culture-bound; they began to realize that Christianity had accumulated much cultural baggage as it developed through the centuries. Problems came to the fore when they attempted to distinguish the essential Christianity from its cultural accretions. The post-twentieth-century adult finds various means of transportation available to her; if she will not visit others, they will eventually visit her. The mono-chromatic culture of the quaint European village has given way to the pluralistic megalopolis, a culture that is a coat of many colors. Increasingly the post-twentieth-century adult finds it difficult not to come into contact with others who are different.

Each of us carries an image of reality, a worldview that is fraught with values and norms. Lacking exposure to foreign images of reality and different worldviews, we tend toward ethnocentrism. We esteem our worldview as superior, our values as absolute. When we seriously encounter other images of reality and their attendant norms and values, we find ourselves in a conflict situation. We may continue to question the validity of foreign images, but we also raise questions about our own image of reality. Insularity brings a comfort of sorts; when we establish relationships with others beyond our purview of the world, we forfeit the easy confidence we have in the value system we assimilated as children. Contact with different ways and different people often prompts us to question not only the different ways and people but our own values as well. In a word, contact with that which is "different" creates a situation that helps us become more critical.

This is not to argue that gullibility and naiveté are absent in the adult population. But we must acknowledge that the post-twentieth-century adult has wide access to knowledge and information, to educational opportunities, and to cultural imperatives that conflict with values that have been handed down to him or her. The cumulative result of this over the past four centuries has been the development of a consciousness in many adults that is both sophisticated and critical.

Individualization

There was a time when most human beings derived their identities largely from membership in a tribe or village community.[11] Consciousness was only minimally individual; each member of the group shared in a collective consciousness, as it were, that was orchestrated by the flow of the seasons, by basic needs for survival, and by common experiences interpreted according to accepted tribal standards. All participated in the same meaning system and in the same store of knowledge. Each person's perceptions of reality were colored and controlled by the tribal lore system. Even the sense of individual death came late on the historical scene. What mattered was not the survival of a member of the tribe, but the survival of the tribe. Cognitive activities and affective experiences were programmed by the tribal milieu.

Just as submersion in nature produced a type of consciousness that did not capacitate a person for the strict differentiation of self from nature, so also submersion in the tribal milieu did not permit the person to differentiate self sharply from the tribe. Thoughts and feelings were legitimate only to the extent they were congruent with patterns of thinking and feeling prescribed by the tribe. In archaic societies there was a profound continuity existing among members of the tribe; members of the tribe were psychologically "one."

The development of individual consciousness did not occur abruptly. While certain epochs can be identified during which human consciousness became qualitatively different, the developmental process leading to individual consciousness as we know it today was agonizingly slow. Present purposes do not allow for a thorough discussion of the individualization of consciousness. It may be stated, however, that post-twentieth-century individual consciousness blossomed forth on a large scale during the Enlightenment. This is not to say that no one previous to the Enlightenment experienced self as uniquely individual; the point made is that the overwhelming majority of adults prior to the past few centuries more often than not viewed themselves as members of a group rather than as individuals.

The individualization of consciousness parallels the development of the philosophical school of individualism. This school of thought emphasized the value of the individual and individual rights. At the same time, adherents of individualism challenged the absolutism of civil and ecclesiastical rulers. In religious matters the philosophy of individualism proclaimed that the individual person does not stand in need of an institutional mediator between himself and God. The philosophy of individualism is obviously reflected in many forms of post-Reformation Christianity. John Dewey observed that individualism is a "product of the relaxation of the grip of the authority of custom and traditions as standards of belief."[12] Except for sporadic instances of individualism in history, notably in ancient Greece and medieval Europe, the individualism we know today, Dewey noted, is a comparatively modern manifestation.

The individualization of consciousness was accompanied with another effect: the heterogeneitization of the adult population. While the division of labor in a tribal or village society provided some degree of individualization (note such surnames as Baker, Chandler, Carpenter, etc.), tribal-village societies were largely homogenous in terms of religious beliefs, mores, knowledge base, and worldview. As consciousness became more and more individualized, the heterogeneity of the adult population increased in direct proportion. As has been mentioned previously, the heterogeneity of the adult population is its foremost characteristic today.

A problem that churches face today is that the culture of the congregation may not only be unappealing to nonmembers, but it may be very difficult to break into. James Hopewell, a former missionary in West Africa who taught at Emory University at the time of his death, spent a sabbatical studying and living among the congregations of two rural churches of different denominational affiliations. After a year, he concluded that the cultures of the two congregations more closely resembled the tribal cultures with which he had worked in Africa than their denominational counterparts. In other words, their distinguishing characteristics were more homogeneously tribal in nature in terms of their norms, idioms, and worldviews.[13]

Post-twentieth-century adults refuse to fit into the tribal mold. They want to set their own goals, make their own decisions, and select the means whereby the goals are achieved and the decisions implemented. Today's adults see life as *their* project. They desire to dwell in unity with others, but not when unity is interpreted to mean uniformity; they desire to live in community but not when community is merely a code word for collectivity that attenuates individual differences. While admitting to a profound need for social interchange, post-twentieth-century adults reject the notion that they need a tribal community, or a surrogate thereof, as an absolute mediator of personal religious meaning. For this reason the post-twentieth-century adult may not apprise the institutional apparatus of a religious tradition as beyond criticism. The post-twentieth-century adult, finally, refuses to surrender to the tutelage of others as Immanuel Kant defined it: Tutelage is the human being's self-incurred inability to make use of his understanding without direction from someone else.[14]

Liberalization

Adult consciousness has undergone a liberalization that goes hand-in-hand with the individualization of consciousness. The post-twentieth-century adult is conscious of self as a self-directing being. What is most individual about anyone is his intentionality, his freedom.

The liberalization of consciousness, on the large scale and as a rule instead of an exception, is also a product of Enlightenment thinking and the sociopolitical transformations that have taken place during the past two hundred years. When we read that people, following Martin Luther's attempt to reform the church, were forced to accept the beliefs of their political leaders for the sake of social order, we may not immediately grasp how far we have come since the sixteenth century. This distance that separates us from the burden of accepting the religious preference of political leaders is brief in terms of history, but immense in terms of significance. The rapid liberalization of consciousness was associated with the rapid decline of the fortunes of political absolutism in the past two centuries. The decline has been swift and definitive. Likewise, the corresponding increase of a sense of personal autonomy among the multitudes of adults, or the thirst for political freedom, has been dramatically accelerated. There was a time when some adults rejoiced in the fact that they were the serfs of a particular duke or earl. That time has passed.

The liberalization of consciousness in the twentieth century has been especially evident. This liberalization was due in large part to economic circumstances that promoted the possibility of greater freedom. A person may enjoy political freedom but will find that opportunities for autonomous thinking and behavior are severely structured by economic conditions. No one who is hungry or without shelter is truly free, despite those who proclaim that political freedom is a fact. Lacking the wherewithal to satisfy basic human needs, a person becomes dependent on the will of others. While poverty yet exists in all industrialized societies, never before have so many people lived comfortable, and even modestly affluent, lives. In relative terms, and in historical terms, millions of adults today are economically secure. They need not endorse someone else's value system to maintain a subsistence level of survival.

Essentially, the post-twentieth-century adult is beholden to no one for the values he espouses; his values are formed in a social context, but he takes pride in shaping his own beliefs. She avoids taking a party line in matters of ecclesiastical discipline. The phenomenon of Roman Catholics, clergy and laity, who openly and in good conscience oppose papal teachings on birth control is a case in point. The post-twentieth-century adult screens and selects religious doctrines and affirms certain teachings not as a matter of capitulation to an absolute religious authority but as a matter of personal choice. The statements of religious leaders, ecclesiastical authorities, and pastors are allowed into the marketplace of ideas, but the post-twentieth-century adult may or may not accept these statements. The post-twentieth-century adult trusts his or her own thinking and experiences more than the thinking and experiences of religious leaders. In the Middle Ages such an approach to the development of personal conscience would have placed a person in grave jeopardy; today the auto-da-fé exists only as a sad memory of bygone days in which the grossest form of dehumanization was practiced in the name of God.

To use Nietzsche's imagery, the post-twentieth-century adult is fully aware that the old despotic god of the past is dead, that the horizon is open, that we can put to sea in the face of every threat, that the sea, our sea, lies open before us, and that such an open sea has never before existed.[15] Fearing neither political reprisal nor economic punishment, and having dealt with the fear of eternal perdition announced by religious leaders as the penalty for disobeying their teachings, the post-twentieth-century adult exercises his personal choices and assumes responsibility for the consequences of these choices. Paternalism is no longer effective. Adults will be adults, even within the context of religious institutions.

Religious Education and the Post-Twentieth-Century Adult

To what extent do religious educators take the post-twentieth-century adult into account? Are educational programs planned and conducted with these adults in mind? The Search Institute Report found that the religious education programs for adults in churches that are effective in developing integrated faith do so in part through development of multicultural awareness and global consciousness.[16] Content focuses upon issues adults face in daily life; the fashion in which programs are conducted encourages critical thinking. On the other hand, Search also reported that these were not well-developed in most congregations!

Let us look at the manner in which most adult education programs are developed by pastors or religious educators. A course of study is determined by the pastor/religious educator; the pastor/religious educator determines what content will be transmitted to the adults. While religious educators hope adults will react creatively with the content of instruction, the main emphasis is on the transmission of a particular body of information. There is a tendency to provide *all* the (simplistic) answers, often to questions that no one is asking, while ignoring the weightier problems of everyday life. The information is nearly always theological or explicitly religious. There is a passionate concern for material resources: video and audio tapes, films, resource kits, and packaged programs.

What does this approach say about the adults who are the target audience of the educational program? It implies that the adults are really children; that they are incapable of selecting topics for study; that they are passive recipients of wisdom bestowed on them from superior others (pastor/religious educator); that their needs, interests, and concerns are not as important as the need of the pastor/religious educator to transmit a particular body of knowledge; that they have no abilities and cannot be trusted to participate in the development of their educational program.

In Search of a Theory

It is our claim that the majority of religious educators of adults have no articulated theory of adult religious education. Lacking such a theory, they unintentionally follow a theory of childhood educational practice, and perhaps not a very good one at that. The unilateral development of an educational program for adults on the part of the educator, and the equating of teaching with the "telling" of something, is a practice that adumbrates and contains, as it were, an outmoded theory of childhood education. The crux of the problem facing religious educators of adults concerns a theory of adult educational practice in the setting of local church, parish, or synagogue. Until a sound theory of adult religious education is developed, much of the activity that goes by the name of adult religious education will continue to be marginal.

Notes

[1] Gordon Allport, *Becoming* (New Haven: Yale University Press, 1955), 21.

[2] There is a real danger in reading life span development reports carelessly. While Daniel Levinson's *The Seasons of a Man's Life* (New York: Alfred A. Knopf, 1978), Roger Gould's *Transformations* (York: Simon & Schuster, 1978), and George Vaillant's *Adaptation to Life* (Boston: Little, Brown, 1977) are helpful in viewing broad general patterns of development in the adult population, we should not assume that statistical norms reported in these studies are anything more than that. Students of life span development should be warned that there are serious problems of research methodology associated with life span studies. See especially, in this regard, L. R. Goulet and Paul B. Baltes, eds., *Life-Span Developmental Psychology: Research and Theory* (New York: Academic Press, 1970), and John R. Nesselroade and Hayne W. Reese, *Life-Span Developmental Psychology: Methodological Issues* (New York: Academic Press, 1973).

[3] Bernice Neugarten, "Time, Age, and the Life Cycle," *American Journal of Psychiatry* 86, no. 7 (1979): 888.

[4] For background reading, refer to Peter Gay's masterful two-volume work *The Enlightenment: An Interpretation* (New York: Alfred A. Knopf, 1968); Will and Ariel Durant, *The Age of Reason Begins* (New York: Simon & Schuster, 1961); *The Age of Voltaire* (New York: Simon & Schuster, 1965); and *Rousseau and Revolution* (New York: Simon & Schuster, 1967). Franklin Baumer's *Religion and the Rise of Scepticism* (New York: Harcourt, Brace & World, 1960) is brief but holds many valuable insights.

[5] By "consciousness" we mean generally what Charles A. Reich meant: Consciousness is not simply "a set of opinions, information, or values, but a total configuration in any given individual, which makes up his whole perception of reality, his whole worldview." Cf. *The Greening of America*, 6th ed. (New York: Bantam Books, 1971) 13. The study of the evolution of consciousness is fascinating, particularly with respect to the interplay between changes in culture and changes in consciousness. A number of writers have approached the topic from different perspectives. See, for example, Karl Jaspers, *The Origin and Goal of History* (New Haven: Yale University Press, 1953); Marshall McLuhan, *The Gutenberg Galaxy* (Toronto: New American Library, 1962); and Julian Jaynes's imaginative and stimulating *The Origin of Consciousness in the Breakdown of the Bicameral Mind* (Boston: Houghton Mifflin, 1976).

[6] Alexander R. Luria, *Cognitive Development: Its Cultural and Social Foundations* (Cambridge: Harvard University Press, 1976).

[7] Martin Heidegger, *Discourse on Thinking,* trans. John M. Anderson and E. Hans Freund (New York: Harper and Row, 1966), 12.

[8] Martin Heidegger *Being and Time,* trans. John Macquarrie and Edward Robinson (New York: Harper and Row, 1962), 210-24.

[9] John Macquarrie, *God and Secularity* (Philadelphia: Westminster, 1967), 51ff.

[10] Will Durant, *The Reformation* (New York: Simon & Schuster, 1957), 160.

[11] Peter Berger and Thomas Luckmann propose a typical society, for heuristic purposes, in which institutionalization is total. All problems and solutions are common; all social actions are institutionalized. All social life is guided by the institutional order. Life is a "continuous performance of a complex, highly stylized liturgy." The authors suggest that primitive societies approximate this type of society to a much higher degree than civilized societies. See Berger and Luckmann's *The Social Construction of Reality* (New York: Doubleday, 1967), 80.

[12] John Dewey, *Democracy and Education* (New York: Free Press, 1966), 305.

[13] See James F. Hopewell, *Congregations: Stories and Structures* (Philadelphia: Fortress Press, 1987). Hopewell died before his research was published. His students and colleagues at Emory University compiled and published his work posthumously. It is a fascinating look at how the narrative of a church's culture develops.

[14] Immanuel Kant, "What is Enlightenment?," *On History,* trans. Lewis White Beck, Robert E. Anchor, and Emil L. Fackenheim (Indianapolis: Bobbs-Merrill, 1963), 106.

[15] Friedrich Wilhelm Nietzsche, *Joyful Wisdom,* trans. Thomas Common (New York: Frederick Ungar, 1971), 276.

[16] *Effective Christian Education: A National Study of Protestant Congregations* (Minneapolis: Search Institute, 1990).

TOWARD A THEORY OF ADULT RELIGIOUS EDUCATION, PART I

Those whose focus is primarily the practice of adult religious education may at this point be tempted to skip two chapters devoted to theory. After all, the complaint of many seminary graduates has been that their education consisted largely of theory with insufficient attention to practical matters. Interestingly, this complaint is most often heard from those having little "field experience" prior to seminary. They fail to understand Dewey's admonition that nothing is so practical as a good theory!

Indeed, in a day when churches took their religious education programs "canned" from their denominational headquarters, the parish educator or pastor needed little theoretical foundation. The primary skill of these program managers was the ability to promote participation in whatever the denomination provided. However, a number of denominational publishers have made severe cutbacks in the materials and programs they provide, and others have become suspect as their materials are seen as primary tools for indoctrination on the current pet theological issue of the denomination. These problems, coupled with a recognition that the local parish is the primary unit for programming according to need, have pushed religious educators back to the "foundations" of their practice. Theory really is the foundation of sound practice!

Yet, some who recognize the need for sound theory in the broader arena of education question whether a sub-field that they see as primarily a means of moral and social intervention rather than a science can justifiably generate theory.[1] Merriam answers such critics by asserting that there is still a need to investigate and conceptualize practice because it "stimulates thinking about practice and brings understanding and insight to the field," thus insuring progress in the field.[2] In reality, as this chapter will subsequently make clear, theory is an unavoidable factor in determining practice.

Theory has been defined in many ways: a principle, a set of principles, the analysis of a set of facts, reflection that is impractical, a plausible explanation of phenomena, a body of axioms or laws, a supposition, a conjecture, a collection of theorems, a paradigm that reflects cultural changes, and so forth. Before attempting a theory of adult religious education, therefore, a brief explication of the term as used in this volume is in order.

Theory

Sometimes it is helpful to examine the etymological roots of difficult concepts. The term theory is derived from the Greek *theoreion*.[3] This word connotes "seeing," "observing," and "beholding," and is related to the notions of "contemplation," "to conclude by observation," "to be interpreted as seen," and "to speculate." In its earliest usage *theoreion* was used in the sense of being a spectator at games, official meetings, or dramatic presentations. In a broad sense, theory suggests a way of interpretative viewing from a particular vantage point or perspective.

An analysis of the lexical entries under *theoreion* reveals many meanings of the word. These meanings have been arranged below into a continuum that moves from a simple connotation to increasingly complex connotations. *Theoreion* can mean:

- a place from which to see
- a place from which to see a variety of events
- a place from which to see a variety of events as a whole or as these events stand in relationship one to another
- a place from which to see a variety of interrelated events in terms of a given reference point
- a place from which to see a variety of interrelated events in terms of a given reference point for the purpose of constructing an explanation of that which is seen.

The connotations move from the simple act of beholding, to beholding a number of disparate events, to the beholding of these events as a system, to observation of the system from a specific perspective, and finally to the act of imposing order and intelligibility on what is observed. But intelligibility is not, in itself, the final goal of theorizing. Intelligibility is an important penultimate goal; the ultimate purpose of theorizing is the action that is evoked by a theory statement.

Four Dimensions of Theory

When we sort out the major etymological elements of the term *theory* we discover that four dimensions of theory emerge:

1. *Theory as Perspective:* a vantage point from which to view something.
2. *Theory as Coherent Vision:* that which is seen from the vantage point; an internal landscape of ideas and feelings; an insight not put into language.
3. *Theory as Proposition:* the vision or insight as expressed discursively; a statement or set of statements that discloses the vision; a theoretical model.
4. *Theory as Practice:* the instantiation or embodiment of propositional theory; the "doing" of the propositional theory and, by implication, the "doing" of the vision.

Theory as Perspective. Initially theory is a perspective from which a person gains a view of a set of variables. These variables may be facts or ideas. The perspective is a vantage point from which a viewer observes a state of affairs. Perspective in turn results from the interaction of tradition and experience. In a real sense "tradition is foundational experience, the kind of experience that orients a person and provides a certain directedness to life . . . All present experiences are interpreted in the light of previous experience, and especially in the light of tradition."[4] Tradition is not determinative in that it does not eliminate choice, but it may serve to provide certain inclinations. Perceptions change with both critical reflection on tradition and with new life experiences. Further, it must be noted that a shift in one's vantage point will yield a *perceptually* different state of affairs. One who views *Les Miserables* from the first row of the orchestra section observes a different scene than his or her fellow theater-goer seated in the back row of the balcony. Analogously, when a person experiences a set of facts and ideas intellectually, the person's vantage point will yield a *conceptually* different state of affairs than a person who is "located" elsewhere experientially.

One's perspective in space and time is not precisely the same as the perspective of anyone else; by the same token one's perspective in terms of life experience is not precisely the same as the perspective of anyone else. John Phillips has pointed out that "it is not the facts which determine our theories, but rather our theories which determine what we take to be so."[5] There is no purely objective theory because there is no absolute point of reference from which to view any given state of affairs. This is because perspective is born in large measure of the various traditions and assumptions with which we are reared and to which we are exposed. Those traditions and assumptions provide "filters," as it were, through which we view and interpret events and experiences.[6]

Theory as Coherent Vision. A perspective on any state of affairs yields a vision. The vision is there; it is present to consciousness in its all-at-onceness; it is integrated, consolidated, whole. In the vision all of the facts and/or ideas are organized into a totality. The vision is coherent. All of the parts that make up the vision are interrelated; each part fits into the vision as pieces of a jigsaw puzzle fit together. The integrity of the vision, however, is compromised when the vision is translated into discursive language.

Theory as Proposition. A vision is translated into language or into the notations of symbolic logic, the principal elements of discursive reasoning. What results is a propositional theory or a theoretical construct. The vision is fragmented as it is translated into discursive form. The vision is mediated or communicated to others not as an intact whole, but in a sequence of statements. Only the major features of the vision survive. It is important to realize that both the perspective and the vision of the theoretician is implicitly contained in the propositional theory.

Theory as Practice. Practice is the actualization of propositional theory (and the vision implicit in propositional theory) *in concreto.* Of course, practice never captures the entirety of any theoretical construct or proposition. As we move from vision to proposition, something is lost; as we move from propositional theory to practice, something is lost. This is not an excuse, however, to engage in practice without propositional theory. Such activity is mere nervous movement and exhibits more than anything else, a certain mindlessness.

Every practice or performance is an embodiment of a theoretical proposition and vision, whether the practitioner is aware of the proposition and vision or not. In the previous chapter it was stated that adult education programs are often developed according to a model of curriculum development taken from an outmoded model of childhood education. By developing a program without paying heed to the concerns of adults in the target population, the educator implicitly affirms the proposition that adults need not be consulted prior to program development as to their concerns and, perhaps, the vision that adults are really large children. The teacher who conducts instruction solely around available films or packaged programs agrees, implicitly at least, with the theoretical proposition that instructional objectives are unnecessary. And implicit in this proposition may be the vision of instruction as purposeless activity. Theory is unavoidable, even for those who never think about theory. All educational practice is undergirded by propositional theory, and each propositional theory represents a particular vision of reality gained from a specific perspective.

Two Functions of Propositional Theory

Propositional theory "does" a number of things. Two of the functions of propositional theory are: (1) the explanatory function and (2) the guidance function.[7] In the prior case propositional theory provides an interpretative explanation of a set of observed facts. Here is an example. Over a period of years Jane has conducted educational programs for adults. She recognizes that many adults seem to enjoy the social dimensions of these programs. She states a theory concerning participation in adult education: "Adults are sometimes motivated to participate in educational activities out of a need for social contact with other adults." Jane analyzed her observations and made inferences based on these observations. A theory resulted. Research later showed that some adults do indeed participate in education out of social need. Her theory was verified. A theory may state an interpretative explanation of the nature of something, of the dynamics of a process, or of the origin of something. The theory is verified only by sound research.

Sometimes there are a number of theories that attempt to explain something. There are, for example, a number of contending theories of learning. What is learning? How does learning occur? No single theory of learning has thus far won the field. This is principally due to two factors: (1) the process of learning is extremely complex and involves an almost indefinite number of variables, and (2) different theorists approach the task of explaining learning from different perspectives and with different philosophical assumptions. Some theories, then, may be unverifiable in an absolute sense. These theories possess different degrees of plausibility. A theory that is plausible (warranted by evidence and logic) should be given credence until such a time as an alternative theory is formulated. If there are several plausible theories concerning the same matter, each person must choose the theory that seems most plausible.

Propositional theory serves as a guide for action. In the previous example, Jane observed adults who enrolled in educational programs and she theorized that some adults participate out of a need for social contact. The theory was verified by research findings. When she develops educational programs for adults, Jane now takes the social dimensions of adult education into more serious consideration. Programs are advertised as affording opportunities for adults to meet new friends as well as presenting occasions for intellectual growth. As a teacher Jane tries to create a more informal atmosphere in her courses and a psychological climate that encourages adults to interact with each other. Further, Jane feels she is able to predict the extent to which adults will derive satisfaction from her courses. Adults will gain more satisfaction, Jane forecasts, from educational activities that occur in an atmosphere that facilitates learner interaction. Precisely because propositional theory is a guide for action, it is also useful for estimating and anticipating practical outcomes.

Theories are called strong or weak in reference to their predictive power. Jacob and Patricia Cohen write that as one moves "from the physical sciences through biology and across the broad spectrum of the behavioral sciences to cultural anthropology, the number of potential causal factors increases, their representation in measures becomes increasingly uncertain, and weak theories abound and compete."[8]

This is to say that it is relatively easy to verify some theories in physics or engineering because the number of variable factors in a given case may be small and easily controlled in a research experiment. This makes for a relatively strong theory. Suppose an engineer theorizes that the angle at which a beam of steel intercepts another beam of steel will strengthen the superstructure of a specific type of building. The theory may be tested without too much difficulty.

On the other hand, suppose you wish to test the theory that adults will retain knowledge longer if they learn by viewing a video as opposed to listening to a lecture. You divide some adults into two groups. One group views a video on a particular topic and the other group listens to a lecture on the same topic. You test the two groups after a month. Those who viewed the video get higher test scores. Does the experiment verify your theory? Of course not. You did not control a number of variable factors in the experiment, factors that may have contributed to the outcome of the experiment. The lecturer may have lacked dynamism; this would have hindered learning in one group. The lecture could have been given when the learners were tired, the video shown when the other learners were alert. Perhaps those adults in the video group had more positive attitudes toward learning; perhaps they had more favorable initial attitudes to the topic. Perhaps the temperature of the lecture hall was too chilly and the learners could not concentrate. Perhaps those in the lecture group were generally less able to retain information presented by any method. Perhaps those in the video group were more test-wise and, therefore, scored higher. The list of variable factors that were not controlled goes on and on. Finally, in some experimental situations there are factors over which the researcher has no control. Suppose a number of people in the lecture group failed to return to take the test, thereby introducing a distortion into the statistical data. Then also there may be unknown intervening variable factors, i.e., there may be factors affecting the outcome of the experiment that no one has even conceptualized.

In the behavioral and social sciences, and in education that is a social practice science, theories are ordinarily weak, not because they are intrinsically faulty but because they address states of affairs that embrace multiple and complex variables. To say that theories in education are generally weak is not to say that these theories are useless. Indeed, one can predict, with a high degree of probability, whether an adult education program will be well-attended simply by examining closely the program development theory of the religious educator. Again, one may predict, with a high degree of probability, the level of adult satisfaction with an instructional activity by questioning the teacher about his theory of teaching adults. And if it is possible to predict these things with a high degree of probability, it is also possible to state which program development approaches and teaching strategies will probably "work."

Prediction in education is not made on the basis of a discovered causal relationship between an educational intervention (e.g., the act of a teacher) and an event usually perceived as an outcome (e.g., the accomplishment of an instructional objective by the learners). Strictly speaking, in the behavioral and social sciences (because of the multiplicity of variables involved in any situation), prediction is made in terms of discovered associations between an educational intervention and an event usually perceived as an outcome. That is, educational research may show that intervention X on the part of the teacher, in situation Y, will be associated with change Z in 80 percent of the learners; the research may also show that such an *association* obtains with a probability of 90 times out of 100.

Prediction in education is not an exact science, but it is better than decision-making based on whim or empty speculation. It is far better than the magical thinking that characterizes the theories of some religious educators, i.e., the assumption that the Holy Spirit mysteriously causes educational outcomes regardless of the words and deeds of religious educators. The so-called blow theory of religious instruction proposes that learning outcomes are attributable to the invisible, and therefore not measurable, work of the Holy Spirit. The theory was given its name by James Michael Lee because its proponents take as a basic proof text John 3:8, "the Spirit blows where he wills."[9] Such magical thinking probably should be classified as largely a defense mechanism. If a program fails because adults did not show up, or if an instructional process is unproductive, it is consoling to believe that things went wrong because the Holy Spirit did not blow.

To sum up: When we speak of prediction in education, we are not speaking of prediction in the same way an astronomer or chemist would speak of prediction. We mean only that the educational researcher is able to forecast the probability that one event is associated with another given certain conditions.

Theory and Practice

Many see theory as something set over against practice. In our view practice is always the embodiment of a propositional theory, whether that theory is articulated or not, and whether the practitioner is aware of the propositional theory or not. Validation of any propositional theory in education, therefore, depends on the propositional theory as it takes its form as practice. If practice leads to anticipated desired results—and there is a concordance between the practice and the propositional theory—the theory is validated to the extent the anticipated desired results occur.

Assume a propositional theory states that teacher behavior ABC facilitates learning on the part of adults. A number of teachers employ behavior ABC and, in fact, discover that adult learning is facilitated. The theory is validated or verified by means of ordinary shared experience. Suppose, however, that someone wanted to verify the theory more scientifically and systematically. An experimental study is conducted. The circumstances surrounding the teaching-learning process are controlled as precisely as possible. The researchers finally announce that teacher behavior ABC facilitates learning on the part of adults with characteristics DEF, in circumstances GHI, nine times out of ten. The practice of employing teacher behavior ABC is verified and, at the same time, the propositional theory is verified. The chart below indicates that research, as it provides evaluative criteria, verifies (or challenges) not only a specific practice and undergirding theoretical base, but also the vision and perspective of the theoretician.

Research: Verification of Educational Practice, Theory, Vision, and Perspective

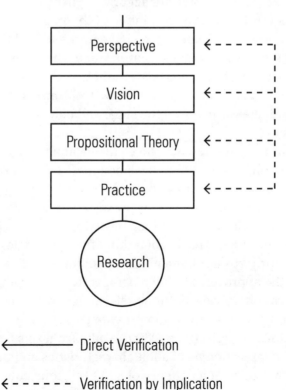

Identifying the Components of a Theory of Adult Religious Education

Speaking of the general field of adult education, Pittman notes that "after half a century, no grand design, no generally accepted set of principles, and no universally accepted definition unites the scholars, practitioners, and institutions of adult and continuing education."[10] While the same may be said of the sub-field of adult religious education, nonetheless, as Nelson points out, theory-building will continue because "A theory helps set goals and priorities, suggests where to start and how to proceed in the educational process and provides criteria for evaluation."[11] If we seek coherent theory of an even more specific sub-field, adult religious education, we must give attention to at least three fundamental notions: (1) adulthood, (2) religion, and (3) education.

Most thinking and reflection about adult religious education has been done by theologians or people who are strongly oriented toward the theological sciences. They have looked at adult education from the standpoint of religion, or more accurately, from the perspective of theology. It is fair to say that a number of theologies of adult education have been proposed. That is, the element "adult" and the element "education" have been placed on center stage while theorists view these elements from a box in the theater labeled "theology." The view from this vantage point, as does the view from any seat in the theater, screens and filters what is on the stage and colors what is seen in a particular way.

It is our purpose to place the element "adult" on stage with the element "religion," and to view these elements from a box in the theater labeled "education." What we propose in the following pages is an educational theory and not a theology of education. Such a theory will attempt to explain what adult religious education is, and it will serve as a guide for practice. This is something that theologies of adult education have hitherto not been able to accomplish. The previous figure indicates the approach. From the perspective of the professional field of adult education we view both the relevant characteristics of adults and the mission of the organization providing educational services, in this case religious organizations. What results from this field of vision and from the juxtapositioning of adult characteristics and the mission of the church is a propositional theory of adult religious education.

The remainder of this chapter will explore adult characteristics germane to the development of a theory of adult religious education as derived from andragogy, as well as the organizational context for providing such education. (Chapter 11 explores developmental characteristics as they impact educational interventions). The next chapter will explore the third element of theory, education, from the perspective of purpose, before proposing a propositional theory of adult religious education.

Adults: The Idea of Andragogy

The evolution of the professional field of adult education was linked historically to an increasingly articulated differentiation between childhood and adulthood begun in the nineteenth century. The professional field of adult education obviously could not have come into existence until it was seen, with some degree of clarity, that adults and children are different in many important respects relating to educational practice. But the differentiation between adults and children is still somewhat problematic. One of the problems facing adult education theorists today is a definitional one. What constitutes adulthood? The problem may be approached from several different avenues.

An adult may be defined in economic terms. An adult is a person who is capable of supporting himself financially and providing for his economic needs. An adult is not dependent on others such as parents for his economic well-being. Another definition stresses the legal aspect of being an adult. An adult is a person who reaches legal majority as defined by a legislative body. What the law states as a matter of legal convenience becomes the criterion that distinguishes the adult from the nonadult.

Culturally the adult may be defined as a person who has negotiated certain rites of passage. In tribal cultures there are certain rituals that demarcate adulthood. Many of these rituals require the candidate for full tribal status to complete specified tasks preliminary to the celebration of the ritual. In a very real sense there are rites of passage in contemporary industrial cultures. These rites of passage are less stylized as rituals but nonetheless mark off adulthood from adolescence and childhood. Included in such rites would be the acquisition of a driver's license, getting married, being accepted as a full-time employee, being able to take out a loan, and so forth. The cumulative effect of these rites bestows adulthood.

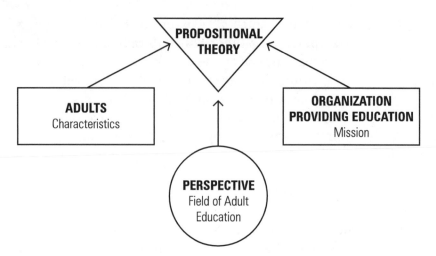

If we approach the definitional problem from the standpoint of the sociology of knowledge, we would say that an adult is a person who is perceived to be an adult by others in society. Adulthood is attained when a general and unspoken consensus forms to the end that an individual is treated as an adult in the various relationships of social interchange.

Adulthood can be defined from the biological standpoint. An adult is any person who is reproductively mature. Quite often in primitive societies biological maturation was celebrated ritually as a sign of a person's passage to full status as a member of the tribe.

Neurologically an adult may be defined as a person whose brain has reached a stage of maturation in terms of synaptic structure. Katchadourian explains the cognitive differences between adults and children by reference to the increased "connectivity" or communicative linkages among brain cells.[12]

Psychologically the adult is defined as one who has reached a certain degree of maturity. Maturity could be understood in the framework of Erikson's schema that outlines various critical periods in life,[13] or from the viewpoints of any number of life span theories. Finally, from the educational point of view, a person could be considered an adult upon finishing the years of schooling mandated by a given society.

It is not difficult to see why writers sometimes offer stipulative definitions of adulthood and avoid definitional formulas that attempt to express the essence of adulthood. The concept of adulthood is agonizingly complex. Even stipulative definitions, however, often turn out to be unenlightening and fuzzy. A definition formulated by a convocation of adult educators evidences the tentativeness and conceptual sloppiness that typifies many definitions: "An adult is a person who has assumed (whether by his own choice or not) some kind of responsibility for self, and perhaps for others, and some degree of independence of parental authority not characteristic to the same degree of adolescents."[14] The definition is hedged by a number of qualifiers and vague terms so as to be practically useless, except perhaps to a convocation of educators who must slap something together for the proceedings of the convocation.

The definitional problem arises because adulthood is not a distinct state of being that can be placed over against another absolutely distinct state of being, i.e., childhood or adolescence. Adulthood, childhood, and adolescence are, instead, modes of being-in-the-world or ways of comporting oneself in everyday life. Adulthood is but one part of a life continuum that includes childhood and adolescence. Because periods or stages along the continuum of development tend to blend into one another, we must be content with differentiating them in broad terms. This is what andragogy attempts to do.

Assumptions Underlying Andragogy

Malcolm Knowles is credited with introducing us to the idea of andragogy in the *Modern Practice of Adult Education*, a book that, particularly in its revision, has become a classic among adult education practitioners. But Knowles credits adult educators in Europe with coining the term to describe a unique approach to teaching adults. The term is derived from the Greek *aner* (stem *andr*) and *agogos*. *Aner* connotes a mature or full-grown man; agogos means "leading." In his first edition, Knowles attempted to contrast pedagogy and andragogy. A pedagogue in common parlance is one who is versed in the art and science of teaching children. In contrast, Knowles described andragogy as "the art and science of helping adults learn." The subtitle of the first edition was "Pedagogy vs. Andragogy." A lengthy debate ensued in the pages of *Adult Education Journal* with an number of highly regarded educators lined up on both sides of the argument, some dismissing andragogy and thus Knowles's ideas as off the mark at best and trash at worst, others steadfastly defended the idea as a needed paradigm for expressing the uniqueness of adult education. Most would agree that the cause of adult education theory and practice was forwarded by the often heated debate.[15]

The mellowing of Knowles's ideas can be seen in the subtitle to the second edition of *The Modern Practice*: *From Pedagogy to Andragogy*, published in 1980. Since then andragogy has continued to be the subject of much debate as well as misapplication.[16] Twenty-plus years after its introduction to the United States, andragogy may best be seen not as a theory per se, but rather as a way of viewing adults and learning. In a sense, andragogy may be seen as a conceptual approach of the adult educator who starts where needed in the process (with pedagogical approaches if necessary) with the intent of moving the adult learner toward learning processes that maximize his or her control over learning. Whether in decades to come anyone remembers the word that stirred adult educators in the 1980s, it is Knowles's analysis of adult life (from which he infers theoretical constructs that serve as the basis for his approach) that is important.

Knowles looks at adulthood in relation to four key categories: self-concept, experience, readiness to learn, and orientation to learning. On these bases he delineates a generic approach to adult education. Each of these bases, of course, are related to the other three. That the self-concept of the adult is different from the self-concept of the child is related to the qualitative difference between adult and childhood experience, to the difference that obtains between an adult's and a child's readiness to learn, and to the difference between the adult's and the child's orientations to learning.

Self-Concept

Adults generally see themselves as independent. They have outgrown the state of dependency that is associated with childhood. Adults have a sense of individual identity: they see themselves as separate and apart from other individual adults, not simply, for example, as children of or extensions of their parents. They view themselves as producers and not simply as consumers; as people who are actively in charge of their own lives, and not as people who passively await superior others to shape their lives. Adults are more self-directing and less other-directed. They are perceived by children and adolescents (either their own children or surrogate children) as being responsible people. The perceptions of these younger people, and the generally deferential treatment afforded the adults by younger people, help adults develop a self-image that emphasizes respectability and responsibility.

Experience

The adult has more life experience than the child; the experience of the adult is of a different sort; the experience of the adult is organized differently than the experience of a child. Knowles points out that a child has not experienced making a living, getting married, rearing a family, being responsible for the welfare of others, and a host of other life situations. The adult has more experience and a qualitatively different experiential background.

Now this also implies that the adult organizes current experiences differently than a child. If an adult and child both experience event X simultaneously, the grasping of the event and its interpretation will be different between them. Event X will be interpreted and appropriated by the adult in terms of her larger reservoir of previous experience; the same event will be interpreted and appropriated by the child in relation to a relatively narrow range of previous experience. It has often been noted that adults usually take longer to complete some timed tests because they must filter test questions through a large store of previously gained knowledge and experience; the child or youth, on the other hand, is not burdened by this elaborate filtering system and may not see the test question from as many different angles. One might even conclude that the texture of experience is different for an adult and child. A newly experienced event is woven into the fabric of existing experience differently. If subjectivity impinges on objects that are known in such a way as to make purely objective knowledge impossible, it may be concluded that adults bring distinctive modes of subjectivity to the act of knowing. Or, as the medieval philosophers stated, that which is known is known according to the mode of the knower.

Readiness to Learn

In speaking about readiness to learn Knowles places emphasis on the work of Robert Havighurst.[17] Readiness to learn is at its peak when the teachable moment arrives. And the arrival of the teachable moment is linked to the accomplishment of a task imposed on people by their relative locus in the life span.

What Knowles addresses here, at least tangentially, is really a theory of motivation. A person is motivated to learn something because in the learning of a particular idea, attitude, or procedure the person is capacitated to complete a task associated with a specific stage in human development. A child, for example, is not required by his life situation to learn how to rent an apartment or buy a house; the provision of shelter is peculiarly an adult concern. A particular life situation or a complexus of events related to a stage of human development sets up learning requirements, expectations, needs, interests, and aspirations that may not be present in other life situations or at other stages of development. A particular life situation gives rise to a definite orientation toward reality. In discussing readiness to learn, then, Knowles also addresses the difference between adults and children in respect to the differential life exigencies.

Orientation to Learning

Adults and children have different time perspectives. Much of what children learn in school cannot be applied immediately in their lives. It is proper to give support to the adage that education is life and not simply a preparation for life. But much of what we learned in childhood is a preparation for adult life and cannot immediately be translated into life situations of children. Children learn to postpone the application of much of what is learned, sometimes to the distant future. The child, then, usually has a subject-centered orientation to learning (rightly or wrongly). She views education as comprising the subjects of reading, writing, arithmetic, etc. Adults ordinarily pursue learning in order to solve problems that crop up in their lives. This is especially true in regard to voluntary adult education. The typical adult wants to learn something that can be applied immediately to the large and small problems he faces.

Brookfield has criticized andragogy as an inadequate theory.[18] Merriam, however, counters that "Andragogy is seen to be not so much an explanatory theory about adult learning as a philosophical stance with regard to the purposes of adult education and the relationship of the individual to society."[19] Instead of presenting it as a philosophy or theory, however, Knowles increasingly came to view andragogy as a set of assumptions guiding the practice of those who would teach adults. Admittedly, andragogy has become a rallying symbol for adult educators seeking a professional identity, and as one colleague put it, we have too long worshipped at the shrine of andragogy. The debate notwithstanding, the concept does clarify the meaning of adult education. In the last analysis, we can readily accept andragogy as a useful conceptual tool for the analysis of adult education and as a source concept from which we may derive guiding principles for program development and instructional processes. We will return to some of these principles in the next chapter, but first we must turn our attention to the other element in our field of vision: the mission of the religious organization that provides educational service.

Religious Mission

If questioned about the purpose of their parish religious education program, most pastors and parish educators would probably respond, "Why, to make better Christians of our congregants, of course." Several problems immediately come to mind in the face of such a seemingly worthy answer, however. First, the response begs another question, "What does it mean to be a better Christian? By what criteria are we to judge 'better?'" With no intent toward cynicism, what is often meant is that we want to make people better church members. Whether the content of the program is oriented toward propagation of theological/biblical knowledge or toward "leader training" to prepare members for service in the congregation, the tacit purpose is preservation of the institution. This requires that parishioners understand the tenets of the institution and its functional procedures. In an era when churches are challenged to demonstrate their relevance, we see more and more effort expended on a mission of institutional survival!

In a lecture years ago, theologian Gregory Baum told a parable that elucidates the danger of narrow definitions of mission. The parable elucidates the danger of narrow definitions of mission. Once upon a time, many years ago, there were two candle shops in a small village. The owners of the shop on Main Street decided to conduct a meeting for the purpose of defining the mission of the business enterprise. After much discussion the owners decided that the mission of the shop was to make and sell candles. The owners of the shop on Broadway Boulevard also had a meeting to frame a mission statement. They decided that the mission of their enterprise was to provide light. Today the shop on Main Street is housed in the same building it occupied many years ago. The only visitors are curiosity seekers. The shop on Broadway Boulevard, however, has expanded into an international corporation. The corporation manufactures all kinds of equipment that aids in providing light for people.

Making Meaning Available

We would assert that the mission of the church is to make meaning available, the kind of meaning that helps adults make sense of their existence and the world around them. Vogel posits that "Sculpting meaning can be soul nourishing for people of faith. It is an invitation to make this journey of faith our home."[20] One of the greatest needs of adults is to understand the meaning of their experience in ways that help them see the movement of God in their lives. How do we do this?

Three New Testament words come to mind: *kerygma*, *diakonia*, and *koinonia*. The kerygmatic function of the church is to announce a message; the diakonic function is to serve those in need; the koinoniac function is to form community. Each function implies the remaining two. This is shown in the chart below.

It is the mission of the Christian church to announce that meaning has been visited upon us in the person of Jesus, that our lives become meaningful by following the way and teachings of Jesus, that Jesus is a sign of promise for all of us, that all things work toward good for those who love God, that the world must be transformed according to teachings of Jesus, that hope is not fruitless if it is anchored in Jesus. The message may be formulated in many ways and in many different discursive fashions. It may also be expressed in "doing" the teachings of Jesus.

Jesus was concerned with the least of his brethren; he was concerned with their needs, even their very mundane needs. Jesus helped people spiritually, but he did not limit his work to spiritual works. This is emphasized strongly in the dramatic scene of the last judgment depicted in Matthew's Gospel. The kingdom is awarded to those who feed the hungry, give drink to the thirsty, welcome the stranger, clothe the naked, care for the sick, and visit those in prison. The "doing" of the teachings of Jesus, serving those who are in need, speaks the message of Jesus in another way.

Building Christian community depends upon sharing and naming common experience and recognition of shared identity. This takes place

A Theory of Religious Education

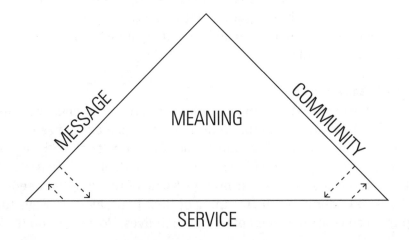

at one level in the observance of the Lord's Supper or Eucharist. At another level, it is the sharing of personal stories, individual and corporate faith pilgrimages, in ways that enable and encourage connections even among disparate paths toward faith that builds the meaningful relationships foundational to community. Vogel emphasizes the importance of such sharing:

> As we share our experiences with others and listen to their stories, we are empowered to reflect and discern, to decide and act; making connections with our own past and present and our future hopes; others' experiences and hopes; and the stories, beliefs, rituals, and values of our faith community helps us make and discover meaning and nourishes our souls.[21]

The mission of the church is to make meaning available by announcing the good news and the teachings of Jesus by serving the people in their needs (secular as well as sacred) and by forming community as we journey along sometimes divergent paths toward faith. This mission statement is brief but serves present purposes. Together with the characteristics of adults articulated earlier, we have a partial foundation for a propositional theory of adult religious education. In the next chapter we examine briefly the attempts to articulate the purpose of adult religious education before setting forth our own propositional theory.

Notes

[1] John Rachal and Sean Courtney, "Focus on Adult Education Research Questions," *Adult Education Quarterly* 36, no.4 (1986): 160-65.

[2] Sharon Merriam, "Adult Education and Theory Building: A Review," *Adult Education Quarterly* 37 (1987): 188.

[3] Henry George Liddell and Robert Scott, *Greek-English Lexicon* (London: Clarendon, 1958), 796.

[4] Leon McKenzie, *Adult Education and Worldview Construction* (Malabar FL: Krieger Publishing Co., 1991), 27.

[5] John Phillips, "Theory, Practice, and Basic Beliefs in Adult Education," *Adult Education* 31, no. 2 (1981): 95.

[6] For a fuller treatment of the effect of such traditions and assumptions on the development of generational perspectives see Douglas Walrath, *Frameworks: Patterns for Living and Believing Today* (New York: Pilgrim Press, 1986).

[7] Theory, of course, has many different functions. Another primary function of theory is that of serving as a basis for research activity. That is, theory assists the researcher in formulating the statement of a research problem and in the design of the research activity. Only two functions of theory are treated since comments about it in the chapter are introductory and do not constitute the principal emphasis of the chapter.

[8] Jacob Cohen and Patricia Cohen, *Applied Multiple Regression/Correlation Analysis for the Behavioral Sciences* (New York: John Wiley & Sons, 1975), 7.

[9] James Michael Lee, *The Flow of Religious Instruction* (Birmingham AL: Religious Education Press, 1973) 174ff.

[10] Von Pittman, "What Is the Image of the Field Today?," *New Directions for Continuing Education* 44 (1991): 15.

[11] C. Ellis Nelson, "Toward the Year 2003," *Religious Education Journal* 79, no. 1 (Winter 1984): 101.

[12] H. Katchadourian, "Medical Perspectives on Adulthood," *Daedulus* 55, no. 2 (1976): 41.

[13] Erik Erikson, *Childhood and Society* (New York: Norton, 1963).

[14] New England Board of Higher Education and Center for the Study of Liberal Education of Adults, *Proceedings of the Conference on the Training of Counselors of Adults*, (1965), quoted in Joan Goldbery, "Counseling the Adult Learner: A Selective Review of the Literature," *Adult Education* 30, no. 2 (1980): 70.

[15] McKenzie made a significant contribution to the debate by pointing out, in response to Houle's assertion that technically children and adults learn things in the same ways, that children and adults may be *metaphysically* the same, but *phenomenologically* different. These phenomenological differences justify a different approach to learning.

[16] For an example of misapplication and misunderstanding of andragogy see chapter five, Charles McCollough, *Heads of Heaven, Feet of Clay* (1983). The author misinterprets andragogy as a method when it is more a way of thinking about people and learning what methods are appropriate in various settings with adults according to their needs and prior learning experience. He also seems to suggest that with its emphasis on self-direction, it may be inappropriate in adult *religious* education, a position that these authors would strongly contest.

[17] Robert J. Havighurst, *Developmental Tasks and Education* (New York: David McKay, 1961).

[18] Steven Brookfield provides a helpful survey of interpretations and applications of andragogy in chapter five, Steven Brookfield, *Understanding and Facilitating Adult Learning* (San Francisco: Jossey-Bass, 1986) 119-22.

[19] Daniel Pratt, "Andragogy After Twenty-Five Years," in Sharon Merriam, ed., *An Update on Adult Learning Theory* (San Francisco: Jossey-Bass, 1993), 21-22.

[20] Linda Vogel, *Teaching and Learning in Communities of Faith: Empowering Adults Through Religious Education* (San Francisco: Jossey-Bass Publishers, 1991), 41.

[21] Ibid., xii.

TOWARD A THEORY OF ADULT RELIGIOUS EDUCATION, PART II
THEORETICAL PROPOSITIONS TO GUIDE PRACTICE

Survey the literature in the broader field of adult education and you will find those who have grand ideas about the ability of adult education to change the world. Certainly adult education and its sub-field, adult religious education, should have worthy goals. Far too many programs targeted for adults have no clear purpose beyond vague shibboleths such as "to make adults better Christians." One of the latest works in adult religious education purporting to be a "handbook" for adult religious educators does not even address the subject of purpose.

The literature in the broader field has paid much more attention to the matter of purpose than the sub-field of adult religious education. Even there, however, one finds wide differences among the various positions on the subject. For example, one of the foremost educators in the field, Eduard Lindeman, long ago made a strong case for social change as the goal of adult education. Lindeman's biographer David Stewart picked up the theme, asserting that "Possibly the most important societal test of the value of education for adults is the extent to which new programs are developed to deal rationally with emerging social problems."[1] Societal change as a goal has had plenty of advocates and continues to be considered viable by writers such as Griffith, Cunningham, and Apps.[2]

On the other hand, Stubblefield sees life fulfillment as the "metagoal" of adult education, asserting that "Adult education that focuses on life fulfillment derives its rationale from the learning motivation of adults: their desire for self-actualization and for the control of their social environment."[3] Knox affirms the value of such a focus, though he divides programs between those with an individual focus and comprehensive programs directed toward organizational and community change.[4] But McGinnis is representative of those who see liberation as the goal:

> Human liberation . . . is the process of man's continuous efforts to create a society in which all people feel themselves to be and are in fact free from all forms of oppression. Thus, individuals moving toward this goal perceive themselves to be increasingly in control of themselves and in harmony with their total environment. They realize their importance in solidarity with others in the struggle to eliminate human exploitation.[5]

Other adult educators are less restrictive in their definitions of purpose. McKenzie, for example, seems to capture the essence of these three arguments when he asserts that adult education in a general sense may indeed help adults achieve their potential, but to the end "that the learners become more liberated as individuals, better capacitated to participate in the life of their communities and institutions, and empowered to create an authentically human future."[6] We shall return later in this chapter to McKenzie's approach to actualizing this broader goal of adult education through construction and examination of worldviews.

Though perhaps an oversimplification, educational programs for adults tend to be guided by the goal to help them "cope," to shape and reshape their own thinking, emotions, and behavior to fit the world as it impinges and intrudes on their lives. Indeed, adults are often heard to plead, "Help me make sense of what is going on around me." The response to this plea, however, is often encouragement to adjust the self to the exterior world, with the ultimate goal of survival. But can adult education (including adult religious education) help adults to envision a future over which they have a greater sense of control, acting upon their world (rather than being acted upon) in such a way as to contribute to the enhancement of the social order while finding greater fulfillment and personal satisfaction? What acceptance of limitations, what understanding of resources, of potential, of political systems would be required? What vision? What inspiration?

Bridging an examination of the purposes of adult education to the sub-field adult religious education, we may borrow Apps's five questions posed originally to clarify the role of adult education.[7] Is the purpose (1) to "pass on culture and help disadvantaged people into the

'mainstream' of society?" (2) to help reform society? (3) to change societal structures? (4) to "help individuals achieve maximum personal
growth?" (5) or is the purpose some combination of all of these? To par-
aphrase and apply these questions to adult religious education, is our
purpose (1) to pass on our religious culture, helping to mainstream the
uninitiated into that culture? (2) to reform society according to biblical
principles? (3) to seek major changes in societal structures so as to
identify the working and grand plan of the Divine? (4) to help people
achieve their potential under God, actualizing His plan (in relation to
others)? Or, (5) is there some combination that captures the essence of
our purpose(s)? The simple response is yes to all of these. Vogel captures the social and personal aspects of purpose but also the spiritual
as she proposes that

> The task of adult religious education is to create settings and processes that
> invite people to journey together—exploring, reflecting, experiencing, and acting
> in and toward faith. Religious education is about hearing and sharing stories;
> about talking together, listening, and making connections; about promise, obedi-
> ence, pathos, and mystery; about sharing hope for the future and seeking peace.[8]

For her the appropriate context for religious education is social as she
proposes as goals "(1) calling individuals to listen and share life experiences and stories as they intersect with one's faith story; (2) building
community through worship, study, witness, and service; and (3) clarifying problems that block justice and then working to bring about a
more just and caring world."[9] Elias assumes the same context as he
avers that "adult education is to take place within a community of disciples who are concerned with both the life of the church and problems
in society."[10] For him, "Adult education has as its purpose to call adults
to be disciples of Jesus Christ and to carry out a ministry within the
church and a mission to the world."[11]

Elias's purpose statement may be more comprehensive than
appears at first reading and may satisfy evangelical religious educators
concerned about what they perceive to be a purely academic approach.
Calling adults to be disciples brings to mind "The Great Commission"
(Matthew 28:19) and includes both the tasks of evangelism and lifelong
learning. Social concerns are addressed in the call to prepare adults for
"a mission to the world." Citing a variety of contemporary social issues,
Griffith asserts that "without an educational approach and the cultiva-
tion of a willingness to examine the issues afresh (with due

consideration to the complexity of the problem), there is little hope that these problems can be resolved."[12] Adult religious education operates within a context that provides a motivation based on a unique spiritual conviction for addressing these concerns.

The scope of adult religious education may be limited by a restrictive viewpoint that addresses only one particular facet. For example, Vogel points out that on the one hand, if a teacher understands, along with Thomas Groome, that Christian religious education is "'a political activity with pilgrims in time that deliberately and intentionally attends with them to the activity of God in our present, to the Story of the Christian faith community, and to the Vision of God's Kingdom, the seeds of which are already among us' this understanding establishes parameters regarding the nature of both content and process. On the other hand, if one understands the goal to be seeking to lead people to a personal conversion experience and to accept Jesus Christ as their Lord and Savior, the parameters for planning and teaching would be less likely to include issues relating to political activity and social transformation."[13]

Finally, in a literature review of attempts to address the issue of purpose in adult education, Beder found typologies falling generally into four categories: to facilitate change in a dynamic society; to support and maintain the "good" social order; to promote productivity; and to enhance personal growth.[14] If these categories are accepted, they find ready support from Scripture, e.g., is not the command to be salt and light not an effort to facilitate change in a dynamic society? Is not good social order maintained by following the admonition to do everything with decency and order? Productivity is certainly implied in the command, "Whatever your hand finds to do, do as unto the Lord." Further, personal growth is enhanced as people "grow into the stature of Christ." Perhaps the challenge to adult religious education is to address the issues of how, in what ways, and where we are to be salt and light. What does it mean to do everything in decency and order, and when is it appropriate to challenge the social order? What are the ethics of productivity? What does it mean to grow toward the stature of Christ, especially in terms of following Christ's example of relationships and ministry to all people in all kinds of need? Is there an area of the adult pilgrimage not touched by these concerns?

We have looked at adulthood and adults in terms of Malcolm Knowles's idea of andragogy; we have examined the church and have formulated a concise mission statement. Our point of reference has been education. We have surveyed attempts to provide a sense of direction by defining the purpose of adult religious education. It is now possible to derive statements of propositional theory regarding adult religious education.

If it is agreed that adults are more self-directing than children, that adults have had more experiences than children, that adults are more independent than children, that adult readiness to learn is related to concerns arising from their life situations, and that adults seek to apply what they learn as soon as possible, the following propositions may be derived:

1. The initial step of program development (curriculum development) is applied research that gains information from prospective learners about their educational needs and interests. This is to say that the religious educator must undertake a needs assessment to determine the main concerns of the adults in the parish or local church. Topics for different courses, conferences, discussion groups, and so forth will be based on data gathered by means of the needs assessment.

A word of caution is in order regarding needs assessment. First, interests and needs are not the same, though they are frequently confused by religious educators. An interest is an expression of some degree of desire, while need connotes a deficit. Religious educators often make the mistake of assuming that because adults express an interest in a topic, they will participate in a program addressing that topic. The religious educator may survey adults (through some means), then proceed to plan programs from the list of expressed interest, only to be disappointed by low (or no) attendance. The adult, however, simply lines the program up against other interests, any of which may be greater.

Where genuine needs are concerned, the religious educator may confuse ascribed needs and perceived needs. Unfortunately, religious educators often observe adults or examine literature describing the life situation of a group of adults (e.g., "characteristics of young adults"), then they ascribe needs to the adults, proceeding to plan programs to address those ascribed needs. However, if adults do not perceive that these needs are real, they will not be motivated to participate. Ascribed needs may be the starting point in the assessment process, but they are never sufficient basis for program planning. For this and other reasons, proposition two is important.

2. Adults should be invited to help the religious educator plan the educational program. Since adults in a given parish or local church are assumed to be experienced and knowledgeable about the parish or local church, the religious educator should invite prospective participants to plan the various course offerings that constitute the program or curriculum. Prospective participants should be brought into the decision-making process regarding the total educational program. This is not to suggest that the religious educator simply turn the planning of the program over to a group of adults. The religious educator, it is assumed, will possess competencies in educational planning. These competencies should be put to use in guiding adults in program planning.

3. Adults should be invited to help the religious educator implement and administer the educational program. This does not mean that adults should be made responsible for setting up the chairs for a workshop! During the course of, say, a fall educational program, several educational activities or courses may be offered. During this time a number of administrative decisions must ordinarily be made. Without surrendering the role of program administrator, the religious educator can bring program participants into the decision-making process whenever feasible. This includes decisions about where, when, and how the program takes place.

4. Adults should be invited not only to provide evaluations of the educational program but should also be involved, as is feasible, in the planning of program evaluation. Program evaluation plans are made prior to the offering of the first course in a given program. Adults should be asked to participate in the planning of evaluation. The religious educator, assuming the religious educator possesses skills in evaluation planning, guides the adults in the planning. Adults who participate in the program as learners should be asked to provide information relating to the worth of the total program. This information may be provided midway through a program, say after three weeks of a fall program of several courses, conferences, etc., and/or at the conclusion of the fall program. Evaluations provided by adults midway through a program allow the program planners to make mid-course adjustments in the program; evaluations provided by adults at the conclusion of a program allow program planners to get ready for the next program, e.g., the spring program or the Lenten program.

5. In the instructional setting, adults must be respected as adults. Teachers who adopt an air of condescension toward adult learners, or who act as if adult learners are inferior or subordinate, will find that most adults react negatively. The adult who participates in what is essentially a voluntary activity (education in the parish or local church) will not return to a situation where he finds his self-esteem challenged.

6. In the instructional setting, adults should be encouraged to be proactive rather than reactive. Within the limits imposed on the teaching-learning situation by the instructional objectives and the selection of instructional techniques, adult learners should not be expected merely to react to what is said by the teacher. The instructional climate should be such that adults feel free to initiate discussions, to introduce new topics, and to participate proactively in the educational activity. This is not to say that the teacher must refrain from proactive participation; it is only to underscore the idea that adults must feel free to act as adults. The adage "Speak when you are spoken to" may be applicable to small children in some situations; it is by no means applicable to adults in the instructional setting.

7. In the instructional setting, depending on the specific instructional objectives and the content of the instruction, adult learners may be resource people for learning as well as learners. This is another way of saying that in many instances the experiences of adult learners can be shared profitably in a group of learners to the end that all present are assisted toward the accomplishment of the instructional objectives. We can learn from one another. This is true for childhood education and, *a fortiori,* it is true in adult education since adults have richer and more variegated experiences.

8. Adult religious education, regardless of its program content, should have as a part of its focus assisting adults to examine, deconstruct, and revise their existing worldviews as a foundation for meaning-making. McKenzie's claim, which was originally applied to the broader field of adult education, can be appropriately and specifically applied to adult religious education, namely that it "can be a major factor in helping adults construct the network of ideas, values, feelings, beliefs, opinions, intuitions, judgments, choices, and actions that constitute a worldview."[15] This proposition is of such importance that the subject will be treated more fully in a later section of this chapter. However, it needs to be stated in this context that our worldviews guide our decisions about actions, our behavior in relationships, our assumptions about what is and is not possible in terms of the effect we can have individually and corporately on the world as we find it, and our regard for the worldviews of others. "The claim that worldviews should make possible an openness to new ideas and experiences, should avoid narrowness of vision, should influence the worldviewer to rely on his or her informed judgment, and should encourage the worldviewer to appreciate the worldviews of others is a claim that exists as a higher order principle. It is substantively different from the claim that a Methodist worldview is demonstrably better than a Presbyterian one."[16]

9. As regards the explicitly religious message of the church, adults must be given choices and options relating to which aspects of the message interest them. The explicitly religious message of the church is multifaceted and contains many separate elements. If we can assume that all these elements relate to the development and/or expression of faith, it may also be assumed that adults are located at different "places" in their development and expression as regards personal faith. Therefore, adults will be interested in (and need) different aspects of the religious according to their personal faith development and expression. An approach of "corned beef and hash for everyone" (which is tantamount to "We don't care what you need, this is what you get because this is what we've got") and programs based simply on what the religious educator or pastor wants to teach are too capricious.

10. Adult religious education, if it is responsive to adult needs, is a form of service. Most religious educators seldom think of adult education in the parish or local church as a form of service. They restrict the scope of educational programs to topics that are explicitly religious and never realize that education can help adults meet some pressing needs. It may well happen that many older adults in a particular parish or local church, for example, could be served as well by a short course on meal-planning than by a Bible study course. The former course, it is maintained, is just as much religious education (in its broad sense) as the latter course.

11. Adult religious education, if it is responsive to adult interests, can contribute to the formation of community. Again, most religious educators think of adult religious education only in limited terms. They do not see educational activity as something that has community formation as its function. Thus, attempts are made in relatively few parishes and local churches to include courses that appeal to the leisure-time interests of adults. A course on the liturgy of baptism, for example, is viewed as appropriately a religious education course; a course on how to bake bread is seen as secular, something best left to the continuing education division of the local college.

12. Adult religious education, in order to be responsive, must acknowledge that any structured program for adults is set in the context of a larger curriculum. Vogel appropriately defines curriculum as "a course to be run, and includes the total life of the community of faith as it teaches and proclaims, worships and breaks bread, and witnesses and serves in the world."[17] Curriculum is much broader than the materials and programs provided for use in the execution of a church's adult education enterprise. Further, the explicit content of a program for adults may be inconsistent with the implicit content communicated through the church's broader curriculum. For example, an adult class on church polity may expound the principles of responsible participation in the affairs of the church, respecting the opinions and contributions of others, and working cooperatively toward common objectives. The curricular context (the congregational environment) of that class, however, may counter such teachings at the point of outward disdain for dissenting viewpoints, acquiescence to power-players in the congregation, and explicit individual efforts to undermine democratically derived decisions. Ideally, formalized adult religious education contributes to the development of a positive curricular context for the life and work of the congregation.

No doubt a lengthy list of theoretical propositions relating to adult education can be derived from Knowles's analysis of adult life. The propositions listed above are, in my estimation, crucial for the practice of religious education. The list may be continued when we look at the delineation of the mission of the church presented above. The mission of the church is to make meaning available. Meaning is made available by means of announcing a message, serving those in need, and forming community. This meaning-making is of such importance as to deserve special treatment, by way of a expansion of proposition eight above.

The Construction of Worldviews and the Role of Adult Religious Education

Proposition eight is of such importance as to demand special treatment. If the mission of the church is to make meaning available, then it is proposed that adult education can facilitate the accomplishment of that mission by helping adults examine, shape, and reshape their meaning perspectives or worldviews as the avenue through which meaning is shaped. As such, worldview construction becomes a transcendent goal of adult religious education. This section is intended to briefly explain the concept of worldview construction and suggest a role for adult religious education in the process of such construction. The material in this section relies heavily on McKenzie's elaboration of the subject in his book, *Adult Education and Worldview Construction*.[18] The reader should consult this work for the background of the concept and fuller explanation of how the process can be facilitated through adult education.

A worldview is not some esoteric concept that one may choose to ignore as out of field or irrelevant to everyday life. It may not be identified as such, but in a real sense one's worldview is the "framework" that provides perspective on life and affects everyday decision-making. McKenzie asserts, therefore, that "Given this realization, this understanding, this sense of being positioned to construct a world, it follows that attentiveness to worldview construction is necessary. This is due to the fact that adult decisions arise out of their worldviews. Their decisions about how they comport themselves and how they live out their lives will be positively creative only to the extent that positive creativity is permitted by their worldviews."[19]

Defining Worldview

What exactly is a worldview? McKenzie defines it as "an interpretation of reality that provides an understanding of the world. Worldviews are constructed in response to the human being's ultimate, penultimate, and immediate personal concerns. A worldview embraces knowledge, ideas, feelings, values, assumptions, and beliefs."[20] As such, it is not something most adults set out to construct with any intentionality. Rather, it develops quite naturally out of lived experience and provides us with a personal understanding of "how things are" in the world (regardless of the accuracy of that understanding—accuracy in this case is relative to the individual and the circumstance). It may be said, however, that a worldview is the ultimate result of trying to "figure things out" for oneself, to quench the thirst for meaning that is the natural quest of humankind. "At the bottom of this," McKenzie avers, "and sometimes amid great turmoil, adults are testing their ideals, values, convictions, beliefs, opinions, feelings, fears, and hopes. They seek an interpretation of their lives that is credible, an interpretation that supplies them with an understanding of their being-in-the-world however fragile and tenuous that understanding may be."[21]

How a Worldview Is Formed

Life experience, and reflection on that experience, is the "stuff" of which a worldview is made. "A worldview is constructed amid all the vicissitudes of life, in a cauldron of laughter and tears, of sweat and pain, of harsh words, penetrating glances, and tender gestures. A worldview takes its shape, texture, and substance not in the seminar room but in the marketplace."[22] As such, it provides an interpretative understanding of the world. In a sense, it may be said that our worldview provides a giant internal screen upon which each new experience is projected. An automatic, typically unconscious search ensues to find a connection between the experience and the existing worldview in order to make it "fit in" to present understandings. In that way, experience may be said to be understood in light of the existing worldview. But what if there is no fit? McKenzie claims that worldviews are never static but are constantly being altered to accommodate new experiences. Some may be rejected out of hand, but usually worldviews are reorganized and reinterpreted in the light of new experiences, depending upon the source and impact of that new experience.

In that vein, Bennis[23] describes three kinds of learning: maintenance, shock, and innovative. Maintenance learning provides experiences that easily fit existing worldviews, and is in fact designed to pass on and reinforce the "accepted" worldview of a culture. Shock learning occurs when the substance of maintenance learning is inadequate (a problem or crisis occurs for which an old solution is inadequate). There is no fit with the existing worldview, and thus there must be reevaluation, reordering, and alterations to the worldview in order to accommodate the new experience. Innovative learning postures one to expect, even to anticipate such change. This type of learning is more likely to facilitate real understanding that results when the existing worldview is deconstructed and reassembled in such a way as to accommodate the new experience. Again, McKenzie: "To use my own nomenclature, thinking strives for understanding by analyzing and synthesizing experience until insights are produced. Relationships are noted; patterns of thought and judgment are related; causes and effects are assigned, connections are made among discrete events, components of a complex reality are recognized and placed in new associations. Resulting insights become a part of the individual's worldview and serve as a basis for the analysis and synthesis of new experiences."[24]

Types of Worldviews

Worldviews may be explicit or tacit and may fall into any combination of five categories, according to McKenzie:[25]

(1) Provisional vs. Fixed
(2) Inclusive vs. Narrow
(3) Active vs. Passive
(4) Critical vs. Uncritical
(5) Disdaining vs. Accepting

Fixed worldviews are open only to congruent views, those that corroborate the existing worldview. A provisional worldview, on the other hand, is open to new and challenging ideas and seeks growth through assimilation of new meanings that are integrated with the old. One's worldview may be provisional with respect to certain meanings while remaining fixed where other meanings are concerned. On the other hand, an inclusive worldview is open to a diversity of new meanings, while a narrow worldview makes a priori decisions to reject potentially threatening input (that which threatens the existing worldview, that is).

People holding a passive worldview rely on an external authority to dictate what is "right," what is meaningful, what is truth. In that sense there is little personal initiative to pursue meaning and truth for oneself. Conversely, an active worldview is always in pursuit of new meanings. "In a sense a passive worldview, i.e., a worldview that absolutizes authority at the expense of autonomous action, is a closed worldview, a fixed worldview. Likewise, an active worldview is a provisional worldview in that it is prepared to evaluate any idea or value whether it is proposed by an authority or not."[26] Similarly, a critical worldview questions and tests new ideas through meditative and deliberative thinking. An uncritical worldview may be rather chameleon-like in that it randomly takes in ideas and values of the prevailing culture with little evaluation of merit, strength, or effect.

One might assume that a fixed, narrow, possibly passive worldview might also be other-disdaining, though McKenzie does not suggest such a conclusion. He does observe, however, that an other-disdaining worldview "appraises the worldviews of others as naive, stupid, or malicious. The understandings of others are dismissed without an adequate hearing or on a basis of a misreading."[27] One could assume these would be the conclusion of those holding fixed, narrow worldviews. Other-accepting worldviews, on the other hand, recognize that we live in a complex world, and there may be some truth in all opposing worldviews. There is a certain humility about other-accepting worldviews, therefore. This does not imply agreement, necessarily, but openness to the possibility that others may have something to teach us.

It is no stretch to imagine numerous combinations of these types of worldviews, though McKenzie does not pursue this train of thought. He does acknowledge that the structural properties of some seem to have higher correlation and compatibility. Can education help adults examine the structural properties of their existing worldviews in order to "unfreeze" and alter them appropriately?

The Place of Education in Worldview Construction

A Christian educator with any experience in the local church will readily acknowledge that one of the problems facing adult Christian education is people who often escape to church to have their worldview reenforced, not challenged. In fact, certain worldviews are unwelcome in some well-known denominational and local church traditions, and are rejected more on philosophical or political than on theological grounds. Thus, in certain religious circles the holder of a provisional, inclusive, active, and other-accepting worldview might find him/herself labeled radical, infidel, and/or persona non grata. The curricula of such churches and their mother denominations are structured in such a way to both combat the threat of such worldviews and to reenforce fixed, exclusively narrow if not consciously passive and other-disdaining worldviews. Maintenance learning (Bennis's category) is their goal. The position of this work, on the other hand, is that innovative learning that results in the development of these alternative worldviews is a worthy goal of adult Christian education! The risks to the Christian educator and the integrity of his/her field are obvious. What approach is appropriate and effective if the risks are faced?

McKenzie suggests the necessity of addressing contradictions, dissimilarities, and polarities between existing worldviews and new experience, a process he calls "deconstruction."[28] This natural process that occurs often quite unconsciously in the face of any new experience (if the experience is compatible with the existing worldview) must become intentional and conscious. He offers participation training as a means for structuring conversation whereby this deconstruction, this critical evaluation can occur.

Examining Worldviews through Participation Training

Participation Training (PT) is a means to enable adults to engage in conversation that probes the understandings of others and allows comparisons between worldviews of others, all in an atmosphere of mutual respect and openness between small group participants.

The purpose here is not to give an elaborate explanation of PT. Rather a sufficient overview is provided that enables the reader to judge whether further examination of the process is in order if worldview construction is deemed a worthy undertaking of adult Christian education. See the references at the close of this chapter for further reading on the subject.

PT began as a design to train adults in ways to develop their own local church adult Christian programs (though the plan had its roots in training programs in industry). Known as the "Indiana Plan," its originator, Paul Bergevin of Indiana University, sought a radical departure from the traditional schooling approach to which most adults were accustomed. (The reader should note that this was the 1950s! PT is still a radical departure from the way most Adult Christian education is conducted). Bergevin and John McKinley, the director of PT Institutes at I. U. until his retirement in the '80s, explain that through PT "Participants learn: 1) to plan and take part in discussions of topics they themselves have selected, 2) to see themselves as they are seen by other members of the group and how their participation influences others, 3) to help others in a group learning situation, 4) to engage in the disciplined expression of ideas, 5) to distinguish, on the basis of experience, what helps or hinders group discussion, and 6) to establish goals, identify discussion topics, and observe group process."[29]

PT as conducted in the '70s, '80s and '90s identified roles, group norms, and specific procedures for discussion. Topics, discussion goals, and outlines are developed by the group and the process itself is examined as well as the topic under scrutiny.

PT as an intentionally structured group discussion process provides a framework for adults to examine the origins of their worldviews, the influencing factors, the similarities and dissimilarities with the worldviews of others, and theoretically the process of worldview construction itself. An examination of the categories of worldviews might be the topic of a PT discussion as a means for introducing the worthy goals of adult Christian education previously mentioned. PT may certainly be one ingredient in the transformational process at the heart of Christian education.

Ideally an adult education program in a local church will encompass three dimensions. Some educational offerings within the framework of the comprehensive program will address explicitly religious topics. Other offerings will focus on educational activities gauged to help adults meet their everyday needs. Still other offerings will center around adult interests, i.e., adult leisure-time endeavors. The comprehensive program may include, for example, a study of the gospels vis-à-vis the life experiences of the adults in the study group, a short course on how to get a job (in a parish where the unemployment rate is high), and a course of study/guided practice on backyard gardening. In other words, some topical areas in the comprehensive program may have nothing to do with religion as narrowly conceived.

It has been noted that John H. Vincent, a leader in the nineteenth-century Chautauqua movement, entertained a broad vision of religious education somewhat analogous to the vision presented here. Vincent maintained that all knowledge (sacred and secular) is sacred to the religious person. Vincent's view was rejected by most religious educators in the nineteenth century on the grounds that everyday adult needs and interests were extraneous to the purposes of the church. Not much has changed since Vincent's time. It is commonly remarked today that adult education programs in local churches must be restricted to the treatment of expressly religious themes. Adult everyday needs and interests, it is averred, should be left to other educational agencies.

What lies at the roots of this narrow view of the purpose of church-based adult education is the assumption that reality should be dichotomized into secular and sacred parts, and that the focus on so-called secular themes cannot contribute to the human and religious growth of adults. In addition, critics of the broad view of church-based adult education do not seem to understand the interpenetrativeness of the three missions of the church.

Religious meaning can be made available to adults not only through the study of religious themes, but also in the "lived experience" of being with other adults in a community of learners. Religious meaning can be made available to people whose everyday needs and interests are addressed in the *context* of the parish or local church. The fruit of such "lived experience" is not to be classified as some secondarily important meaning. The religious meaning made available to adults *en passant* in, say, a course on backyard gardening may be more profound and powerful than any meaning derived from the discursive study of an expressly religious theme. An individual adult may experience the meaning of community and the meaning of agape in a course on financial planning, and not at all experience these meanings in a discursive study of the gospels.

There is another way of saying this. In every educational activity there is a manifest content and a latent content.[30] The manifest content is the ostensible subject matter: that which is apparent or in the foreground. The latent content subsumes those processes and interactions that conduce to tacit learning; the latent content enfolds, permeates, and backgrounds the manifest content. We often distinguish between process and product without ever reflecting that the product is in the process, to some extent, and that the process is in the product. Process and product are logically distinct but existentially inseparable.

Discursive knowledge is the outcome of analytic reasoning. Prehensive knowledge is the result of grasping the gestalt of a particular context in such a way that the context becomes, in part, the content of education. This is not to say that prehensive knowledge is unconscious or preconscious. "Tacit integration," as Michael Polanyi calls it, "may often take place effortlessly unnoticed by ourselves. But all this does not make a subsidiary state an unconscious one."[31] Prehensive knowledge may be subsidiary when the focus of consciousness is on knowing *this* object, but knowledge of this object would be impossible without a prehensive grasp of the context in which this object is known. That is to say, we know things discursively only in relation to the context of our knowing and the context of the things that are known. To put the matter simply, the context of any educational activity holds a message for adults as well as the content of education. By "context" is meant the complexus of elements (people, sponsorship of the educational activity, interpersonal transactions, and so forth) integrated as a functional unit in which the whole is greater than the properties of the summed elements.

Two other objections are sometimes mentioned as arguments against including so-called secular topics in church-based adult education programs. First, it is stated that most parishes do not possess the financial resources to maintain comprehensive programs that can compete with programs offered by other educational agencies. Second, some religious educators have honestly stated that they are not personally inclined to discuss anything except religious themes in adult education activities.

No doubt some parishes and local churches are not able to afford comprehensive programs. Most parishes, it is suggested, have arranged their priorities in such a way as to preclude the possibility of a comprehensive adult program. In the first instance, the problem can be solved through the collaborative effort of churches in a specific neighborhood. In the second instance, some parishes would do well to reassess priorities. If adult education is truly a value, programs can be supported; if adult education is merely something valued as a topic for discussion, programs will never be implemented in any event. And while a host of educational agencies offer adult education activities, it should be remembered that most adults prefer the convenience of participating in educational activities situated in familiar surroundings and in their own neighborhoods. Local churches have less to fear from competition in providing educational services than do other agencies.

When a religious educator states that he does not prefer to treat so-called secular matters in a parish program, it seems apparent that such a remark proceeds from something other than an effective concern for adults. It will do no harm to suggest again that some religious educators use adult programs to satisfy *their* needs rather than the needs of adults. Or, perhaps such a preference on the part of the religious educator may be traced back to the false dichotomy between the sacred and the profane.

Notes

[1] D. Stewart quoted in William Griffith, "Has Adult and Continuing Education Fulfilled Its Early Promise?," *New Directions for Continuing Education* 44 (San Francisco: Jossey-Bass, Winter 1989): 7.

[2] Griffith, "Adult and Continuing Education"; Phyllis M. Cunningham, "Making a More Significant Impact On Society," *New Directions* 44; Jerold Apps, "What Should the Future Focus Be for Adult and Continuing Education?" *New Directions* 44.

[3] Harold Stubblefield, "The Focus Should be on Life Fulfillment," in B. W. Kreitlow et al., *Examining Controversies in Adult Education* (San Francisco: Jossey-Bass, 1981), 19.

[4] Alan Knox, "Designing Comprehensive Programs in Adult and Continuing Education," *New Directions* 44: 48.

[5] Paul St. Clair McGinnis, "The Focus Should be on Human Liberation," in Burton Kreitlow, ed. *Examining Controversies in Adult Education* (San Francisco: Jossey-Bass, 1981), 24-25.

[6] Leon McKenzie, *Adult Education and the Burden of the Future* (Washington D.C.: University Press, 1978) iii.

[7] Jerold Apps, "Developing a Belief Structure," ed. Chester Klevins, *Materials and Methods in Adult and Continuing Education* (Los Angeles: Klevens Publications, 1982), 29.

[8] Linda Vogel, *Teaching and Learning in Communities of Faith* (San Francisco: Jossey-Bass, 1991), xi.

[9] Ibid., 76.

[10] John Elias, "Towards Adult Faith: Adult Education in Faith in the Catholic Church in Australia Today," a working paper published in 1983 for the National Catholic Education Commission, quoted in *Religious Education* 84, no. 1 (1989): 92.

[11] Ibid.

[12] Griffith, "Adult and Continuing Education," 7.

[13] Vogel, 67.

[14] Hal Beder, "The Purposes and Philosophies of Adult Education," ed. Sharan B. Merriam and Phyllis M. Cunningham, *Handbook of Adult and Continuing Education* (San Francisco: Jossey-Bass, 1989).

[15] Leon McKenzie, *Adult Education and Worldview Construction* (Malabar FL: Krieger Publishing Co., 1991), 112.

[16] Ibid., 133.

[17] Vogel, 144.

[18] McKenzie, 112.

[19] Ibid., 138.

[20] Ibid., 14-15.

[21] Ibid., 14.

[22] Ibid., 4.

[23] Warren Bennis, *On Becoming a Leader* (Reading MA: Addison-Wesley Publishing Co., 1989), 75-79.

[24] McKenzie, 60-61.

[25] Ibid., 66-70.

[26] Ibid., 68.

[27] Ibid., 69.

[28] McKenzie defines deconstruction as "a process that occurs outside of educational settings, although educational strategies can be developed to help learners develop their world views. Deconstruction refers also to the critical evaluation of experiences, and to the analysis, and pari passu the destruction, of meanings by a world viewer. Lastly, deconstruction as used here relates to hermeneutics, to the construction of an interpretive understanding of the world in the broadest and most inclusive sense of the term" (32).

[29] Quoted in McKenzie, 77.

[30] The distinction between manifest and latent content was made many years ago by John McKinley, a colleague of McKenzie's at Indiana University. James Michael Lee frames the distinction in terms of process and content: "Process . . . is not simply a way to achieving content; process is itself an authentic content." See Lee's essay, "Process Content in Religious Instruction," *Process and Relationship,* ed. I. Cully and K. Cully (Birmingham: Religious Education Press, 1978), 22ff.

[31] Michael Polanyi, *Knowing and Being* (Chicago: University of Chicago Press, 1969), 194.

APPROACHES TO PROGRAM DEVELOPMENT

Theory is initially a perspective that permits a coherent vision of a set of variables. The vision or image is translated into a statement that conveys the vision discursively to others. The discursive statement or propositional theory may then be expressed in action or performance. Perspective yields vision, vision becomes theoretical proposition, and theoretical proposition is expressed in deeds.

We may also look at this sequence in reverse. Every set of deeds is an instantiation of propositional theory, unless the deeds are random and ungrounded in thought. Propositional theory vaguely suggests, in turn, a particular vision. This vision is gained from a specific perspective. It is quite impossible to turn away from theory, except in the case of random actions that are not rooted in reflection. A teacher, for example, who is given over to the practice of using gimmicks in his or her classes, is acting out a theoretical position, i.e., that teaching is principally a matter of using gimmicks. When we analyze any set of manifest behaviors we may be able to infer the theoretical basis from which these behaviors derive.

In this chapter we consider five different approaches to the development of adult education programs in parishes and local churches. The word "program" is used in the sense of curriculum. Any grouping of short courses, discussion meetings, conferences, etc., that are conducted within a specific short-term time frame constitutes an educational program as a part of the larger curriculum of the church. Thus, in many parishes and local churches there is the fall adult education program, the Lenten adult education program, and so forth. Each approach to program development is examined in such a way that inferences can be made about the propositional theory that undergirds the program development process. Finally, each of the approaches is subjected to a critique.

Program Development: Five Approaches
Satisfying the Educator's Needs: The Preemptive Approach

The adult education program at Old First Church consists solely of a series of lectures on ecclesiology. The pastor, director of religious education, or minister of education (hereafter the religious educator) attends a summer workshop in graduate religious education and is favorably impressed with the lectures given by a theologian who had authored a popular book on ecclesiology. The religious educator decides unilaterally to replicate these lectures in the parish. Adults in the parish are recruited to participate in the implementation stage of program development: registering enrollees, setting up the chairs, providing coffee and donuts, cleaning the lecture room, and so forth. They are excluded, however, from the program planning phase. If an evaluation is to be conducted, adults are also excluded from evaluation planning.

If the religious educator holds any degree of coercive power, he may attempt initially to require the attendance of adults at the lecture series. Since religious educators generally lack such coercive power, and given the essentially voluntary nature of parish adult education, the religious educator attempts to influence adults to attend by means of a selling campaign. Adults are reminded of the necessity of staying close to God, fulfilling their obligations as Christians, or some other similar sales approach. The educational product has been manufactured, so to speak, by the religious educator without reference to the concerns of the adults. The religious educator in this scenario is well-intentioned and no conscious attempt has been made to neglect the concerns of adults, but the religious educator simply believes that an effective educational program may be described as transferring important content to the minds of adults.

This program development process, under analysis, discloses the preemptive theoretical approach of program development. The religious educator is utterly fascinated by a particular topic or subject matter. It is usually this fascination with a particular topic and not the conscious desire to preempt adults from consideration that inclines the religious educator to adopt, explicitly or implicitly, the preemptive approach. The program emerges out of the need of the religious educator to teach something and not out of a study of adult needs and interests. So strong is the need to teach something that the subject matter becomes the primary focus of the program. The needs and interests of adults are sometimes not even secondary to program development; the needs and interests of adults are sometimes not considered at all.

The immediate goal of the program may be announced as "bringing people closer to God through a better knowledge of the church." While this may be the ostensible goal, and while the religious educator may sincerely believe this is the goal, an outside observer would conclude, and rightly so, that the immediate goal of the program is to satisfy the need of the religious educator to share what he has learned at a popular conference.

The religious educator exercises a dominative or persuasive management style.[1] That is, the religious educator makes all decisions respecting program development and announces these decisions (dominative style) or makes all decisions respecting program development and then tries to persuade adults that these decisions are best (persuasive style). The religious educator takes the role of a friendly autocrat if the dominative style is used, the role of salesperson if the persuasive style is employed. This implies corresponding roles for the adults: They are expected to be loyal subjects or willing buyers of an educational service.

Deducing Adult Needs: The Ascriptive Approach

At Trinity Church the adult education program is limited to a series of audio-visual presentations on the topic of the responsibilities of Christian parents. The religious educator is attentive to the needs of adults in the parish, and these needs play an important part in program development. On the basis of general knowledge of the adult population the religious educator ascribes certain needs to the adults and determines which of these needs are most important. (On some occasions the religious educator determines that two or three topics will address adult needs. Adults may choose to participate in one of the educational activities or in all of them.)

The religious educator identifies educational needs or interests on the basis of general knowledge of adults in the parish. That is, the religious educator deduces adult needs from a global apprehension or subjective impression of the adult population. No attempt is made to validate this impression empirically through the systematic gathering of data from the adult population or from a randomly-selected sample of the population. Adults are usually asked to help with the administrative details of implementing the program, but their help is not solicited in planning the program.

The procedures involved in the development of the program for Trinity Church point to an underlying theory base, the ascriptive approach. The religious educator ascribes needs to adults, selects program topics, and hopes that the ascription of needs has been adequate. Frequently, particularly in larger parishes with heterogeneous populations, the needs ascribed to adults by religious educators are neither primary nor urgent, nor do these ascribed needs actually apply to large segments of the adult population. In such cases the religious educator is forced to become a product salesperson. If the religious educator happens to be wrong in his assessment of adult needs, the program will not be perceived as worthwhile by many adults. The religious educator is confronted with an almost impossible task, something akin to selling the proverbial refrigerator to the proverbial Eskimo.

The management style or decision-making style associated with the ascriptive approach is occasionally dominative; more often than not the persuasive style is employed, i.e., decisions are made solely by the religious educator and the religious educator attempts to persuade adults that the decisions are valuable.

Credit must be given to the religious educator at Trinity Church in that she is interested in adult needs and interests as a basis for program development. But ultimately this interest is vitiated by a lack of needs assessment data. Lacking empirical data about adult needs, the religious educator usually selects program topics that hold a high degree of appeal for her. As in the preemptive model, but to a lesser extent, concern for program content is high.

The expressed goal of the program is always couched in ambiguous language: "bringing adults closer to God," or "helping adults deepen their faith." The religious educator may have every intention of accomplishing such a goal, but more fundamentally the immediate goal of a program grounded on the ascriptive model is the satisfaction of needs ascribed to the adults by the religious educator. What eventually happens is that the program is built upon the untested perceptions of the religious educator and not really on adult needs. There are some areas of overlap between the preemptive and ascriptive approaches. The distinguishing feature of the latter approach may be found in the intention of the religious educator to address adult needs and interests. As it usually happens in practice, however, this intention is frustrated because it is assumed the identification of needs and interests can be made easily on the basis of the unverified and uncritical impressions of the religious educator.

Adults as Parish Members: The Diagnostic/Prescriptive Approach

The content of the adult education program at St. Paul's may not differ substantively from the content of programs in other parishes. What distinguishes the St. Paul's program is the manner in which it was developed. First, the prospective clients for the program are viewed principally in the organizational context. That is, they are seen primarily as parish members. While there may be some concern for their individual educational needs, the emphasis is placed on educational needs as these reflect problems in the parish community. The educational program is directed chiefly toward the amelioration of organizational problems; individual needs are considered largely in terms of the individuals' membership in the parish. McKinley has stated this succinctly: "Diagnostic procedural models . . . are used to discover educational needs of a social system—usually an organization, a subunit of an organization, or sometimes a community. They are termed 'discrepancy models' because they either assume the existence of, or attempt to identify, the gap or discrepancy between 'what is' and 'what ought to be' in the system."[2]

Second, the religious educator strives to determine the felt needs of adults in the parish, utilizing adults as data sources. Data are collected from adults either by means of a representative panel, interview of randomly selected adults, and/or by means of a parish survey. This procedure clearly distinguishes the model from the approaches presented above.

Third, the data are not immediately translated into program goals. The statements of educational need uncovered by the research are treated as felt needs that are symptomatic of real organizational needs. Felt needs are identified in the research process. The religious educator organizes information about felt needs (data relating to symptoms) in such a way that patterns or syndromes emerge. On the basis of these syndromes the religious educator infers certain problems that may be ameliorated or resolved by an educational program. The felt needs identified in the research, in other words, are transformed—via the mediation of the religious educator's inferences—into real organizational needs and thence into program objectives. What is assumed is that the educational program should be responsive to adults insofar as they are members of the parish, and that individual felt needs may not always address real needs or problems at the level of the parish as a social system.

The model is sometimes called the medical model of program development since it assumes that problems analogous to disease entities are present in the organization. The religious educator is placed in the role of a physician-diagnostician who collects and interprets data, makes inferences, and prescribes an educational remedy.

The management style implied by the model is consultative. The religious educator consults the adults in the parish and seeks information from them. This information is refined in terms of the religious educator's total supply of data; the information is also manipulated and serves as the basis for the religious educator's diagnostic inferences and prescriptive judgments.

The religious educator assumes that a sales pitch is not necessary to attract adults to the program. The program needs promotion, to be sure, but not in the sense of the so-called "hard sell." Program promotion simply apprises adults of the existence of the program. If the religious educator's diagnosis is correct, and if the educational prescription addresses real problems in the parish, it is also assumed that adults will already be inclined to participate.

A potential for a subtle error exists in the approach when the religious educator lacks understanding of his own motivations. It could very well happen that the religious educator would undertake parish research and data analysis with a hidden agenda. This is to say, the religious educator could merely use the relatively elaborate procedure required by the approach as a cover to justify teaching what he learned at summer school. It is possible to employ the procedures of the diagnostic/prescriptive approach with a mentality that is more congruent with the preemptive or ascriptive approaches.

Responding to Market Demand: The Analytic/Subscriptive Approach

The adult ministry at Mt. Vernon includes a wide range of educational opportunities from, for example, a discussion group on the gospels to a parent effectiveness workshop, from a reflection-action social justice project to a short course on basic home repair, from lessons in square dancing to an historical study of early Christianity. An examination of the various courses within the overall program does not reveal a unifying thread even to the most discerning eye.

The religious educator begins program development with research aimed at identifying individual needs, interests, and wants. If enough adults show interest in any given topic, the religious educator recruits a group leader from the people interested in the topic. The religious educator helps the leader recruit resource people who are knowledgeable about the topic and resource materials that pertain to the topic. Adults in each interest group become involved in planning, implementing, and evaluating the learning activities.

The major work of the religious educator is the task of market analysis. The religious educator gathers data that elucidate individual wants; the religious educator also determines the extent to which a given topic holds appeal for adults in the parish. If it is likely an adequate number of adults will participate in, say, a square-dancing class, the religious educator subscribes or underwrites the learning activity on behalf of the parish. On the other hand, perhaps only one or two people are interested in square dancing. In this case the religious educator steers the people in the direction of the nearest dance course in the community. Thus the religious educator must determine the feasibility of offering a particular learning activity on the basis of collected data.

The goal of the total program is the satisfaction of individual wants. In this the model differs from the diagnostic/prescriptive model, which views adults largely in terms of parish problems. The religious educator consults adults by means of the research process. The resulting data, however, are not interpreted as required by the diagnostic/prescriptive model but are taken at face value. The *felt* needs, interests, and wants of adults are assessed as equivalent to *real* needs, interests, and wants. Adults are perceived as self-directing, intelligent people who know what they want. The expertise of the religious educator is challenged not in the act of inferring real needs from felt needs, but in conducting a thorough market analysis and in the administration of the program.

Religious educators may flinch at the idea that they must take the role of market analyst. There is a widespread idea that market analysis refers only to the world of commercial enterprise, and that marketing is a process unworthy of any organization save the commercial organization.[3] This belief, of course, is not true. Market analysis refers to the likelihood and extent to which people will be responsive to a product or service, whether that product or service is sold or provided gratis. Market analysis attempts to determine the inclinations and disinclinations of a particular segment of the adult population vis-à-vis a product or service. Applied to adult education, market analysis is a process by which the program developer searches out a potential within a given population. If the research suggests a potential is present for a particular learning activity, the learning activity is planned and promoted; if there is only a marginal potential or a negative potential, the labor of the educator is put to better use. Market analysis, then, does not denote hucksterism, nor does it refer to making a sales pitch. It simply means getting in touch with potential clients in order to determine what these clients want.

Talent Inventory: The Cafeteria Approach

To all appearances the adult ministry at Parkway Church is similar to the Mt. Vernon program. The program encompasses a variety of topical areas. Some educational activities address explicitly religious topics; other educational activities emphasize a sharing of mundane knowledge and skills; still other activities focus on adult leisure-time endeavors to the end that community is formed. The Parkway program is distinguished principally by reason of the religious educator's unique approach to program development.

The program development process is initiated not by searching for educational needs, interests, or wants, but by taking inventory of the human resources in the parish who are willing to share their knowledge and skills with fellow parishioners. In essence, the religious educator embarks on a talent search and hopes to identify people who will volunteer to act as the "faculty" in the overall program. By satisfying the contributive needs of adults—the need to share one's expertise with others—the religious educator hopes also to satisfy many of the needs, interests, and wants of adults in the parish. The religious educator is mostly a broker of instructional relationships, someone who brings teachers and learners together.

The parish talent roster or listing of volunteer teachers includes anyone in the parish who wishes to teach anything. The roster may include, of course, those responsible for biblical-theological-liturgical education. After the inventory has been completed, the religious educator underwrites or subscribes to the various course offerings by publishing a prospectus that lists topical areas, the names of volunteer teachers, and the times and places of the initial meetings. Parishioners are asked to complete a registration form that is returned to the religious educator. This permits the religious educator to make administrative decisions relating to the overall program. The religious educator may also function as a resource person for the volunteer teachers by helping them plan and organize the instructional process.

The approach is appropriately called the cafeteria model and is widely followed by many agencies that provide adult education in community settings. Many university continuing education programs, for example, follow the cafeteria model. Courses are developed not to meet the identified needs of adults in the community but are planned on the basis of the availability of university faculty or others who wish to teach evenings or weekends. Individual courses are set before the public much in the same way food items are set before the public in a cafeteria line. Many continuing education programs are successful, not necessarily because the programs have been developed in terms of research data, but because in any large-size adult population there will usually be sufficient numbers of adults who will elect items from the educational cafeteria. Even programs that are managed poorly appear to succeed, given a large enough market potential.

If no one registers for a particular activity in the parish cafeteria program, or if too few register, the religious educator notifies the volunteer teacher. Some items in a cafeteria line are untouched; some course offerings in a parish cafeteria educational program will not be elected. The extent to which a cafeteria-style program will attract participants cannot be estimated ahead of registration.

The management style of the religious educator in the context of this model is adaptive: The religious educator adapts to the decisions of both volunteer teachers and learners. The adult population is viewed as containing many who have profited from previous experience and have gained special knowledge and skill. Prospective adult learners are seen as self-directing individuals who are capable of choosing wisely from a variety of options placed before them.

The Five Approaches: An Assessment

Which of the five approaches to program development listed above are appropriate for adult education in the parish or local church? Each of the approaches may be evaluated in terms of the assumptions of andragogy, which has matured to the point of being honored more for its practical application than as a theory. Merriam asserts, "Because of its intuitive validity and because the assumptions underlying andragogy are and have been easily translated into practical guidelines and mandates, andragogy is here to stay."[4] We will thus turn our attention to the five approaches in relation to andragogy. We will then consider them against the backdrop of motivational theory.

It will be recalled that Malcolm Knowles developed the idea of andragogy according to the framework of the differences between adults and children in (1) self-concept, (2) experience, (3) readiness to learn, and (4) time orientation.

Five Approaches to Program Development

Approach	Principal Focus	Immediate Goal	Roles of Educator	Education Managment Style	Roles of Adult Learner
I. PREEMPTIVE	A content area that meets a need of the educator	Satisfaction of the educator	Autocrat. Salesperson.	Dominative/ Persuassive	Dependent Subject
II. ASCRIPTIVE	A content area that meets needs of adults ascribed by the educator	Ostensibly the satisfaction of needs of adults as ascribed by the educator	Benevolent autocrat. Salesperson.	Dominative/ Persuassive	Dependent Subject
III. DIAGNOSTIC/ PERSCRIPTIVE	Organizational needs. Individual needs related to member-ship in the organization	A more effective organization, better members of the organization	Diagnostician. Physician.	Consultave	Member of the organization. Data source.
IV. ANALYTIC/ SUBSCRIPTIVE	Individual needs, interests, wants	Satisfaction of adult learners	Market analyst.	Consultave	Adult as self-directing individual. Data source.
V. SUBSCRIPTIVE (Cafeteria)	Individual needs, interests, wants	Satisfaction of adults as teachers and/or learners	Broker of instructional relationships.	Adaptive	Adult as self-directing individual. Resource Person.

Adults are typically more self-directing than children; adults have more options available to them and a greater range of choices. As a consequence, adults generally conceive of themselves as more independent than children. In most samples of the adult population, a relatively wide range of skills and competencies can be found. Adults have more expertise than children; adults have had more experiences and qualitatively different experiences. The educational needs and interests of adults are ordinarily associated with their life situations. Adults tend to participate in education because the educational activities have direct bearing on their places in the adult life span.

Adults are usually problem-oriented in terms of participation in education. They seek educational activities that promise immediate application of learnings to a variety of small and large problems. Children, rightly or wrongly, are directed toward the study of subjects or specific content areas such as English, mathematics, history, and so forth. This brief review of andragogy suffices as a groundwork for the evaluation of the five approaches to program development.

Andragogy and the Five Approaches

If the assumptions of andragogy are used as a criteria for evaluation, it must be concluded that the preemptive approach is not consistent with sound principles of adult education. In fact, the preemptive approach is not even congruent with sound principles of childhood education. The dominative management style, which insists strongly on the prerogatives and judgment of the religious educator, creates a stifling atmosphere that alienates many adults and rejects the self-concept of adults as independent and mature people. Adults are not only foreclosed from decision-making regarding program development, but they are not even consulted regarding their concerns. This model has survived to the end of the twentieth century, but it belongs in the past. The democratization of adult consciousness that has occurred over the past four hundred years makes it unlikely adults will participate in programs that grow out of modus operandi more germane to feudal society. Adults are free, and church-based adult education is essentially voluntary.

Since the instructional process tends to reflect the program-development process, one must also question the kind of learning that takes place in such programs. A transference of knowledge from the mind of an authority to the minds of the relatively few adults who will participate in programs based on the preemptive approach may take place. It is doubtful, however, that this knowledge will be internalized by adults or made a part of themselves. The mere transference of knowledge does not ordinarily contribute to the growth of a person as a creative, critical, and mature individual.

In the ascriptive approach the religious educator at least considers the potential clients of educational services. But the religious educator's fixation on particular content areas vitiates an effective concern for people. Adults are not consulted; they are not approached as data sources. The value placed on the religious educator's unverified impressions of the adults in the parish is overblown, and perhaps even tinged with arrogance. The bald ascription of educational needs to adults, without any kind of decisional research, bespeaks an attitude of self-importance on the part of the religious educator that is seldom justified. It also bespeaks a failure to recognize the complex tasks of the program-development process. Program development is not something one does on the spur of the moment within the sheltered confines of an ivory tower or ivied manse.

The last three approaches—diagnostic/prescriptive, analytic/subscriptive, and subscriptive (cafeteria)—meet the requirements of the assumptions of andragogy. In the cases of the analytic/subscriptive and subscriptive (cafeteria) approaches, this is fairly evident. Further discussion is necessary to show the compatibility of andragogical assumptions with the diagnostic/prescriptive model.

Some people, when first introduced to the idea of andragogy, begin to see educational programs as oriented exclusively to the satisfaction of the concerns of individual adults. Knowles explicitly states, however, that adults are members of organizations and wider communities, and that this membership should be kept in mind during the program development process.[5] The diagnostic/prescriptive approach *emphasizes* adults as members of a specific organization or community and *de-emphasizes* adults as individuals. The analytic/subscriptive and subscriptive approaches *emphasize* adults as individuals and *de-emphasize* their membership in a particular community. What is at issue here is a matter of focus or emphasis. The prescriptive approach does not deny that adults are individuals, nor do the analytic/subscriptive or subscriptive approaches deny that adults are members of specific communities.

The diagnostic/prescriptive approach is sometimes needed in certain parishes or local churches. As members of a parish organization, adults must take corporate responsibility for the needs and problems of the parish. But as individuals, adults are often unable to gain a wide enough perspective on these needs and problems. It falls, then, to the religious educator as diagnostician to collect data relating to parish problems, and to prescribe education remedies. The prescription of particular educational activities to remediate organizational problems is congruent with the assumptions of andragogy.

Motivation Theory and the Five Approaches

One of the tests of the success of most adult education programs is the degree to which they are accepted by adults. If a program is not well-attended, all other things being equal, the program could be flawed in its development. To express this differently, poor attendance is sometimes associated with the use of a program development approach that ignores motivation theory. As in everything else, one ignores theory at his own hazard.

The approaches to program development described above should be measured not only against criteria stipulated by andragogy, but also in relation to motivation theory. But which motivation theory? A number of different theories have been formulated to explain human behavior.[6] Of these theories, one stands out as especially applicable to adult participation in educational programs. It is called the expectancy theory of motivation. The remainder of this chapter is devoted to an explanation of the theory and to a critique of the five program development approaches with the expectancy theory of motivation as criterion.

According to the expectancy theory, a person is motivated to perform in a desired way if he believes there is a linkage between the effort he puts forth and the desired performance (Will this effort lead to the desired performance?), and if he believes also there is a linkage between the desired performance and a reward (Will the desired performance actually lead to the consequence of a reward?). When a person believes or expects that no amount of effort he expends will lead to a desired performance, the person will not be motivated to expend effort. A worker, for example, will not expend effort if he does not know how to perform in the desired way. Likewise, when a person believes or expects that no amount of desired performance will result in a reward, he will not be motivated to expend effort. A worker may know how to perform but does not see how performance is related to a reward. "I'll get paid whether my performance is excellent or marginal; why should I worry about excellent performance?"

What constitutes a reward is a function of the individual's perception. A reward is that which is perceived as a reward. What is rewarding for one person may not be rewarding for another. The notion of reward should not be interpreted in a crass sense. Money may be a reward for some people under certain conditions. For other people the reward may be a sense of achievement or personal growth. For still others the reward may be the knowledge that a noble cause or ideal has been served. To say that people act to obtain rewards is not the same as stating people are selfish, ego-centered, or materialistic.

The diagram on the following page applies the expectancy theory to participation in adult education. An adult puts forth effort to participate in education because she expects that participation is worth the effort that must be expended. After initial participation she continues to participate week after week because she expects that participation will lead to a reward. On the other hand, an adult does not participate because he perceives participation is not worth the effort required; he may initially participate and then terminate participation if he expects participation will not lead to a reward.

The controlling variable is the reward variable. As we have noted, a reward is that which is perceived to be rewarding. This underscores the necessity of building programs on research data that reflect adult concerns. The research data indicate what adults in a given population perceive to be rewarding. (Also underscored is the need to evaluate the instructional process formatively—as it goes on from one week to another—to determine if participants continue to perceive a linkage between participation and an expected reward. If full-fledged evaluations are not in order, the instructor must at least be sensitive to the reactions of the participants.)

The preemptive and ascriptive program development approaches must be faulted precisely because neither of the approaches require the religious educator to investigate adult perceptions of reward. Indeed, in the preemptive approach the program is developed on the basis of what is rewarding to the religious educator. The religious educator's global apprehension of what *might* be perceived as rewarding by adults serves as the basis for program development in the case of the ascriptive approach. Neither of the approaches directs the attention of the religious educator to the question of adult motivation. It is little wonder that the rates of participation in programs developed according to these models is generally very poor.

The Expectancy Theory of Motivation and Adult Education

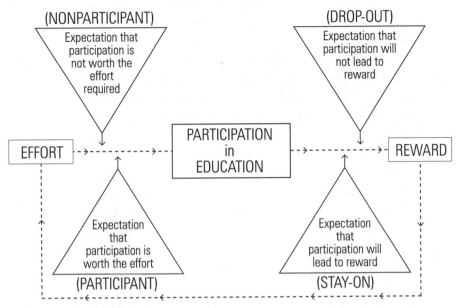

While the preemptive and ascriptive approaches virtually ignore the issue of adult motivation, the analytic/subscriptive and subscriptive approaches feature the motivation issue prominently. These approaches direct the attention of the religious educator away from the a priori determination of program content and toward those who are potential program participants. The preemptive and ascriptive approaches tend to be content-oriented; the analytic/subscriptive and subscriptive approaches tend to be person-oriented.

The diagnostic/prescriptive approach looks at reward in terms of the reverse side of the coin; that is, reward is viewed as the avoidance of punishment. In a certain sense the problems of a community to which one belongs can be punishing. In collecting data about parish problems that may be remediated by education, the religious educator is actually collecting data about situations that make membership in a parish less than rewarding. The diagnostic/prescriptive approach requires that reward-punishment data are collected, and that programs be developed in light of these data. In this respect the approach is congruent with the expectancy theory of motivation. In another sense, however, there is a discrepancy between the diagnostic/prescriptive approach and the expectancy theory.

The expectancy theory, as with most theories of motivation, emphasizes the individual qua individual. The diagnostic/prescriptive approach to program development, however, looks principally at adults in a parish as members of the parish community. Faced with a program developed according to the diagnostic/prescriptive approach, adults in the parish must view themselves chiefly as members of the parish community (and less as individuals) before they will move toward participation in the program. That is, the expectancy theory indicates that people move toward a desired end when they perceive that end to be rewarding. As an individual, I may find it more rewarding to attend a high-school football game than a group discussion in the parish hall. When I value my membership in the parish community more than my individual wants, however, I may find it more rewarding to attend the group discussion. When the diagnostic/prescriptive approach is employed, therefore, the religious educator must convince the adults in the parish that participation in the program will be rewarding; that while the educational program addresses *community* problems, the solution of these problems will bring *individual* benefits.

Generally speaking, the religious educator can expect better rates of participation in programs that are developed according to the analytic/subscriptive and subscriptive approaches. This is not to say, however, that the diagnostic/prescriptive approach is inappropriate. Given the exigencies of a particular parish or local church, there are times when the remediation of community problems takes precedence over the satisfaction of individual concerns. In a parish or local church that has a long history of racism and discrimination, for example, the mission of the church would require that this problem be addressed. Adult education in the context of the parish or local church is always different from adult education in other contexts even when such a difference is not immediately evident.

A Model for Congregational Adult Religious Education

Perhaps no other period in the history of religious education has seen more interest in alternative models of church-based education than the present. In fact, among Catholic religious educators there is an "Alternative Models Network" where sharing of new approaches takes place through a newsletter and occasional conferences. CEN (Christian Educator's Network), a Protestant network of educators, holds an annual conference at Scarrett College and passes on ideas, approaches, and models through an occasional newsletter. Even among conservative evangelicals, discontent with old denominationally designed programmatic approaches runs high. This discontent leads their educators by the literal thousands to flock to annual conferences by "new paradigm" churches such as the Willow Creek Community or Saddleback Community Church to hear about new efforts to assimilate new members and nurture all members in the faith.

Unfortunately, one thing nearly all these educators share is preoccupation with the ascriptive or diagnostic/prescriptive approaches to program development (we want to be optimistic enough to believe they are beyond the preemptive approach). Thus, models and programs profiled in articles, newsletters, or conferences are designed, promoted, operated, and evaluated *by staff ministers* with little involvement of those for whom the models and programs are designed.

The model profiled here meets the criteria set forth in this chapter in at least three ways. First, it fits the analytic/subscriptive and the subscriptive approaches. Rather than focusing on learners as organizational members, for example (which may lead to conformity in theology, doctrine, philosophy and ecclesiology), it focuses on the wants, interests and needs of adult learners. The educator functions as consultant/facilitator assisting adults to manage the developmental process themselves (which is also why it is called a "congregational model" since the locus of control is with participating adults in the congregation). Second, the model is consistent with andragogical assumptions about adult learners and adult learning. Adults are seen as capable of being self-directing, possessing rich resources in terms of life experience and previous study. And third, the model provides a medium through which the principles of Participation Training may be practiced. Adults themselves are the source for determining the data upon which step is predicated. Further, control increasingly becomes the domain of participating adults as they move from data generation to determination of program direction and operation. The model operates as follows.

Just as Hopewell[7] observed that each church has its own "culture," each church operates according to certain basic assumptions that run the gamut from theological (e.g., how God attempts to relate to people) and educational (the place of education and how people learn) to personal and global concerns (which include systemic considerations). While some of these are related to the larger realm of denominational affiliation, most are uniquely nuanced to the individual congregation. The beginning point in this model, therefore, is identification, through reflective dialogue, of these assumptions. Use of the nominal group process may enhance consensus building around assumptions common to the congregation.[8]

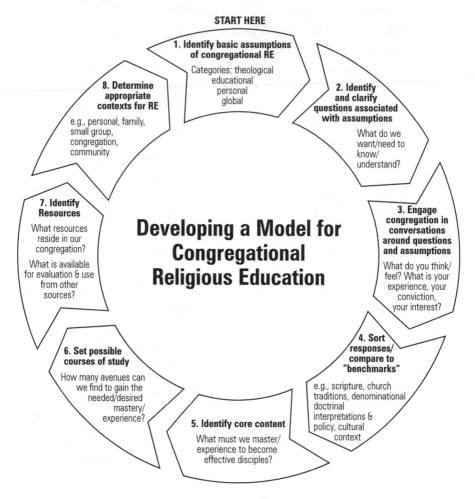

In continued reflective dialogue, questions related to these assumptions are identified and clarified (What do we want or need to know and understand about these assumptions and their origins?). This step may be brief and is preliminary to a lengthier discussion of individual and congregational experience with these assumptions, as well as the convictions upon which they rest, and participants' interests in pursuing answers to questions thus identified. Responses are recorded so they can be duplicated and distributed for the next step during which they are sorted and compared to "benchmarks" such as Scripture, church traditions, doctrinal interpretations of the affiliated denomination, church polity, and the cultural context of the congregation. Such sorting and comparison is done in small groups by participating adults and engenders lively discussion and debate. As will be seen in subsequent treatment of transformative learning, such debate is not only welcomed but may encourage the critical reflection that is foundational to perspective transformation.

Adults are taking more responsibility and exercising more control as the process continues, exemplified in the next step by their cooperative identification of core content areas implied by results of the previous step. Once again, the Participation Training process is conducive to such interchange. The question upon which adults focus in step five is "What must we master or experience in order to become effective disciples?" Examination of responses in step four may result in several categories of content that include both personal and corporate concerns. These categories provide the beginning of a possible "curriculum map" to which the courses in the sixth step may be added.

Step six involves setting possible courses of study, but includes consideration of the variety of avenues that may enable adults to gain the needed or desired experience and mastery. Determining possible courses carries no assumption or prescription concerning methodology or contexts. Sample courses are included under the core content categories identified on the sample curriculum map. Step seven can be more difficult for participating adults and calls for the consultative role of the religious educator who is in touch (as much as possible) with available resources. However, these resources include not only what is available from the denomination and other literature and resource providers, but include the human resources resident within the church and community. For example, a Virginia church staged a Christian parenting conference at the request of its adults, who were involved from the program's inception in the planning, promotion, and operation. A current author was flown in as featured speaker and conference leader, but numerous church members were involved in seminar leadership, as public school teachers, professional psychologists, counselors, and others from within the congregation contributed their skills and insights. Some of these seminars were led by church members utilizing curriculum materials available from their denomination. (Note again that this church's approach is consistent with the subscriptive approach to program development.)

The final step in this model consists of determining all the possible appropriate contexts in which the courses may be pursued. Results of this step may include more traditional small-group, congregational, or classroom settings, but may also include individual, family, mentoring, or even computer-based approaches. Churches who are not so provincial in their perspective may include community-based opportunities or offerings of neighboring churches, thereby expanding the available resources to their own adults. (It has always been somewhat of a puzzle as to why each congregation feels it must be self-sufficient, often thereby duplicating the resources and offerings of other nearby churches).

As with other such models, this congregational model of adult religious education is dynamic in that it functions continuously, with ongoing or at least periodic revisiting of assumptions, questions, content, courses, resources, and contexts. In fact, the reflective dialogue that hopefully will characterize steps one through five may actually provide the heart of the adult curriculum!

Some Thoughts on Curricular Approaches

Faith traditions, and even individual churches, take various approaches to structuring and researching their religious education efforts. Roman Catholics determine broad themes to be studied, publish those themes for the benefit of numerous resource developers, and leave it largely to local parishes to select resources to support those themes. Southern Baptists not only predetermine subject matter in most areas of religious study, but they write and publish their own materials, strongly urging churches to be faithful consumers, thus insuring not only a profitable bottom line but doctrinal purity as well. Other traditions fall somewhere in between, with individual churches often making their own choices of themes to be studied and resources to be studied. Unfortunately, many church-based religious education ministries are program and resource driven. That is, they purchase "canned" programs and resources from their denomination (and occasionally from other providers), rigidly following uncritically the prescribed content and procedures for the prescribed duration (often sixteen to twenty-three weeks). Such programs and resources often are wedded almost inseparably to a lock-step cognitively-oriented approach to content delivery. A common approach is to take a book or series of lessons on a given subject deemed (usually by a denominational leader) worthy of study, then superimpose elementary learning approaches such as workbook-type, fill-in-the-blank activities.

Some churches have attempted to customize curricula through a college-type approach by offering "semester" length courses on a variety of subjects, often based on the pet interests of students *or* the interest or self-avowed expertise of teachers. Two problems are inherent in this approach, though neither are insurmountable. First, there is usually no mechanism to insure balance. Thus, what is offered is often the "sugar sticks" that planners think will attract adults, with little thought of how any offerings fit into a curriculum plan. Second, relying on the unexamined, self-proclaimed expertise of a teacher invites all kinds of strange ideologies and theologies (its seems, for example, that nearly every church has at least one authority on the book of Revelation who is more than willing to hold forth on the subject for weeks and months on end).

While admittedly not adequately addressing the element of praxis, the "curriculum map" on page 155 is an attempt to demonstrate what an "integrated" approach to Christian adult education for a church might look like. It is integrated in the sense that it includes both a serious consideration of content areas deemed appropriate and consistent with a church's faith tradition and includes the freedom for adults to choose and control (with guidance) what and how studies are conducted. Core content in the sample curriculum map is based upon the participate validated assumptions and benchmarks identified through legitimate group process. These provide the parameters within which individuals, classes, and groups may select subjects and avenues of study. This model is consistent with the planning model offered in chapter 7 and uses elements of the participation training model discussed there. It respects the ability of adults to determine the content of study and to be self-directed in appropriate settings.

Core areas of study in this particular model are Biblical Knowledge and Understanding, Christian Heritage and Hope, Life Together, and Applied Spirituality. Core areas are subdivided into subject areas, and sample courses contributing to each subdivision are listed below that area. If made freely available to the congregation in some published form, the map may truly become the curriculum guide for the adult education ministry. It should be considered neither restrictive nor all-inclusive. If we trust adults to make intelligent, consensus-based decisions, classes of adults may use the guide for making choices about what the group studies together in their weekly Sunday school classes. Weekday discipleship groups may use the same guide to select their studies. The religious educator, in cooperation with staff colleagues, may make choices about church-wide studies based on the guide. An individual may consider what he or she is studying on Sunday morning, in the Tuesday night group, and what the church is offering in seminars on Wednesday night and decide to undertake an individual study selected from the guide. The pastor may even consult the guide for preaching suggestions in order to support the adult curriculum.

The adult religious educator in a church using this curriculum map or guide functions in two ways (in addition to facilitating the planning process that developed the guide initially). First he or she consults with classes, groups, and individuals in making selections to insure balance. For example, "Last time you studied _____, and before that ____. For the next six weeks you may want to look at ____. Please remember that the group has not yet selected a study from ____." If the educator keeps a database of courses chosen by various adult groups and even individuals, such tracking is relatively simple.

The second function of the educator is to secure resources for selected studies. Adults cannot be expected to keep abreast of the wealth of available resources. The educator, therefore, constantly researches print, media, and human resources that support the courses and subjects represented in the curriculum map categories. For nearly all categories and courses, multiple choices are available that give individuals and groups an opportunity to select resources that fit their preferred approach or avenue of study (whether it be video, lecture, or group discussion, for example). The more difficult task for the adult religious educator, of course, is to evaluate to the extent possible all resources recommended for use in his or her church. Again, this is an area where educators would do well to share expertise, evaluations, and the resources themselves.

A Three-Year Curriculum "Map" for Congregational Religious Education

BIBLICAL KNOWLEDGE AND UNDERSTANDING

Understanding the Bible

Central questions:

How did we get our Bible?

How was the Bible written?

Why is the Bible important today?

What are the themes of the Bible?

Why are there so many translations?

How can I properly interpret the Bible?

How can I study the Bible effectively?

What resources are available?

Possible courses of study:

The Historical Development of the Bible

The Canonization of Scripture

Bible Lands: A Survey

The Literature of the Bible

A Survey of Bible study resources

Biblical Interpretations: An Introduction

Old Testament Studies

Central questions:

What is the relevance of the Old Testament?

How can I understand the Old Testament?

How should I read the Old Testament?

Possible courses of study:

The literature of the Old Testament

Interpreting the Old Testament

Central characters of the Old Testament

New Testament Studies

Central questions:

What is the relation of the NT and OT?

In what context was the NT written?

How should I read the NT?

What is the relationship of the gospels?

Possible courses of study:

The structure of the NT

The Parables of Jesus

The Miracle Stories

The Beatitudes

The Gospels

CHRISTIAN HERITAGE AND DOCTRINE

Historical Development of the Church

Central questions:

What are the biblical roots of the Church?

How did the Church develop in the Bible?

What is the purpose of the Church?

Why are there so many different versions of the Church?

Possible courses of study:

The New Testament Beginnings of the Church

The Development of the Early Church

The Medieval Church

The Reformation

The Church in Early America

A Survey of non-Baptist Faith Traditions

The 21st Century Church

Our Baptist Heritage

Central questions:

Where are our Baptist roots?

What are the different Baptist groups?

What is unique about Baptists?

How do Baptists relate to each other? To other faith traditions?

What is the future of the Baptists?

Possible courses of study:

A History of Baptists in Europe

A History of Baptists in America

Strains of Baptist Thought and Doctrine

Issues Facing Baptists Yesterday and Today

21st Challenges for Baptists

Christian Doctrine and Baptist Interpretation

Central questions:

What is doctrine?

What is the difference between Doctrine and creed?

On what doctrines do Christians agree? Differ?

What are the major Christian doctrines?

What do Baptists believe?

Possible courses of study:

A Survey of Christian Doctrine

Major Creedal Statements

Baptist Interpretations of Major Doctrines

Thinking Critically About Issues of Belief

Church Membership

Central questions:

How does one become a member?

What is the meaning of church membership?

What are the responsibilities of church members?

What are the privileges of church membership?

Possible courses of study:

Qualifications for church membership

The meaning of church membership

Roles and responsibilities of members

Church Polity

Central questions:

How does my congregation make decisions?

What is unique about Baptist polity?

How does my church organize for ministry?

Possible courses of study:

Baptist Polity and Practice

Our church's relationship to national bodies

Decision-making processes in our church

Guiding documents in our congregation

Functions of the Church

Central questions:

How can a church be true to the NT?

What does a NT church do?

What is true worship?

What is our responsibility in evangelism?

What is the place of Christian education?

How can I identify my gifts for ministry?

Possible courses of study:

A biblical perspective on church functions

Learning to worship effectively

Music in the life of the church

The ordinances as worship

A survey of Christian education ministry

A New Testament study of Spiritual Gifts

Becoming a caring congregation

The Nature and Mission of the Church

Ethical Decision-Making

Central questions:

How does my faith affect my decision?

What is a criteria for making ethical decisions?

Can I know God's will in making decisions?

How can I develop a personal code of ethics?

Possible courses of study:

Relating faith to life

Principles for ethical decision-making

Developing a personal code of ethics

Case studies in ethical-decision making

Christian Perspectives on Ethical Issues

Central questions:

How can I balance family and work?

How can I maintain a healthy family?

How can I influence community and national decision?

How do I discern a Christian perspective on contemporary issues?

Possible courses of study:

Identifying Christian perspectives on Contemporary Ethical issues: some guidelines

How to communicate with your political leaders

Planning a personal course of actions for local and national influence

The Church in the World

Central questions:

How can I practice spiritual discipline?

What is our responsibility in evangelism?

What is "missions"? What is the history of missions in our church?

How can I become involved in missions?

How can I prepare my family to be "in the world" but not "of the world"?

Possible courses of study:

A Short History of Evangelism

A Short History of Missions

An introduction to the Spiritual Missions

Developing Personal Stewardships

Christian Parenting

Caring for Aging Parents

Ministry Opportunities in our Community

Case Studies in Contemporary Evangelism and Missions

Conclusion

What emerges out of this discussion is clearly indicated. The religious educator is advised to utilize program development approaches that direct attention to the concerns of adults in the church. This is a central message of both andragogy and the expectancy theory of motivation. This may be taken as bad news by some religious educators. It is much easier to develop a program by selecting program topics in a somewhat arbitrary fashion.

Programs developed according to the diagnostic/prescriptive, analytic/subscriptive, and subscriptive approaches entail much work and some competence in social science research techniques. Again, we are confronted with the need for greater competence on the part of the religious educator in the field of adult education and in the area of applied research. A problem arises for religious educators who have had no opportunity to gain social science research skills in a systematic way. How can they possibly conduct, for example, a survey of the adults in their parishes when they know next to nothing about questionnaire construction, random sampling, or the statistical interpretation of the data they collect? There is nothing wrong with religious educators studying theology, but theological studies do not prepare religious educators as educators, and more precisely as adult educators who must necessarily be firmly grounded in social science research competencies. Nor do theological studies prepare religious educators as instructors, administrators, or audio-visual specialists. The problem, at its root, has been stated previously. The academic preparation of adult religious educators must involve them thoroughly in the field of adult education. Until such involvement occurs for large numbers of religious educators of adults, church-based adult education will remain an enterprise with marginal impact.

If the adult religious educator has the freedom and is bold enough to break with denominationally prescribed curricular approaches, he or she may actually facilitate the liberation of adults in the congregation to help plan the adult education program and develop the curriculum to support the program. Such is not an easy task, however. Realistically, the educator will have to provide at least maintenance attention to the traditional program while developing "new wineskins" for a new approach. And because traditional approaches tend to be thoroughly engrained, it is unrealistic to expect one-hundred percent enthusiasm, support, and participation, at least in the beginning stages of implementation. This should not deter the educator from attempting such a revolution, but should encourage us to be willing to start small with even a handful of adults who are willing to try something new. Difficult and challenging as it might be, a hunch says it will be exhilarating for the educator as he or she begins to function truly as an educator, assessing needs, nurturing and facilitating growth in independence and reflective thinking, and evaluating and building resources.

Notes

[1] Valuable information relating to leadership and management styles has been developed within the field of organizational behavior. Much of this information is applicable to the management of adult education programs. Cf. W. B. Eddy, W. W. Burke, V. A. Dupre, and O. South, eds., *Behavioral Science and the Manager's Role* (Washington D.C.: NTL Institute for Applied Behavioral Science, 1969). See also the book of readings edited by B. Hinton and H. Joseph Reitz, *Groups and Organizations* (Belmont CA: Wadsworth, 1971).

[2] John McKinley, "Perspectives on Diagnostics in Adult Education," in *Adult Education: The Diagnostic Procedure*, ed. Leon McKenzie and John McKinley (Bloomington IN: Indiana University School of Education Bulletin, 1973), 74.

[3] A complete explanation of the concept of marketing is contained in Phillip Kotler's *Marketing for Nonprofit Organizations* (Englewood Cliffs: Prentice-Hall, 1975). See also Travis Shipp's "The Marketing Concept and Adult Education," *Lifelong Learning: The Adult Years* 4, no. 7 (1981): 8-9.

[4] Sharon Merriam, "Taking Stock," in S. Merriam, ed., *An Update on Adult Learning Theory* (San Francisco: Jossey-Bass, 1993), 109.

[5] Malcolm S. Knowles, *The Modern Practice of Adult Education* (Chicago: Association Press, 1980), 66-67.

[6] A good summary of the various theories of motivation may be found in Martin J. Gannon, *Management: An Organizational Perspective* (Boston: Little, Brown, 1977), 195 ff.

[7] James F. Hopewell, *Congregations: Stories and Structures* (Philadelphia: Fortress Press, 1987).

[8] For a description of the nominal group process, write the authors at P.O. Box 8568, Richmond, VA 23226.

LEARNING
THEORETICAL CONSIDERATIONS

This chapter opens with an affirmation for the reader. Many who began this book have already laid it aside as simply not practical enough to meet the existential needs of the moment. "You don't understand," they might protest. "I am looking for something that *works*. I am looking for something that gives more credit to the Spirit, that relies less on 'secular' theory and helps me understand the biblical model of education." With no intention to offer an apologetic, we would respond with an admonition that is seldom acknowledged by those with an avowed "practical bent." First, anyone concerned with education (religious or otherwise) is concerned with learning theory, for whatever method used, whatever is deemed as *working*, is based on an underlying theory. Theory is inescapable. Without conscious consideration of that theory, where do we go when what works today doesn't work tomorrow? Theoretical discussion may not seem holy, but practice that is not linked to propositional theory eventually degenerates to mindless activity (of which we already have plenty that passes for religious education and leads many adults to conclude that the church is not a viable provider of quality learning experiences). Further, while fully acknowledging the work of God's spirit in guiding transformation, we would claim that God is the author of all truth, whether discovered by a theologian or a scientist. As for a biblical model of education, we all await enlightenment as to what that looks like, exactly. The only thing that comes close to suggesting models are perhaps the Shema (Deuteronomy 6), Jesus' intuitive approach (primarily conversational), and the witness of Acts, which observes that "the disciples went from house to house teaching and preaching" (no mention of classrooms or schooling).

But an affirmation was promised: if you are still reading you are among those serious religious educators who have a heartfelt desire (dare we say *calling*?) to find not only something that works in terms of leading people to deep faith, but that is based on a sound understanding of who adults are, how they develop and learn, and how to apply that understanding to practice. So congratulations! Keep reading.

Because volumes have been and will be written dealing singularly with the issue of learning theory and we are limiting our consideration to one chapter, only three important issues relating to the concept of learning are discussed below. First, the relationship between the concepts of education and learning are examined more fully than in chapter 2, and a general topology of learning is outlined. This issue is pursued because many religious educators of adults are unable to define, even operationally, adult religious education. Quite often they use the words education and learning interchangeably. While we would not pose as the final arbiters of how words should be used, we would suggest that the prevailing distinction (in the field of adult education) between education and learning would make discourse about learning more precise.

Second, the concept of the learning process is analyzed. We view the learning process at several different levels of meaning. Two of these levels of meaning are discussed. Learning is a process by which a person appropriates events previously outside of his experience base. At another level of meaning, learning is a process of self-construction.

Third, the notion of transformative learning is reviewed. Transformative learning provides a medium for helping adults change their fundamental orientations toward reality (their worldviews).

Education and Learning: Four Types of Learning

The concept of education is open to many different interpretations. "Part of the problem involved in talking and thinking about education," states one commentator, "is the variety of definitions of education which is offered to us on all sides. We are, in fact, literally bombarded with a multitude of competing definitions."[1] A sampling of these definitions will underscore the significance of this observation.

Harry Broudy defines education as the process or product of a deliberate attempt to shape experience through the management of learning.[2] William Frankena suggests that the term education may denote: (1) the activity of teaching the young, (2) what goes on in the child in the process of being educated, (3) what the child acquires out of the process, and (4) the discipline that studies the three foregoing elements. Aside from his predilection to think of education strictly in terms of children, Frankena's definition is helpful for casting light on some of the denotative senses of education.[3] John Laska states that education is the deliberate attempt by the learner or by someone else to control a learning situation for the purpose of bringing about the attainment of a goal.[4]

Thomas Groome means by education "the deliberate and intentional attending in the present to the future possibility of the total person and of the community. Education is a concerted attempt by people called educators to enable others with themselves to confront the limit situations of life and push beyond them."[5] James Michael Lee avers that education "is the broad process whereby persons learn something. Therefore a person is always in the process of being educated at every moment of his waking life, and in a panoply of situations."[6] Maria Harris reminds us that even forms and contexts teach.[7] Education and learning in this description appear to be synonymous.

Charles Melchert takes a different tack and sees the need to examine the concept of education with more focus. He refuses to deal with the concept as anything that happens to anyone. He suggests that a concept "so broadly taken offers no help in clarifying distinctive or unique features." He offers six criteria for the purpose of structuring the concept: (1) The concept of education implies intentional activity; (2) it implies something valuable in that the educated person is changed for the better; (3) it involves knowing in depth and breadth; (4) it refers to a relatively long period of time; (5) it implies interpersonal interactions; and (6) education implies wholeness in that it involves the whole person.[8]

In the field of adult education a clear distinction is usually drawn between learning and education. This helps to clarify both concepts. Adult learning is seen as a continuing mode of adult activity permeating the categories of human experience while adult education "refers to organized and sequential learning experiences designed to meet the needs of adults."[9] J. Roby Kidd distinguishes learning from education. He states that learning may go on with or without conscious plan or direction. "It is thus most easily distinguished from education by the fact that the latter word suggests the conscious planning or organization of experience. Education is planned learning."[10]

Coolie Verner, one of the leaders of the modern adult education movement in America, offered a more complex definition. "Adult education is the action of an external educational agent in purposefully ordering behavior into planned systematic experiences that can result in learning for those for whom such activity is supplemental to their primary role in society, and which involves some continuity in an exchange relationship between the agent and the learner so that the educational process is under constant supervision and direction." [11]

We shall come back to the distinction between education and learning shortly. It would profit us more, at this point, to look at four types of learning. The chart on page 164 indicates some of the characteristics of these types. The types of learning are: (1) random experiential learning, (2) other-managed experiential learning, (3) self-managed learning, and (4) teacher-facilitated learning.

Random Experiential Learning

Random experiential learning, according to Paul Bergevin, is characterized by an absence of planning, a lack of definite purpose or goals, the quality of being accidental (as taking place in everyday activities outside of a school context), and lacking the guidance provided by an instructor.[12] Barring brain damage or some other unusual circumstance, we cannot avoid being influenced by a multiplicity of factors that exist in our environment. By merely walking down the street, a normal person will learn something. The person may have no intention to learn. Random experiential learning is usually the immediate effect of "having" an experience. That is, the experience is neither analyzed nor studied discursively. This type of learning involves no direction or monitoring from another person. No one validates or tests learning outcomes. Learning is episodic and, to a high degree, involves the peripheral consciousness.

The distinction between peripheral and focused consciousness is based on Michael Polyani's hypothesis of tacit knowing. As knowers we possess a dual orientation toward that which is knowable.[13] This dual orientation yields simultaneously explicit knowledge (related to focused consciousness) and tacit knowledge (related to peripheral consciousness). An example will elucidate the difference. A person looks at a book in his bookcase. He reads the title on the spine of the book. His vision is focused on the book and targeted on the spine of the book. Peripherally he also sees other books in the bookcase, the person sitting in a chair to his left, the vase on top of the bookcase, and a host of other objects within the field of peripheral vision. What is "there" in the peripheral field frames the book that is the object of focused vision. What registers in his brain structure is the gestalt: everything in both the focused and peripheral visual fields.

The analogy of a visual field illustrates the field of consciousness. When we learn anything, the context in which we learn as well as the explicit content of learning constitutes the totality of "that which is learned." We appropriate not only an explicit content but also a contextual content. This contextual learning activity, furthermore, results in learning that is tremendously influential in shaping and changing us. The impact of contextual learning is all the more powerful since this kind of learning is not reflected on; it is almost subliminal in that it is beyond the threshold of focused consciousness.[14] This is not to say, however, that random experiential learning involves peripheral consciousness solely. What is noted here is that peripheral consciousness is perhaps involved in random experiential learning to a greater extent than it is in other types of learning.

Other-Managed Experiential Learning

Perhaps the best example of other-managed experiential learning can be found in a person's participation in a religious ceremony or ritual. Assume that an adult wishes to be baptized. The adult intends primarily to gain membership in the church, to gain grace, or to achieve a number of possible religious goals. During the process of the ceremony the adult may learn quite a bit, but learning is not a primary objective of the participation in the ceremony. In fact, there is usually no explicit learning objective at all; religious objectives are ordinarily the sole explicit objectives.

Anyone who has participated in a well-managed liturgical celebration knows how forceful such an experience can be. The point is not that adults do not learn from participating in liturgical celebrations, but that learning is something that occurs in the background. It is probable that for the larger part of human history, religious meaning was made available to people not in a logical, discursive manner, but through the instrumentality of symbolic events that carried messages which did not require discursive interpretation. It has been only in relatively recent times, in terms of human history, that theological talk about a liturgical event has taken precedence over the event itself. This may be attributed to pastoral ministers who have a tendency to place more confidence in their explanations of the liturgical event than in the power of the symbols that are explained.

There is no planned sequence of learning activities in other-managed experiential learning. There is generally a planned sequence of liturgical activities. This is to say that the activities are apprised as something other than learning activities. Frequently the learner receives guidance from a liturgical leader; the liturgical leader is not viewed as a teacher but as a key agent in the liturgy. The adult is not tested as to what he learned from participation in the ceremony. There is no validation procedure by which a participant knows he actually achieved a learning objective.

Four Types of Learning

Random Experiential Learning	Other-Managed Experiential Learning	Self-Managed Learning	Teacher-Facilitated Learning
Unintentinal learning	Intention to achieve something other than a learning objective	Intention to achieve a learning objective	Intention to achieve a learning objective
No planned sequence of learning activities	No planned sequence of explicitly labeled learning activities	Sequence of learning activities planned by learner	Sequence of learning activities planned by learner and teacher
No guidance from another	Guidance from a leader	Occasional guidance from others, no guidance from a teacher	Guidance from a teacher
No validation of learning	No validation of learning	Nonsystematic validation of learning	Nonsystematic to systematic validation of learning
No learning objective	No explicit learning objective. Learning objective implicit in ritual activity.	Explicit learning objectives. Limited in number and scope.	Explicit learning objectives. Wider in number and scope.

Self-Managed Learning

The third mode of learning is called self-managed learning. Researchers in the field of adult education have shown that the majority of adults in their samples were involved in learning projects or self-managed learning.[15] It has been estimated that approximately three-fourths of the adult population undertake learning projects of a minimum duration of seven hours per project during the course of a year. These adults generally desire to set their own pace of learning, use their own style of learning, and keep their strategies of learning flexible. While research data in the area of self-managed learning are probably skewed by bias in the selection of sample subjects and by prompting bias during interviewing,[16] it appears that a rather large proportion of the adult population is involved in self-managed learning.

Self-managed learning implies an intention to engage in a learning activity qua learning activity and conscious objectives for learning. Since this type of learning occupies a relatively short time frame, the learner's goals are limited in number. Learning activities range from episodic to sustained. A person may spend an hour or so learning something; on the other hand, a person may devote many hours to the achievement of a learning objective over a period of several weekends. The guidance of a teacher is not sought; information is sometimes sought from another person who serves principally as a resource person. Learning is typically discursive. Learning outcomes are validated in terms of the learner's consequent experience. If someone wishes to learn how to make a pudding, the proof of the pudding will be in the eating. So also will be the proof of the learning. On some occasions a more formal system of validation comes into play, e.g., a person may study on his own in preparation for testing out of an academic course of study. This latter eventuality, however, is not common.

Teacher-Facilitated Learning

The most common form of the fourth type of learning is strongly associated with the traditional classroom setting. The learner entertains an active intention to learn and clear-cut objectives are identified. The sequence of learning is planned by a teacher or by a teacher and learners in collaboration. Discursive reasoning and reflection are predominant. A teacher guides the learning process. A teacher ordinarily helps assess the extent to which objectives have been reached. Teacher-facilitated learning usually implies a sustained and long-term activity, and a variety of learning outcomes may be attained within the scope of the activity.

While there is no officially sanctioned nomenclature within the professional field, it seems commonly accepted by most theorists in the field that teacher-facilitated learning is called education. To extend the term education to all types of learning merely introduces confusion into theoretical discourse about education. If education means everything—if education is descriptive of all types of learning—then education means nothing. Of course, teacher-facilitated learning could be called schooling, but most adult educators would react negatively to such a suggestion. Schooling, rightly or wrongly, conjures up images in the minds of many of school desks lined up in neat rows and a dominating instructor telling things to pupils. Most instructional activities in adult education, as distinct from higher education (college and university adult education), are nontraditional in that the typical classroom situation does not obtain.

Coolie Verner's definition of adult education as involving an external agent seems to be the definition of choice. The external agent could be called a teacher, facilitator, leader, or counselor. Such an external agent is crucial to the definition. Note also that the agent is an educational agent. In other managed experiential learning an agent may be present but the agent is properly a liturgical agent. We may say that it is educational to take a walk through a certain parish. We may also say that participating in a liturgical celebration is educational. A person who undertakes a learning project on his own is involved, we may say, in an educational pursuit. But our language would be inexact; we would be using the term educational only in a very loose sense.

The use of language in respect to the words education and learning has many implications at the level of theoretical discourse about education and learning. But there are also implications for the practice of adult education in the parish or local church. A pastor once observed that adult religious education was defined so broadly by some that it seemed to include everything that happened in his parish. "I am beginning to believe," he said, "that the Lord's main mission was to promote adult education and that adult education is the hub of all parish activities. Does the term adult education embrace everything that happens to conscious adults?"

Adult education is not everything. It is not a blanket concept that should be thrown over the entire local church. The term adult education should be applied only to programs in which an educator brings a degree of expertise to the task of structuring and facilitating learning. This includes classroom sessions, workshops, conferences, group discussions, lecture series, demonstrations, and a host of other activities that may be construed as belonging to the category of teacher-facilitated learning. An adult may learn something by merely walking through the church, but the adult educator is not a tour guide who promotes random experiential learning. Learning may take place when an adult participates in a liturgical event, but the adult educator is not necessarily a liturgist. Nor should the adult educator feel responsible for the self-managed learning that occurs among parishioners, although the adult educator may promote such learning at every opportunity. Simply put, education and learning must be differentiated. All education implies learning; not all learning implies education.

The Learning Process

An interesting book edited by Donald Vandenberg, *Teaching and Learning,* contains a number of philosophical or theoretical essays on learning.[17] Learning is described variously as problem-solving, enquiring, appropriating, symbolizing, acquiring, actualizing, experiencing, acting, feeling, co-disclosure, becoming, working, socializing, loving, unifying, criticizing, understanding, and hearing. What is marvelous about the selections in the book is that each description of learning makes sense given the perspective of each author. What is undeniably frustrating is the knowledge that the concept of learning is so rich in possible meanings. The concept of learning may never be fully and completely delineated. Be that as it may, an attempt must be made to deal with the complex process of learning. One's concept of learning controls one's idea of teaching. To go even further, it is quite impossible to think seriously about teaching without first reflecting seriously about learning.

Learning is an appropriative process and a process of self-construction. These processes are logically distinct but existentially inseparable. We may talk about appropriation and self-construction as two different things; both appropriation and self-construction, however, are the same process viewed from different levels of understanding.

Learning as Appropriation

Learning is a process by which the "experience base" of a person is developed through the appropriation of "experience events" previously outside the person's experience base. The definition is somewhat awkward, but for a purpose. The concept of experience has a twofold connotation. It is crucial that experience as a base or reservoir be distinguished from the experiencing of an event. Let us now redefine learning after stipulating that the notion of experience base, for definitional purposes, is equivalent to the notion of person. Learning is a process by which a person develops through the reflection on and appropriation of new experiences. (This reflective process will be further explored shortly when we consider transformative learning).

When the word appropriation is used there is an immediate danger that it will be apprised as denoting the spectator theory of learning. There are two fundamental theories of learning; the spectator and the participant theories. The spectator theory maintains that the learner (subject) simply assimilates stimuli (objects). There is a gulf between the learner and the stimuli; the stimuli bridge this gulf and present themselves to the learner. The learner receives the stimuli. The theory can be traced, in part, to John Locke who envisioned the mind of the subject as a blank tablet. Environmental stimuli produce marks on the tablet. If we change the environmental stimuli, we also produce a change in the learner.

While the spectator theory of learning accounts for the environment and external stimuli as factors in the act of learning, the theory does not take into account the activity of the learner (beyond merely receiving external stimuli). Specifically the spectator theory of learning does not deal with the intentionality of the learner. Nor does the theory deal with two operations of intentionality: perception and interpretation.

Experiments in perceptual psychology have shown that the learner or subject, in the act of perceiving an object, "works over" objective stimuli.[18] What is perceived are not objective stimuli pure and simple, but objective stimuli that have been screened, selected, and shaped according to the sensory predilections of the subject. Quite often we hear and see what we expect to hear and see. If a teacher, for example, addresses a complex statement to twenty students, in all probability twenty slightly different messages will have been received. Each of the students will repeat the message with different nuances. Perceptual bias explains this occurrence to some extent, but it may be explained further by noting that in the act of learning the learner is actively interpreting the object of learning.

Objective stimuli are perceived according to the perceptual mode of the receiver. Stimuli are selected, screened, and shaped in the act of perception. Beyond the perceptual level, at the conceptual level, the learner interprets that which is learned. The *intentional* appropriation of objective reality implies that the learner introjects meaning into that which is learned and changes the meaning of the stimuli, to some degree, in the very act of encountering these stimuli. The twenty students in the foregoing example will not only hear or perceive the teacher's message differently; they will also vest what they hear with individual meaning. In the act of learning we come into touch not with bare facts or external realities in themselves. Instead we come into touch with phenomena that are joint products of external realities and the intentionality of the learner.

The diagram on the next page contrasts the spectator theory of learning with the participant theory. The participant theory of learning places the responsibility for learning within the learner in a way the spectator does not. In the framework of the spectator theory the learner is responsible for assimilating "pure" stimuli from the external world. Following the participant theory the learner is responsible for appropriating phenomena. Phenomena are stimuli that have been "worked over" by the learner, stimuli that have been screened and shaped perceptually and interpreted conceptually. Phenomena are stimuli that have been subjectivized.

To rephrase this in terms of the concept of experience, when we experience an event we color the event by means of our intentionality. That intentionality, in turn, is itself shaped and influenced by all of our previous experiences taken as a whole. (Mezirow calls this the creation of meaning schemes). The quality of the present experience is related to the sum of all of previous experiences. This experience, here and now, is constructed in terms of our entire reservoir of experience. "No stimulus or cue *has* a particular meaning or significance," insists Alvin Mahrer, "it is invested with meaning or significance by the persons who actively structure these intrusive components of the external world." Mahrer mentions that in most theories of learning external stimuli "cause" the person. In his theory the person defines the stimuli.[19] The experience base of a person, therefore, defines the event that is experienced.

The appropriative process is not the mere process of receiving something. It does not imply simple passivity on the part of the learner. In a very basic sense the learner is responsible for what is learned. Erich Fromm states that most models of human behavior are founded on principles of instinctivism (which proposes we act in response to internal stimuli or instincts) or behaviorism (which proposes we act in response to external stimuli). He adds that most writers in the area of human behavior are not aware of the philosophical implications of their theories. He also states that both instinctivism and behaviorism exclude the person from consideration. "Whether man is the product of conditioning, or the product of animal evolution, he is exclusively determined by conditions outside himself; he has no part in his own life, no responsibility, and not even a trace of freedom. Man is a puppet, controlled by strings—instinct or conditioning."[20] Fromm's desire for a model of human behavior that admits the intentionality of the learner is satisfied by the participant theory of learning and by the school of thought known as phenomenology, which furnishes a philosophical ground for the participant theory of learning.[21]

The Learning Act: A Comparison of Two Theories

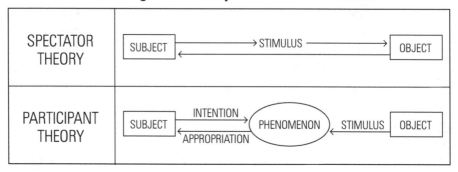

Learning as Self-Construction

The learner is at the center of the learning process as an active participant in determining what changes will occur in himself as a consequence of learning. He is not merely a malleable subject who is easily molded according to a predetermined form. This point of view has long been held in the field of adult education. Howard McCluskey, one of the founding fathers of the adult education movement in the United States, wrote:

> The mistake of the original S-R formula has been its reductionist oversimplification of the highly complex nature of the learning process. By over-emphasizing both stimulus and response as well as their external character, it has reduced if not ignored the unique importance of the person (the intervening variable, O) as the agent receiving and often originating the stimulus as well as the one giving the response. A more valid version requires the insertion of an O between the S

and the R, thus reinstating the learner as an indispensable factor in understanding and influencing the learning process.[22]

The learner is not only central to the appropriative process, as we have seen above, but is also the key to understanding learning as growth or development.

Each event that becomes an experience event (an event that is appropriated and, therefore, colored by the subjectivity of the learner) is evaluated in terms of the experience base of the learner. But the converse is also true: The experience base of the learner is enriched and altered, to some degree, with the appropriation of each experience event. Or, as John Dewey stated, learning is the reconstruction of experience.[23] When the experience base changes, of course, the person changes. In the act of appropriating (perceiving and interpreting) the event, the learner changes the event; in the act of appropriating (actively receiving) the event, the event changes the learner.

Some of the changes associated with learning occur imperceptibly over a long period of time. We change to some degree simply by living and learning experientially. But we also change as a result of planned learning such as self-managed learning projects and as a consequence of participating in teacher-facilitated learning. In these latter instances it can be seen more clearly that we become directly and consciously involved in the process of self-construction.

If you desire to reach a particular learning objective (to change in respect to some cognitive, affective, or motor performance outcome), you may enroll in, say, a workshop. The workshop facilitator arranges a series of events gauged to foster the desired changes. The experience of these events shapes and fashions your experience base. To put the matter in another way, you are (to some degree) a different person as a consequence of what you have learned at the workshop. You have consciously altered your experience base. With the help of the workshop facilitator, you have been busy in the work of self-construction.

It is not the teacher or facilitator who changes the learner. It is the learner, relying on the teacher's expertise in structuring events for experiencing, who changes himself/herself. The teacher is not a sculptor who manipulates pliable learners but rather a helper.

Implications
The full implications of the above perspective on learning are presented in the following chapter. A few things may be noted here, however, to

good advantage. It seems that the religious educator who holds the spectator theory of learning, either explicitly or implicitly, will place a great emphasis on the message (objective stimulus) that is to be received by the learner. Teaching will be viewed fundamentally as telling something to someone; the content of this telling will become all important. The effective teacher will be seen, above all else, as a content specialist. Little attention will be paid to the learner of the instructional process. Those who accept the participant theory of learning will tend to place an emphasis on the learner, the perceptual processes of the learner, the interpretations placed on the manifest content of instruction by the learner, and on the instructional process.

Those who see learning as self-construction will tend to think of the teacher as a facilitator, as someone who structures learning experiences that are gauged to help the learner attain instructional objectives. Those who do not view learning as self-construction on the part of the learner will be sorely tempted to think of teaching in terms that are more magisterial (The term is used pejoratively!). The teacher will be apprised as a master, a ruler, or a content authority who actively changes the learner by speaking to the learner authoritatively. Unfortunately there is a pronounced tendency among some religious educators to think of teaching as authoritative speech. Such ideas probably derive from absolutist notions of the teaching function of the church. The church teaches via religious leaders, by issuing proclamations, edicts, or announcements. Learning is thought to be equivalent to listening and accepting what has been announced. As theologians and curriculum developers pursue their ideas about the teaching function of the church in the future, they would be well served to ask first what learning is. Nor would they go far wrong to ask this question of learning theorists.

Other implications of learning as an appropriative and self-constructive process will be noted in the next chapter. Three implications can be stressed here, however. First, adult education programs in parishes and local churches will never be effective as long as adults do not participate in selecting the learning objectives. Second, learning is not simply the receiving of a lecture or sermon; teaching is not merely the telling of theology. Third, adults will never grow or develop along the lines prescribed by religious values until they decide to grow and develop. This last consideration leads us to the idea of perspective transformation through a process called transformative learning.

Transformative Learning

In the first edition of this book, Mezirow's idea of "perspective transformation" was held up as having promise both for the wider field of adult education and particularly for adult *religious* education. At that time Mezirow was still developing his theory, and critique and debate over both the theory and the research upon which it was based were just beginning. In subsequent years a number of adult educators took up the debate in the Forum section of the *Adult Education Journal*. Cranton provides a brief summary of the debate citing various points at which colleagues took Mezirow to task.[24] As might be expected, this elicited both a substantial defense by Mezirow and a sharpening of transformational theory. The latter was enhanced both by Mezirow's further reflection and subsequent replication of his research in various settings, largely by his graduate students in adult education.

The publication of Mezirow's *Transformative Dimensions of Adult Learning* in 1991 represented a bolder and more articulate explication of his theory and its application, though the debate has not ended.[25] It is even clearer that both the theory and development of transformational processes have important implications for adult religious education. Thus a brief consideration of transformational learning and its application are in order. At this point it should be noted that one must follow closely Mezirow's use of his technical terminology, which is central to the whole concept (meaning perspectives, reflective discourse, perpective transformation, transformational learning).

Briefly stated, according to this theory transformative learning occurs as our meaning perspectives are transformed through reflective discourse. The process and the theory is not that simple, however. Cranton provides a concise description:

> By the time they reach adulthood, people have acquired a way of seeing the world, a way of interpreting their experiences, and a set of values. Although adults continue to acquire new knowledge and skills, they often must integrate new experiences with prior learning. When this integration does not occur easily and contradictions or dilemmas result, the prior learning must be examined and some adjustments made. Individuals can reject the contradictory new information or revise their previous views. This, simply stated, is the process of reflection and transformative learning.[26]

Those ways of seeing the world, the ways we interpret experience, and the resulting set of values constitute our meaning perspectives.

Examining and adjusting prior learning involves reflective discourse and results in perspective transformation. Reflection on experience is crucial to transformative learning, as it is to Lewin's four-stage learning model upon which Kolb developed his theory of learning styles.[27] Mezirow explains: "We may reflect on *content* or description of a problem (or problematic meaning scheme), the *process* or method of our problem solving, or the *premise(s)* upon which the problem is predicated. . . . Reflective learning involves the confirmation, addition, or transformation of ways of interpreting experience. Transformative learning results in new or transformed meaning schemes or, when reflection focuses on premises, transformed meaning perspectives."[28] Thus, according to Mezirow, "Perspective transformation [that is, transforming meaning perspectives] is the process of becoming critically aware of how and why our assumptions have come to constrain the way we perceive, understand, and feel about our world; changing these structures of habitual expectations to make possible a more inclusive, discriminating, and integrative perspective; and finally, making choices or otherwise acting upon these new understandings."[29]

Mezirow has stuck to his contention drawn from the original research among twenty-three women who were returning to college, that the process of transformation involves ten phases, as follows:

(1) A disorienting dilemma (such as illness, divorce, empty nest, retirement)
(2) Self-examination with feelings of guilt or shame
(3) A critical assessment of epistemic, sociocultural, or psychic assumption
(4) Recognition that one's discontent and the process of transformation are shared and that others have negotiated a similar change
(5) Exploration of options for new roles, relationships, and actions
(6) Planning a course of action
(7) Acquisition of knowledge and skills for implementing one's plans
(8) Provisional trying of new roles
(9) Building of competence and self-confidence in new roles and relationships
(10) A reintegration into one's life on the basis of conditions dictated by one's new perspective.[30]

Two further items should be noted as they answer earlier questions previously not addressed in early explanations of the theory. Mezirow points out the social nature of the process. For example, he states that the disorienting dilemma that begins the process is precipitated by others (even though elsewhere he suggests that it may begin by reading a book, leading us to assume that it may involve not a person but an instrumentality). Further, they facilitate our exploration of alternative perspectives, support us, and engage with us in the necessary rational discourse.[31]

Another question Mezirow addresses is the permanency of the transformation that occurs. He boldly states, "Although slippery and subject to diversions and self-deception, the transformative learning process is irreversible once completed; that is, once our understanding is clarified and we have committed ourselves fully to taking the action it suggests, we do not regress to levels of less understanding. Reaching this point of full understanding and commitment can be extremely difficult, however, and many people do regress before they reach this point."[32]

Mezirow has provided the basis for a new perspective on adult development and learning. Others have suggested that consciousness changes as a person moves through the life span. However, he has presented a yet-to-be surpassed conceptual tool for dealing with adult development and learning. If the human being is the animal who receives and makes meanings, there is no better way to investigate human beings than in terms of meaning perspectives.

Transformational Learning and Adult Religious Education

To address the rich implications of the concept of perspective transformation and how such occurs (transformational learning) requires a further consideration of the concept of *meaning* and the affect of learning on meaning. Mezirow sees learning as "a process of construing or appropriating a new or revised interpretation of the meaning of one's experience as a guide to decision and action."[33] But meaning is an *interpretation* of experience. Further, the meaning resulting from such interpretations may relate to ultimate questions of a metaphysical nature. Jarvis explains, "Underlying the history of religious thought is the quest for meaning: cosmologies, theologies, and church doctrine all seek to provide answers to that fundamental question of creation and existence 'Why?' but this is also the question with which all learning begins."[34] There are, however, meaning structures that are more "tribal" in nature, developing as a result of the socialization process of the culture into which one is born. As Jarvis points out, every society contains systems of meaning that are expected to be passed on from generation to generation.[35] These meaning systems are assumed to be necessary if members of that society are to make sense of their world. For the most part they are acquired uncritically at a very young age, largely as a result of formal education. Gradually, however, these meaning schemes, gathered ostensibly from everyday learning, are shaped into meaning perspectives that result from both education and life experience (and interpretations of experience). Changes in meaning perspectives are very significant and are akin to a type of religious experience for Mezirow.

Jarvis summarizes the relationship of meaning-making to learning in this way:

> "The desire to discover meaning seems quite fundamental to humanity and where there is ignorance, then there is questioning. In answering those questions there is learning, seeking sometimes to interpret the meaning that others have placed upon those experiences and to make sense of those meanings in the present."[36]

If the reader is attempting to synthesize the theoretical propositions thus far explored, as well as to find *something* of practical use, it may be helpful to review at this point the section of chapter six on worldview construction. Indeed, the concepts of perspective transformation and worldview construction have much in common and ostensibly address the same concerns. Thus, it will be remembered that worldviews (meaning perspectives?) are a result of tradition, early nurture, and early experience. Further, both development and change in worldview is a social process, involving interaction (reflective discourse?) with others, both within and outside formal learning settings.

While deriving his conclusions from assessment of a wider array of adult education theories, Stubblefield nonetheless summarizes the religious implications of both the theories of transformational learning and worldview construction:

> . . . theological and moral concerns are embedded in adult education philosophy and practice. Education for becoming and doing takes the form of moral education, for an explicit normative system informs the diagnostic and prescriptive process and addresses the central question of how to create educative processes that would empower adults to live responsibly and in freedom.[37]

"Empowering adults to live responsibly and in freedom" are certainly at the heart of these theories. But are these not implicit in the purposes of adult religious education? As was stated in chapter 6, the mission of the church is to make meaning available, and adult religious education can facilitate discovery of meaning by helping adults examine their meaning perspectives and worldviews. In fact, since meaning perspectives and worldviews are the stuff out of which values and decisions for life arise, it may be said that worldview construction via transformative learning may be the medium for bringing the gospel message to fruition. Transformation is certainly a biblical concept. Romans 12:2 admonishes us not to conform to the world around us, but rather to "be *transformed* by the renewing of our minds." Was not Jesus sharing both a meaning perspective and a worldview in his famous "sermon on the mount," and was not his intention to inspire transformation of the minds and spirits of his hearers?

The implications for learning are clear, and yet to some this whole notion will smack of preoccupation with method over message. "We just need to teach the Bible" has been an oft-voiced cry of those who believe we have been too bound to secular theories of education. Yet, the very cry implies the necessity of method, for *how* will we teach the Bible? The inevitable choice of method will be made out of our meaning perspectives and worldviews!

The findings of Search Institute in their research on congregational factors affecting faith maturity have been cited numerous times already in this work. The reader is reminded that one factor reported by participants in the study was a *critical thinking climate*. It is no stretch to assume that such a climate is characterized by reflective discourse. Such interaction takes place in the context of the factor cited by participants as being the most influential in their faith development: participation, over time, in an effective Christian education ministry. And recall that the characteristics of such an effective ministry, from the actual observation of researchers, included a global perspective and intentionally treating issues of concern to the daily lives of adults. To extrapolate an application of McKenzie's types of worldviews (see again chapter six), this would imply a provisional worldview that is open to new and challenging ideas; one that is inclusive of a diversity of new meanings; an active worldview that constantly seeks new meanings; a worldview that critically questions and tests new ideas through meditative and deliberative thinking. We would affirm Vogel's reminder, "For Christians' transformation grows out of encounters with Jesus

Christ and is an ongoing process. As people receive the gift of God's self-giving love, they are called to live out of love rather than fear, to give rather than control, to serve rather than to accumulate power or money or possessions, to be open to alternative ways of experiencing and understanding what God calls us to be and do."[38] The intersection of Vogel, Mezirow, and McKenzie are clear. To observe that achievement of what God calls us to be and do involves perspective transformation and construction of a Christian worldview does not constitute unholy reliance on secular methodology.

Notes

[1] Jonas Soltis, *An Introduction to the Analysis of Educational Concepts* (Reading MA: Addison-Wesley, 1968), 2.

[2] Harry Broudy, *Building a Philosophy of Education*, 2d ed. (Englewood Cliffs: Prentice-Hall, 1961), 8.

[3] William K. Frankena, *Philosophy of Education* (New York: Macmillan, 1965), 2.

[4] John A. Laska, *Schooling and Education: Basic Concepts and Problems* (New York: Van Nostrand, 1976), 7.

[5] Thomas Groome, "Christian Education for Freedom: A 'Shared Praxis' Approach," in *Foundations of Religious Education*, ed. Padraic O'Hare (New York: Paulist, 1978), 10.

[6] James Michael Lee, *The Shape of Religious Education* (Birmingham: Religious Education Press, 1971), 6.

[7] Maria Harris, *Fashion Me a People: Curriculum in the Church* (Louisville: Westminister Press, 1989), 169.

[8] Charles Melchert, "What is Religious Education?," *The Living Light* 14, no. 3 (1977): 339-42.

[9] U.S. Department of Health, Education, and Welfare, *Perspectives of Adult Education in the United States and a Projection for the Future* (Washington D.C.: DHEW Publication [OE] 73-09100, 1973), 1.

[10] James Robbins Kidd, *How Adults Learn* (New York: Association, 1973), 17.

[11] Coolie Verner, *A Conceptual Scheme for the Identification and Classification of Processes* (Chicago: Adult Education Association, 1962), 2-3.

[12] Paul Bergevin, *A Philosophy for Adult Education* (New York: Seabury, 1967), 60.

[13] Michael Polanyi and Harry Prosch, *Meaning* (Chicago: University of Chicago Press, 1975), 71. See also Harry Broudy's essay, "Tacit Knowing as a Rationale for Liberal Education," in *Education and Values*, ed. Douglas Sloan (New York: Teachers' College Press, 1980), 50-66.

[14] For a fuller treatment of the impact of context or environment on learning see Lee, *The Flow of Religious Instruction* (Birmingham: Religious Education Press, 1973), 65 ff.

[15] For a review of research see Allen Tough, "Major Learning Efforts: Recent Research and Future Directions," *Adult Education* 28, no. 4 (1978): 250-63. See also Patrick Penland, "Self-Initiated Learning," *Adult Education* 29, no. 3 (1979): 170-79.

[16] Preliminary research undertaken by Travis Shipp and Leon McKenzie suggests that many adults are prompted inadvertently by interviewers to a socially acceptable response, i.e., subjects are only too glad to state they are active learners when they suspect the interviewer wants to hear this

response. Notwithstanding the presence of such prompting bias in the data of most researchers who use the interview technique, it seems the majority of adults are active learners. Prompting bias, of course, can be controlled through a number of subtle interviewing tactics.

[17] Donald Vandenberg, ed., *Teaching and Learning* (Urbana: University of Illinois Press, 1969).

[18] The best single volume in this respect is Arthur W. Combs, Anne Richards, and Fred Richards, *Perceptual Psychology* (New York: Harper & Row, 1976). In the course of explicating the significance of perceptual psychology, the authors review a large number of important studies in perception.

[19] Alvin Mahrer, *Experiencing: A Humanistic Theory of Psychology and Psychiatry* (New York: Brunner/Mazel, 1978) 189.

[20] Erich Fromm, *The Anatomy of Human Destructiveness* (New York: Fawcett Crest, 1975) 95-96.

[21] For an excellent treatment of phenomenology see Quentin Lauer, *Phenomenology: Its Genesis and Prospect* (New York: Harper Torchbooks, 1958).

[22] Howard McClusky, "An Approach to a Differential Psychology of the Adult Potential," in *The Adult Learner: A Neglected Species*, Malcolm Knowles (Houston: Gulf, 1973) 145.

[23] John Dewey, *Democracy and Education* (New York: Free Press, 1966) *76* ff.

[24] P. Cranton, *Understanding and Promoting Transformative Learning: A Guide for Educators of Adults* (San Franciso: Jossey-Bass, 1994).

[25] See, for example, Mark Tennet's critique in "Individual and the Social in Mezirow's View of Development and Transformation," *Adult Education Quarterly* 44, no. 1 (fall 1993): 34-42.

[26] Cranton, 22.

[27] See David Kolb, *Experiential Learning: Experience as the Source of Learning and Development* (Englewood Cliffs NJ: Prentice-Hall, Inc., 1984).

[28] Jack Mezirow, *Transformative Dimensions of Adult Learning* (San Francisco: Jossey-Bass, 1991) 117.

[29] Ibid., 167.

[30] Ibid., 168-69.

[31] Ibid., 194.

[32] Ibid., 152.

[33] ———, "Transformational Theory," *The 29th Annual Adult Education Research Conference Proceedings* (Calgary: University of Calgary, 1988) 223.

[34] Peter Jarvis, "Meaning, Being and Learning" in Peter Jarvis and Nicholas Walters, *Adult Education and Theological Interpretations* (Malabar FL: Krieger Publishing Company, 1993) 95.

[35] Ibid., 97.

[36] Ibid., 102.

[37] Harold Stubblefield, "Soul, Self and Learning," in Jarvis and Walters, *Adult Education*, 138.

[38] Linda Vogel, *Teaching and Learning in Communities of Faith* (San Francisco: Jossey-Bass, 1991) 135.

TEACHING
AN ANALYSIS

The concept of education as a field of study includes a diversity of special functions, all of which are directed ultimately toward the teaching-learning process. In distinguishing education from learning, in previous pages we have employed the word education in a more focused sense—the instructional sense. Education, in the instructional sense, involves the agency of a teacher who ideally helps others learn. This learning takes place in a systematic rather than random fashion. What imposes order or system on the learning is an instructional plan that identifies specific learning objectives, human and material resources for learning, teaching-learning techniques, and a particular sequence of events gauged to assist the learners in the attainment of the objectives. The instructional plan is implemented in a desired psychosocial climate conducive to learning. The teacher is responsible for initiating this climate and for supporting adult learners in the maintenance of the climate. Instructional interactions take place between teacher and learners, and among learners. These interactions are governed by the interpersonal relationships that obtain in the instructional setting. These interactions in relationship give rise to the old saw that in any instructional setting often more is "caught" than "taught." Galbraith characterizes these interactions as a transactional process, described as a "democratic and collaborative endeavor whereby facilitators and learners are engaged in a mutual act of challenge, critical reflection, sharing, support, and risk-taking. The essence of the transactional process is collaboration. Facilitators and learners are full partners in the learning experience."[1] The role of the teacher, essentially, is to function as a manager of the instructional situation. This does not render inappropriate the designations "facilitator" or "lead learner" preferred by some adult educators. The instructional situation is the complexus of all factors that constitute the learning environment.

This chapter is built around four pivotal concerns relevant to the instructional situation: (1) the management of instruction, (2) instructional planning, (3) teacher-learner relationships, and (4) an ideal climate for adult learning. It should be noted that emphasis upon teaching in this chapter does not intend to place the teacher at the center of the teaching/learning enterprise. There is truth to the old saw that says what the teacher does to teach is not as important as what the learner does to learn. To clarify this contention we should address the issue of what teaching is not. Teaching is not, in most circumstances, telling things to learners.

Teaching as Telling

Leroy Ford, a retired professor of religious education, produced many helpful training tools for lay teachers. He was adapt at illustrating via cartoon the various principles about teaching and learning that he addressed in his materials. A favorite drawing illustrated the "hole in the head" theory of learning, and showed a learner sitting passively in his chair with a funnel stuck into his head. The "teacher" was dutifully pouring knowledge into the funnel.

There was a time, before the Gutenberg revolution and the large-scale availability of printed materials, when teaching consisted largely in telling things to learners. In preliterate societies the storyteller would recount the elements of the tribal myth to his listeners. The tribal myth contained the essence of a particular culture—the values, beliefs, and norms sanctioned by that culture. The duty of the teacher was to tell something in a form that helped learners remember; the chief duty of the learners was to remember the tribal myth, live according to its dictates, and be able to transmit the myth to the next generation.

A shift occurred in literate pre-Gutenberg societies. The teacher was perceived to be a master of special knowledge; the *magister* was a content specialist who told what he knew to learners. The *magister* remembered what he had heard from his teachers and this was written down in copious notes; the *magister* shared his notes, plus a commentary, with his students. In the medieval university, for example, discussions and critical inquiry were a part of the learning process, but necessity required (if the learners were to have any sort of a library at all) that a large amount of time be spent by the teacher dictating a basic text. A standard text such as the work of Peter Lombard, for example, became the course outline and provided the teacher with an opportunity to compose a lecture that consisted mainly in a series of glosses on the text. Teaching as telling was acceptable because this approach was an effective way of transmitting ideas from one generation to another.

But even after printed materials and books became available to students, most teachers continued to read standard texts to students. Immanuel Kant received wide acclaim at the University of Koenigsburg because he departed from this teaching custom. Instead Kant lectured from his own notes and spoke from his own mind. Kant moved from telling the approved text to students to telling his own thoughts, a practice frowned on by the civil authorities who tried to keep tight rein on creative thinking and critical inquiry. Kant's step was small and in the right direction, but the step away from the standard text as course context and course outline did not evidence a substantial departure from the narration model of teaching.

Teaching as the stimulation of inquiry was alive in the past, but teaching as telling was the preferred mode of instruction. It is no wonder, then, that in common parlance, as reflected in lexical definitions, teaching is viewed as an activity of imparting something to someone. Nor is it a wonder that many teachers today are chained to standard curriculum materials (in adult as well as in children's classes) and equate instructional success with "finishing the lesson" or telling all the content they can about a particular topic. Teaching has come to mean, in common parlance, telling subject matter to others. The good teacher is an effective teller; the good learner is an effective listener. Illustrations abound, but here is a personal one.

A friend in a midwestern city is a competent businessman and considerable scholar with regard to the Scriptures. He teaches a one-hour young adult Bible study class on Sunday mornings in the church we both previously attended. He spends literally hours each week preparing his lesson from the curriculum materials and accompanying commentary. On Sunday morning the co-educational class of adults sits appropriately in a semi-circle. The teacher sits at the front with his Bible and legal (seventeen-inch) pad of copious notes spread on a small "teacher's table." During the hour-long Bible lesson, occasional questions will be raised by students, and the teacher is always courteous to allow questions and discussion when initiated by class members.

However, when questions are answered, he returns immediately to his notes, and picks up exactly where he left off before the question or questions were posed. For, you see, his goal is to *cover the lesson*. In his mind, he has not been a successful teacher unless he has covered the lesson, which means getting to the end of his several pages of legal pad notes. This class has more than once filed quietly in through the side door to the sanctuary balcony well into worship. Why? Because too many questions were asked that particular day, delaying the teacher in reaching his goal of covering the lesson.

From the time of Socrates' maieutic method to the present day, we have not lacked for astute men and women who regarded teaching as something infinitely more complex than narration, but neither have we lacked for those who assumed that teacher preparation consisted in the mastery of a content area and the subsequent retelling of this content to others. To be fair (though not to excuse), there is truth to the adage, "We tend to teach the way we were taught." Most churches have traditionally relied upon lay teachers, who while perhaps possessing a gift for teaching, nonetheless lack adequate training for their task. Their only models were *their* teachers, and telling being the extant model, the tradition is passed on. (The same can be said of "Teaching Pastors" trained theologically but not pedagogically.)

Paulo Friere's *Pedagogy of the Oppressed* constituted a devastating attack on the concept of teaching as telling.[2] What he wrote did not come as a revelation to reflective educators. Adult educators in particular viewed Friere's work as adding little to what they already knew,[3] but Friere did publicize widely the case against teaching as telling.

Friere pointed out the connection between what he called the banking system of education and the intention of teachers to domesticate and control learners. For such teachers, teaching

> becomes an act of depositing, in which the students are depositories and the teacher is the depositor. Instead of communicating, the teacher issues communiques, and makes deposits, which the students patiently receive, memorize, and repeat. . . . In the banking concept of education, knowledge is a gift bestowed by those who consider themselves knowledgeable upon those whom they consider to know nothing. Projecting an absolute ignorance onto others, a characteristic of the ideology of oppression, negates education and knowledge as a process of inquiry.[4]

Teaching as telling, it could be said, can make a cognitive imperialist out of the teacher, a colonizer of learners' minds, and a manipulator of their lives.

Friere's rhetorical style, of course, made him overstate his case, or at least oversimplify the issue. Education may suffer from narration sickness (either because of the teacher's intent to dominate, the teacher's readiness for ego-tripping, or because the teacher does not know what to do except narrate), but there are times when the impartation of information is appropriate. Three Greek words for knowledge suggest three connotative senses of the term knowledge and three kinds of learning. The word *techne* refers to learning how to do something; *episteme* refers to the learning of factual knowledge; *sophia* refers to the learning of normative principles or values. The words are pregnant with subtle nuances; it suffices here to distinguish among "learning how," "learning that this is such," and "learning what one ought to be."

Now, the best way to teach someone how to do something is to show the person how, arrange a demonstration, and schedule practice sessions. It is not advised that the teacher structure an inquiry process concerning the reinvention of the wheel, unless of course the teacher wishes the learner to gain experience in inquiry and learn something about the invention process. Likewise, factual knowledge may be imparted by simply stating the facts. A teacher may sometimes arrange that learners discover facts in an effort to whet their appetites for further discovery, but all things being equal, the most efficient way to help someone learn a fact is to state the fact to that person. Impartation of knowledge may also be involved in the teaching of normative principles or values, as when a teacher states the value as a fact, e.g., stating the Bible forbids idolatry. But the telling of values to adults in expectation that they will accept these values is foolish. Personal adult commitment to a given value or principle is not the function of having a teacher narrate that value or principle. If a group of adults is told, "You should believe such and such" or, emphatically, "You must believe such and such," one may occasion (at most) mere outward observance of this belief, but the adults will not learn the value in the sense of permitting their lives to be governed by the value. And even if the teller lays out a rational and logical argument in the telling of the value, he or she should not expect a commitment to the value on the part of the listeners. (Knowles used to like to differentiate between teaching adults and teaching children by saying children were involved in *faith* learning: they just had to have faith that someday they would need what the teacher was telling them. Adults, he rightly pointed out, are not very interested in *faith* learning.) Rationality and logic are not convincing for many people. Merely telling a principle or value to adults results only in their learning of a fact: that they have been told that they should believe such and such.

This fallacy of identifying teaching with telling is critically important for adult religious education for two reasons: (1) Religious education is concerned ultimately with the commitments adults make to religious values and principles, and (2) religious educators of adults, by and large, equate teaching with telling, education with the formation of adults, and adult learning with the submissive acceptance of that which is told. At least one major denomination known for its emphasis on religious education is quite concerned about lack of evidence that all its tradition of teaching and education seems to be making little difference in the lives of its members. Biblical literacy is appallingly low. Their answer is to redesign curriculum materials rather than to examine their assumptions about teaching, their underlying educational philosophies, and their overreliance on didactic methodologies. The approach assumes that if people are not *acting* better, the answer is to get them to *think* better, and the way to do that is to throw more content at them. The curricular approaches reinforce the teacher-centered (teaching as telling) approach to learning (if, indeed, this can be called learning at all). If the desired outcome of the religious education of an adult is a more vital commitment on the part of the adult to specific religious values, the acquisition of a particular orientation toward reality, and the development of a specific religious way of being-in-the-world, then it is important for religious educators of adults to know that the simple telling of theological and scriptural things to adults does not accomplish these ends.

Managing the Instructional Situation

The teacher is the manager of the instructional situation. James Michael Lee's definition of teaching is apposite here: "Teaching is that orchestrated process whereby one person deliberately, purposively, and efficaciously structures the learning situation in such a manner that the specified desired learning outcomes are thereby acquired by another person."[5] Management of the instructional situation refers to the structuring of the learning situation and the orchestration of the process whereby learners achieve the objectives of instruction.

Management Style

Daniel Pratt demonstrates the old admonition that "what you are speaks louder than what you say." In his research among adults and their teachers in several cultures, he concluded:

> . . . it is clear that learners experience more than the mechanics of teaching activities, that is, the roles, rules, and procedures of teaching methods. They also experience the teacher's ideas and judgment as to which information will be examined, what sources will be respected, and whose frames of reference will guide the emergence of knowledge. In short, learners experience all aspects of a teacher's conceptions of teaching, that is, their beliefs and intentions, as well as their actions. What is learned will be determined as much by those beliefs and intentions as by the activities used.[6]

As a manager or leader, the teacher of adults is called upon to determine a prevailing managerial or leadership style. And it follows that the style chosen will say as much about the educational philosophy of the teacher and his/her assumptions about learners. And it will be a part of the "hidden curriculum" from which adults learn. In the chapter on program development, five approaches of program development were outlined. Each of these approaches was based on a specific kind of decision on the part of the program developer. Managerial decisions are also required of the teacher in the instructional setting. The teacher's management style relates essentially to the degree of control the teacher will exert and, correspondingly, to the degree of freedom permitted the adult learners. This decision determines answers to two important questions: (1) To what degree will the adult learners be responsible for the determination of instructional objectives, and (2) to what degree will the adult learners be responsible for the general planning of the learning experience?

The teacher who adopts a *dominative* decision style will select instructional objectives unilaterally. This is tantamount to determining the specific content of the instruction without reference to the expressed needs and interests of the learners. Instructional planning will take place without regard for the predilections of the learners. The teacher's control of the instructional situation will be very high, while the degree of responsibility enjoyed by the learners will be very low.

Following the *persuasive* style of decision-making or management, the teacher will determine instructional objectives unilaterally and plan the instruction unilaterally. The teacher will then offer a rationale for the decisions that have been made and will attempt to persuade the adult learners of the appropriateness of these decisions. Teacher control will be high to moderate; the degree of freedom allowed to the learners will be moderate to low.

The teacher who operates according to the *consultative* decision style will have outlined instructional objectives and an instructional plan prior to meeting the learners for the first time. But the objectives and plan serve principally as a basis for discussion and negotiation. The teacher is willing to change the objectives and modify the instructional plan in the light of suggestions from the learners. Since a greater degree of flexibility enters the instructional situation, the control of the teacher and the freedom of the learners are virtually balanced.

The *consensual* decision style requires that the teacher become a member of the group of learners. The determination of the instructional objectives and the planning of the instruction are the work of the group. The degree of learner freedom will be high; the degree of control exerted by the teacher will be low. The teacher may serve principally as a resource person, a catalyst of group cohesion, and a facilitator of group consensus.

Finally, the teacher who adopts a *compliant* decision style largely abdicates instructional responsibility. The degree of learner freedom will be very high; the degree of teacher control will be very low. The teacher becomes a member of the group but functions neither as an agent of consensus nor as a leader. The climate is totally egalitarian. At most the teacher is an occasional resource person who furnishes factual information solicited by the learners in the group.

Which decision style should be adopted by teachers of adults? There is no easy answer to this question. The research concerning the management of the adult instructional situation is both sparse and inconclusive, owing to the great number of variables that come into play in the research problem. As Brookfield observes, "Classrooms are not limpid, tranquil ponds, cut off from the river of social, cultural, and political life. They are contested spaces—whirlpools containing the contradictory crosscurrents of struggles for material superiority and ideological legitimacy that exists in the world outside."[7] The age and sex of the teacher, the age and sex of the learners, the size of the group of learners, the kind of content to be treated, the amount of time allowed for instruction, the personal qualities of the teacher and learners, the social climate of the instruction, the relationship that obtains between teacher and learners, and the experience base of the group of learners are but a few of the variables that must be accounted for in research relating to the association between learning and teacher management style.

The most sophisticated research to date suggests that both ends of the continuum of decision style, the dominative and the compliant styles, are not facilitative of learning. Highly controlling teachers "may elicit resistance and resentment on the part of their students, and thereby a withdrawal from active involvement in the subject."[8] On the other hand, the permissive end of the continuum may not provide the minimal direction necessary for learning.

It has been maintained previously that many post-twentieth-century adults tend to be relatively sophisticated individuals who are wont to exercise their freedom in many areas of life. In the foregoing chapter we noted the centrality of the place of intentionality in adult learning. We have also reviewed the major elements of Knowles's andragogy paradigm: Adults generally see themselves as independent rather than dependent; they have much life experience; the motivation to learn derives from the challenges of adult life situations; adults are more likely to learn in order to resolve specific problems and are not too interested in learning subject matters.

Given these considerations it is not difficult to understand why many adults would be resistant to the highly controlling teacher. Likewise, it is clear that some kind of structure, direction, and order is necessary in the instructional situation. Anarchy in the instructional situation is similar to anarchy in the civil situation: Nothing gets done when no one is responsible for getting things done. The appropriate decision style, then, is relative to the exigencies of the instructional situation. The persuasive, consultative, and consensual styles are preferred.

Overall Purpose

The management of the instructional situation also calls for a decision on the part of the teacher regarding the overall purpose of instruction. The overall purpose of the instruction refers to the fundamental logic of instruction and is distinct from the concept of instructional objectives. Zvi Lamm uses three concepts to indicate three distinct patterns of instruction.[9] Each pattern derives from a different logic of instruction and adumbrates a distinct instructional purpose. The concepts are imitation, molding, and development.

The imitation pattern of instruction has as its purpose imitative learning. Learners are expected to copy and echo the content of instruction. This pattern requires an authoritarian climate in which the teacher functions, according to Lamm, as an autocrat. The teacher insists on a strict adherence to what is taught. Learners assimilate what is taught with accuracy and attention to detail. When children are trained in social roles they learn according to the imitation pattern of instruction.

The logic of molding also requires firm control of the instructional situation by the teacher. The overall purpose of this pattern is served when learners are shaped and formed according to normative principles dictated by a particular culture. Molding initiates learners into a culture.

The logic of development directs learners to think critically, to use their imaginations, and to be innovative and daring. This instructional pattern requires a climate of freedom. The teacher serves as a supporter of learner self-actualization.

Lamm emphasizes that what is learned in the instructional process is "not a function of the contents that are presented for learning, but of the style in which they are taught."[10] This is somewhat of an overstatement. The contents presented for learning are ordinarily learned, but at a deeper level the entire instructional situation—including the teacher's style—is learned. When adults are asked to imitate, when they are the subjects of a molding process, or when they are expected to act creatively as a means of self-actualization, they learn something about themselves and lay hold of the values implicit in the logics of imitation, molding, or development.

The patterns of instruction identified by Lamm, reflecting three distinct overall instructional purposes, pose a dilemma for religious educators of adults. Most religious educators of adults—save those who prize the memorization of biblical passages or theological formulas—would probably agree that the imitation pattern of instruction is inappropriate for adult learners. The patterns of molding and development, however, pose a dilemma. On the one hand it can be maintained that adults are to be formed and shaped according to the values, doctrines, and disciplinary practices of a particular religious tradition. The overall purpose of such instruction is to make the adult learner a good Baptist, Lutheran, Roman Catholic, or so forth, or to make the adult learner more loyal to a particular religious worldview. On the other hand it can be maintained that adults should engage in critical reflection, that the unexamined faith no less than the unexamined life is not worth living, and that adults should critically evaluate the values, doctrines, and disciplinary practices of a particular religious tradition. This dilemma is but a manifestation of a perennial philosophical problem, the problem of the one and the many.

The problem may be restated in different language: Is the overall purpose of the religious instruction of adults the molding of the learners in a particular way of life so as to serve the community, or is the overall purpose directed toward the self-actualization of the individual? To err on the side of the many is to forestall the development of the individual; to err on the side of the individual is to imply that particular religious traditions, and the communities parametered by these traditions, are unimportant.

The dilemma is real, but its solution is not impossible. The teacher is involved in a dialectical situation. At times, circumstances will demand that instruction should stress molding; at other times, the circumstances will indicate that instruction should emphasize individual development. Lamm defines instruction as "actions resulting from choices between contradictory goals and contradictory means, which are made in accordance with the data of the situation in which the instruction takes place."[11] It is not advised that teachers attempt to harmonize the molding and development patterns or to dismiss one or the other as invalid. The teacher must be able to determine the limitations and possibilities of each event in the series of events that constitute the instructional process. The teacher must be willing to remain poised in a dialectical tension between the two patterns of instruction, and be able to decide for one or the other pattern as instructional events flow and unfold.

It is not unfair to state that most instruction that occurs in the context of the local church or parish has molding as its overall purpose. Many religious educators are prone to follow the logic of molding to the near exclusion of the logic of development. The motive is often indoctrination that produces uniformity of belief and behavior (and a predetermined idea of a good church member!). Teaching is often confused with preaching.[12] Religious educators must be strongly advised, therefore, to pay more than lip service to the logic of development. Individual development must be a real possibility, at the appropriate times, in any instructional process that occurs in the context of the local church. Adults must be permitted the freedom, and even encouraged to exercise the freedom, to question, criticize, deny, raise new hypotheses, and pose discomfiting problems. To deny adult learners the possibility of such freedom is to dismiss the intentionality of the adult. As we saw in the previous chapter, the intentionality of the adult holds the central place in the learning process.

No doubt religious educators will always be able to recruit adult learners who are content to be shaped and molded, to be directed by another and, alas, manipulated. But is it a service to these adults to allow them to think of themselves as subjects to be molded? It is also true that religious educators will never be able to recruit other adults, perhaps the majority, for an instructional process that conveys the message that they are children.

Instructional Planning

The design of instruction is as important as the instructional process itself, for it is the implemented design that imposes structure, order, and system on the process. Education, in the instructional sense of the term, is planned learning. Lacking an instructional plan, therefore, any gathering of adult learners merely offers the occasion for random experiential learning. The instructional plan, it must be noted, is not simply a topical outline of what is to be presented to the learners. Content specialists very frequently think they possess an instructional plan when they outline the information they wish to impart. An instructional plan looks to the major elements of the teaching-learning process.

A number of formats for instructional planning have been developed by adult educators. These formats can be as simple as the one delineated by Paul Bergevin and John McKinley[13] or as complicated as the PERT (Program Evaluation and Review Technique) system explained by Malcolm Knowles in the first edition of *The Modern Practice of Adult Education*.[14] The PERT system identifies a multitude of elements and charts out the instructional process in relation to a time schedule. The Bergevin-McKinley format prescribes six basic steps: (1) the identification of a real educational need or interest, (2) the translation of the identified need or interest into a topic, (3) the formulation of instructional goals, (4) the choice of human and material resources that will be brought to bear in the learning situation, (5) the selection of instructional techniques, and (6) an outline that organizes the instructional process in a definite sequence of events. The format presented below is a modification of the Bergevin-McKinley format. Complicated "systems" approaches to instructional planning seldom hold practical utility for teachers.

Step # 1—Formulation of Instructional Objectives

The determination of educational needs or interests, and the development of a course of study based on topics derived from these identified needs and interests, is properly an operation relating to program or curriculum development. An instructional offering is a single instructional session or series of sessions. A program may consist of a single offering or a number of offerings. A program typically is limited to a particular time frame. The fall program at a local church, for example, runs from September to November. The program includes six course offerings; the topic for each of the course offerings is based on survey data that identify adult educational needs and interests. Each course offering, in turn, may range from one to many sessions. Instructional planning is concerned with structuring the process for single sessions. If a teacher meets a group of adults on four consecutive Thursday nights, the course offering will have four sessions. An instructional plan should be developed for each session. The number of sessions comprising any course offering is contingent on the estimated amount of time needed to reach the instructional objectives.

Nothing is more misunderstood in the entire planning process than the proper formulation of instructional objectives. Many teachers write objectives that express: (1) the general topic of the instruction, (2) what the learners will be doing during the instruction, (3) what the teacher will be doing, or (4) a very general outcome of the instruction.[15] Objectives such as these are useless for the planning process. Further, these kinds of objectives do not lend themselves for evaluation of the instruction. We shall discuss this latter concern below.

Entire books have been written on the formulation of instructional objectives.[16] Findley Edge spent an entire seminary teaching career helping religious education students become adept at this task (in such a way that they could train lay teachers in the process). His *Teaching for Results* became a classic among lay and professional religious educators. His emphasis, as ours, is that instructional objectives should be formulated in terms of desired learning outcomes. These outcomes must be amenable to some kind of measurement. Finally, the objectives must attain a satisfactory level of specificity. Thus, the objective "At the conclusion of the session the adults will have a deeper faith" is not an instructional objective. It is simply a pious utterance. Such an utterance offers no guidance for planning since it is so general, and since the outcome expressed cannot be measured. Specificity and concreteness are necessary qualities of the properly formulated instructional objective. Without specificity and concreteness the teacher will not be able to bring focus to the instructional plan and, eventually, to the instructional process. In the absence of focus, the instructional process is very likely to become submerged in a morass of undisciplined chatter.

A parenthesis needs to be added here. Care must be taken to formulate instructional objectives precisely. The success of instructional planning hinges on adequately stated objectives; the systematic flow of instruction depends ultimately on properly phrased objectives. But in the course of the instructional process the teacher should not pay slavish obeisance to the objectives. Occasions arise when adult learners begin to grapple enthusiastically with serious topics that may be extraneous to the instructional objectives. This enthusiastic concern of adult learners must take precedence over the attainment of predetermined objectives. The possibility of serendipity must not be foreclosed out of an unbending commitment to instructional objectives. This is to say, in other words, that the teacher must be willing to change objectives in midcourse when a diagnosis of the situation indicates the appropriateness of a change.

James Michael Lee has pointed out that teaching is an art as well as a science.[17] The teacher who devises an instructional plan takes a scientific approach to teaching. When the same teacher exercises informed judgment and permits a departure from the instructional plan, he brings artful insight to the situation. The teacher's judgment in such an instance should be grounded on his sense of the possibilities of the moment, possibilities that cannot always be anticipated in an instructional plan. In summary, the teacher should not be a technician who blindly follows blueprints but rather a creative architect who is able to take stock of a situation for the purpose of introducing promising modifications of the instructional plan.

Step #2—Selection of Resources

There are two kinds of resources for learning: human and material. A human resource is a person whose experience qualifies him to speak vis-à-vis a particular topic. Quite obviously the teacher can be ordinarily listed as a resource for learning. At times a guest expert may be called upon to present a point of view, to share his expertise with the learners, and/or to provide a stimulus for learning. Frequently the adult learners themselves are resources for learning.

Many instructional situations involving adult learners would be enhanced if the instructional planner viewed adults not simply as potential recipients of knowledge but also as sharers of their experiences and knowledge. What is at issue here is the teacher's advertence to the fact that adults may be able to contribute something to the learning situation. Failure to account for this fact in instructional planning deprives the instructional process of potentially valuable resources for learning. Such a failure may also be symptomatic of the teacher's tendency to adopt an assumption of Friere's pedagogy of oppression: projecting an absolute ignorance on learners.

At times more is at stake than advertence to the fact adults may have something to contribute. No doubt there are teachers who believe that they, as representatives of the scribal class, possess the truth. The experience and powers of critical judgment of the learners are discounted; the experience and critical judgment of the teacher are apotheosized. On many occasions the teacher's knowledge of the manifest content of instruction will be far more developed than the knowledge of the learners, but this does not imply that the teacher's life experience (the experiential frame of reference that serves as a basis for interpreting the meaning of knowledge) is better than the life experience of the learners. Nor does it imply that the teacher is necessarily better equipped for critical judgment.

Material resources may range from a piece of chalk, a felt marker, or a book to elaborate computer-assisted technologies. While a listing of possible material resources is outside the scope of this chapter, it is nevertheless necessary to comment briefly on material resources in education.

If the great failure of most teachers of adults is the neglect of properly formulated instructional objectives, the second greatest misadventure is building the entire instructional process around a material resource. This is true not only of religious educators but also of adult educators in whatever context they may function. A video or audio tape, a pre-made set of overhead cells, or whatever, become ends in themselves and not means to accomplish an objective derived from a study of adult needs and interests. Material resources and self-contained "packaged" programs may be used or abused. Quite frequently they are abused. Instructional "things" tend to become the centerpieces of the instructional process and the teacher feels excused from the task of instructional planning. (This is probably to the delight of some publishers who pride themselves on "giving you everything you need," in effect encouraging teachers to be lazy in their preparation.) The first great failure (neglect of instructional objectives) is therefore related to the second great failure (an almost mindless fascination with the "things" of instruction).

Make no mistake: curriculum materials (and other teaching aids) are very seductive. Their siren call is to stick to the letter of the prescribed outline. This seduction carries over into materials provided for learners as well. More than one good content resource has been turned over to an ill-trained consultant to develop learners' "workbooks" that entail little more than fill-in-the-blank responses requiring little or no reflection or interaction with the concept in question.

Simply stated, the horse must go before the cart. Material resources should be selected only after the instructional objectives have been formulated and they should be considered just that: *resources*. If the material resource does not directly help the learners achieve the objective, it should not be used.

Step #3—Selection of Techniques

An instructional technique is basically a way of organizing the instructional situation for communication. Among the more common techniques are the lecture, role play, group discussion, video presentation, simulation game, panel, forum, and symposium. These may be employed in a variety of combinations.[18]

Three criteria govern the selection of techniques in instructional planning. First, the techniques must be relevant to the instructional objectives. The teacher may judge, for example, that active participation of the learners and a sharing of personal experiences is most appropriate for the attainment of a given objective. In this case techniques that foster a high degree of learner interaction will be selected. Second, the techniques must be compatible with situational constraints. If one hour is allowed for the attainment of an objective that calls for the mastery of factual knowledge, the teacher would avoid time-consuming techniques that involve learners actively and settle for a lecture or video presentation. Third, the techniques selected will be congruent with the teacher's general orientation to instruction and will be appropriate for the accomplishment of secondary (but important) outcomes. This criterion needs further amplification.

Bruce Joyce and Marsha Weil have outlined sixteen different approaches to teaching-learning that they call "models of teaching."[19] These sixteen approaches are grouped in four families. The four families represent what may be called four philosophical orientations to teaching-learning:

(1) The social interaction orientation emphasizes the importance of the social relations of the learners during the course of the instructional process. Social interaction is viewed as a vehicle for the development of the learners as members of a community of learners and for the learning of subjects. The group discussion approach, wherein the learners function as a body, exemplifies this orientation.

(2) The information-processing orientation emphasizes the ways "people handle stimuli from the environment, organize data, sense problems, generate concepts and solutions to problems, and employ verbal and nonverbal symbols."[20] This orientation underscores the importance of problem solving, creativity, and the processing and integration of information.

(3) The personal orientation looks closely at the personal life of the learner and the processes by which the individual organizes and interprets reality. Emphasis includes the emotional life of the learner and the learner's self-concept and individual development.

(4) The behavior-modification orientation inclines the teacher to regard solely the external behavior of the learner. Attempts to change external behavior are made through the use of a schedule of reward/punishment reinforcers.

There is some overlap among the orientations, particularly among the first three. What distinguishes the orientations one from another, in practice, is largely a matter of differential emphases. This is not to say the differences are negligible or trivial. In any given circumstance the teacher may wish to promote one of the above orientations through the choice of instructional techniques, thereby structuring the learning to achieve secondary outcomes over and above the attainment of the stated instructional objectives.

Let us suppose a teacher wishes to help learners attain a specific instructional objective, say, the ability to explain a complex concept. This ability could possibly be gained by the learners as a result of listening attentively to a lecture presented by the teacher. Suppose, however, the teacher wishes also to help the learners gain the ability of working effectively with others. This secondary outcome of the instruction, it is decided, would best be served by the technique of group discussion. In this instance the group discussion technique is apprised as a means of accomplishing both the stated instructional objective—explanation of the complex concept—and as a means of accomplishing the secondary outcome: gaining a greater competency in working with others.

The selection of instructional techniques is not as easy a matter as would appear at first glance. One does not simply choose a particular technique as one selects a piece of candy from a sampler of chocolates. The selection of instructional techniques must be carried out in the light of serious thought; the use of a particular technique should be based on a developed rationale. The teacher must know what techniques are available, assess the compatibility of likely techniques with the instructional objectives, and evaluate promising techniques in relation to the specific group of learners before selecting one technique above the others.[21] And, we should point out that it is at this point that teachers often face an ethical dilemma: Is the content worth knowing, are these techniques the most appropriate for this content, or am I focusing on this content and using these techniques because I know I can provide an entertaining session on the content?

Step #4—Sequencing of Instructional Events
The sequence of instructional events is a written outline that: (1) coordinates the planned resources with the planned techniques and (2) identifies the main events in the instructional flow. The outline brings resources and techniques together conceptually in a temporal order, i.e., the order in which the unfolding of the instructional process is planned.

We must emphasize the importance of flexibility at this point, and the willingness to revise plans as the plan begins to "come together." The teacher may discover, for example, as planning proceeds, that a video assumed to be appropriate for use in a given lesson no longer "fits" (contributes to the learning objective). Methodologies are constantly changing in the course of planning as we make decisions about what approaches will move us toward the desired outcomes.

During this step in the planning process the teacher attempts to anticipate the phases of the instructional process or the separate events that coalesce to constitute the entire process. This is the place to be concerned about "who does what." There is nothing wrong with describing what the teacher and learners will be doing during the instruction, but this description is apt only after objectives have been formulated and resources and techniques identified.

The teacher brings to the task of sequencing the powers of critical intellect and imagination. Intellect is responsible for the systematization of instructional events; imagination aids the teacher in creating an anticipatory "playing through" of the instructional session. This operation of creative imagination links the abstract plan to an anticipated real-life situation. The instructional situation anticipated in the imagination of the teacher may deviate in some respects from what actually occurs, but the envisioning of what will probably occur, occasioned by the design of sequenced instructional events, can heighten the sensitivity of the teacher to the instructional situation. Preparing a sequence of events on paper is not nearly as important as the internal process experienced by the teacher during the sequencing. The outline of events, therefore, serves as a guide to the actual conduct of instruction and also as a device that attunes the teacher to the instructional process as an integrate series of events. The sequencing operation equips the teacher, as it were, with a form or pattern. The pattern is internalized by the teacher and functions as a frame of reference for interpreting events as they unfold. This internalized pattern aids the teacher in ordering instructional events and prevents the instructional process from degenerating into mere random talk.

Step #5—Evaluation Planning

The final step in instructional planning is the design of an evaluation procedure. Evaluation is necessary to minimize the possibility of instructor illusion regarding the outcomes of an educational activity and to provide the instructor with information that may be used for instructional improvement. Evaluation need not take place after every session of an educational offering. For example, a course conducted on five consecutive Tuesday nights need not be evaluated each Tuesday night unless the instructor suspects that data yielded by such evaluations are needed to improve the instruction. Ordinarily it suffices to evaluate learning sessions summatively, i.e., at the conclusion of the last session. When a course offering is of relatively long-term duration, it is advisable to gather formative data midway through the offering for possible mid-course correction. Summative data are then collected after the last session. In any case evaluation plans should be sketched for each session. The instructor may wish to undertake an unscheduled evaluation of a session because of its apparent extraordinary success or failure.

Two mistakes must be avoided in regard to evaluation. It is possible to err by defect and evaluate instruction too infrequently or not at all; it is also possible to make evaluation so extensive and frequent as to dilute the impact of the instruction.

Fundamentally, two orientations may be taken toward evaluation. Evaluation may assess the degree to which instructional objectives have been met. Such an evaluation would perhaps utilize a test of some kind. Since adults generally have an aversion to tests, however, (left over from previous formal education) the teacher may say, "Let's pause and take this quick inventory," and allow adults to score their own inventories. Role play or case study analysis are good tools for evaluation as well. Or, the instructor could unobtrusively assess the degree to which objectives are met through an analysis of what is stated during class discussions. In some cases it is permissible simply to ask the adults to assess the degree to which the objectives have been met. In most instances of voluntary adult education the learners are quite candid in providing evaluative data.

The second orientation looks at the impressions and reactions of the adults in terms of a number of variables: physical comfort during instruction, the pace of instruction, the techniques and resources used during the instruction, the psychological climate, and so forth. Both orientations are valuable and can provide the teacher with fresh perspectives on the quality of the instruction. Some of the techniques included in the subsequent chapter on program evaluation are applicable to instructional evaluation as well.

A parenthetical observation needs to be made here. On occasion the question as to the relevance of instructional evaluation in religious education has been raised. "Isn't it presumptuous to evaluate the outcomes of religious instruction? After all, the outcomes are really the work of the Holy Spirit." Other religious educators fear that evaluation of religious instruction takes religious instruction out of the spiritual realm. We would assert that it is presumptuous not to evaluate religious instruction on the grounds the Holy Spirit is responsible for instructional outcomes. It is presumptuous—a sin of excessive hope as Thomas Aquinas pointed out—to leave everything up to the Holy Spirit. This kind of thinking, carried to its logical conclusion, would have everyone sitting around waiting for a divine illumination. It is our point of view that the evaluation of instruction is the most spiritual thing in the world, if by spiritual we mean the use of the good sense God has given us.

Instructional planning need not be the special preserve of the teacher. The teacher should know the steps involved in instructional planning and should have an instructional plan in hand. This does not mean, however, that the written plan is to be treated as something carved in stone. In many instances the adult learners can be invited to participate in modifying elements of the prepared instructional plan. In so doing they invest themselves more in the instructional situation and thereby strive more enthusiastically to achieve the instructional objectives.

The Teacher-Learner Relationship

The central relationship between teacher and learners is the helping relationship. The teacher, ideally, helps adults learn; adults are the recipients of this help. This matter seems relatively simple, but appearances are deceptive. There are different kinds of help; help is not always helpful.

There are at least four different kinds of help. Each of these kinds of help is expressed in one of the following statements of a teacher to a learner regarding the operation of a machine:

(1) "I'll help you by doing it for you."
(2) "Just watch me and do what I do."
(3) "Sometimes people get the machine to work by experimenting with the blue levers."
(4) "This is a difficult job. Where do you think we should begin?"

The teacher's comments refer to the operation of a machine, but the *forms* of help represented by each statement are applicable to a variety of teaching-learning situations. In the first case the teacher does the work for the learner, but the learner discovers nothing about the work process. In the second instance the teacher demonstrates a specific technique, but the learner may never discover whether a different technique is more effective. The third statement is supportive and prompting; the teacher's statement allows for some initiative on the part of the learner. Finally, the fourth statement is also supportive and frames a problem for the learner. There may be times when each form of help is appropriate, but generally the first and second approaches are counterproductive in dealing with adult learners. (These approaches may also be counterproductive in many areas of childhood education. Our focal concern, however, is adult education.)

Jack R. Gibb has pointed out that help is not always helpful.[22] The recipient of help may be made to feel dependent, less able to make decisions, less self-sufficient and resourceful, less venturesome, and more concerned with conformity than with creativity. It is suggested that the first two forms of help described above, if employed consistently, may work to the disadvantage of adult learners. In the very act of intending to help, adults learn the teacher may unintentionally make them feel less adult and less self-directing. It is interesting to note that Allen Tough's research into the actual learning projects of adults revealed not only that most adults are active learners, but that when teachers are present they often *get in the way* of *learning!*[23] How can the teacher guard against inappropriate forms of help?

Arthur Combs and his associates conducted research studies on the helping relationship to determine the perceptions and beliefs of effective helpers (teachers, counselors, professors, nurses, and Episcopal priests).[24] A summary of the findings are pertinent here. The helpers maintained beliefs about their professions, about what people are like, about themselves, about the purposes of help, and about approaches to the helping process. It was hypothesized that these beliefs found expression in the external behavior of the effective helpers.

The effective helper was characterized not only by a specialized body of knowledge relevant to the helper's field of endeavor but also by a firm commitment to the meaning of that knowledge. That is, the effective helper believes strongly in what he is doing with the special knowledge. One could say, perhaps, that the effective helper exhibits a devotion toward what he/she is about.

The effective helper believed that the people helped had the capacity to deal with their problems; that these people were friendly and well-intentioned; that they possessed dignity and worth; that they were creative and dynamic rather than passive and inert; that they were trustworthy and dependable; that they were sources of satisfaction to the helper rather than sources of frustration. The beliefs of these helpers, of course, color the external behaviors of the helpers, establish a psychosocial climate in which they work, and set up positive expectations vis-à-vis those who are helped. What Combs may have found was the phenomenon of the self-fulfilling prophecy: People respond according to what is expected of them.

Effective helpers were found to entertain specific beliefs about themselves. They identified themselves with others rather than seeing themselves as withdrawn or apart from those who received help; effective helpers believed they were adequate to meet the challenges of the helping relationship; they saw themselves as trustworthy, reliable, and dependable; they viewed themselves as being wanted as opposed to feeling ignored by others; they envisioned themselves as being worthy of respect as opposed to being people of little consequence. Intuitively it makes good sense that helpers with a high positive self-regard would regard others highly and expect the best from them. Beliefs about others are usually inseparable from beliefs about self.

As to purposes, effective helpers wanted to free rather than control people; effective helpers tended to view reality from a broad perspective as opposed to taking narrow perspectives; they were likely to reveal their feelings instead of hiding them; they were involved with people and did not remain aloof; they were more concerned with facilitating the process of search than accomplishing a preconceived solution; they were more altruistic than selfish. Again, the beliefs of effective helpers correspond logically with their beliefs about others and themselves.

Finally, effective helpers, in their approaches to tasks, were more concerned with people than with objects, events, rules, and regulations. Effective helpers were more interested in how those who were helped see reality than they were with objective facts. In a word, effective helpers were empathetic. Effective helpers tried to experience reality in the same way those who were helped experienced reality.

One may assume that teachers are sincere about helping adult learners. What counts, however, in the matter of being an effective teacher is not sincerity, but the kinds of actions that characterize the teacher's part of the teacher-learner relationship. These actions are rooted in the system of beliefs the teacher brings to teaching. The beliefs described by Combs are the necessary, but not sufficient, bases of effective teaching. That is, effective teaching cannot ordinarily be expected of someone who does not possess a suitable belief system, but the belief system of itself does not assure that effective teaching will occur. Teachers must also possess the full range of competencies related to instructional management, instructional planning, and communication.

Combs's research also pointed out that effective teaching is related to the effective use of self as an instrument of teaching.[25] It follows that the helpful teacher has a good sense of self and exhibits a certain sense of vulnerability in terms of openness to change in self as effected by interactions in the teaching-learning enterprise. Parker Palmer, in the introduction to another of his wonderful books on teaching says in his introduction:

> Teaching, like any truly human activity, emerges from one's inwardness, for better or worse. As I teach, I project the condition of my soul onto my students, my subject, and our way of being together. The entanglement I experience in the classroom are often no more or less than the convolutions of my inner life. Viewed from this angle, teaching holds a mirror to the soul. If I am willing to look in that mirror and not run from what I see, I have a chance to gain self-knowledge—and knowing myself is as crucial to good teaching as knowing my students and my subject.[26]

This means essentially that lists of behavioral traits and physical attributes that purport to identify effective teachers are generally useless. A person may be short or tall, have a soothing or rasping voice, give the appearance of joviality or seriousness, or be subtle or straightforward, and it does not make much difference as far as teaching effectiveness is concerned. The effective teacher is one who uses self as an instrument of teaching and does not attempt to take on a recommended personal style, a set of prescribed mannerisms, or someone else's ideals. To claim that an effective teacher must be humble, magnanimous, outgoing, etc., is to ignore the fact that there are some highly effective teachers who fail to meet these ideals.

This brings us back to the beliefs of effective helpers noted by Combs. These beliefs must be real; they must be internalized. It is not enough, for example, for a teacher to say he believes adults are creative and resourceful. The test of such a belief is in the assessment of the way the teacher conducts the instruction, whatever the teacher's personal style or "virtues" might be. A teacher who provides no opportunities for adults to be creative and resourceful, all things being equal, does not really believe that adults are creative and resourceful.

A Climate for Adult Learning

Some psychosocial climates or environments are more conducive to learning than others. As manager of the instructional process, the teacher is responsible for initiating the structures that permit the creation of an appropriate climate for learning. Writers in the field of adult education have provided descriptions of what they perceive as ideal climates for learning. Evaluative data relating to instruction and collected over a period of years suggest that the ideal climates described by Malcolm Knowles,[27] and by Paul Bergevin and John McKinley,[28] merit our attention.

The ideal climate for adult learning emphasizes: (1) the physical comfort of the learners, (2) freedom of expression, (3) mutual trust and respect, and (4) shared responsibility for learning activities and outcomes.

Physical Comfort

Teachers of adults sometimes forget that as adults get older they experience deficits in visual and auditory acuity. As adults get older they are more susceptible to glare; they are unable to hear certain tones. Further, they begin to lose muscle elasticity after age thirty. The peak of bone density occurs around age thirty-five. Tendencies toward arthritis are evident in some adults after age forty. While there is a wide variation in the rate of physical decline in the adult population, it is clear that the aging process takes its toll on some adults as early as the third and fourth decades of their lives.[29]

With these things in mind the teacher of adults must be alert to the physical setting of instruction. Care must be taken that the lighting arrangement is adequate and that acoustics are good. Adults should not be expected to sit in chairs designed for children. Adults should be encouraged to speak up when they feel the temperature is too cool or too warm.

Alertness to factors in the physical setting of instruction is recommended not to provide adults with pampering luxuries but to insure they will not become distracted during instruction. One can hardly concentrate on the matters at hand if physical arrangements contribute to discomfort or even pain. The physical setting of the instructional situation can do much to enliven or dampen spirits and to channel the attitudes of adults in one direction or another. Paul Bergevin, professor emeritus of adult education at Indiana University, was wont to repeat that trivial things are never trivial in adult education. The wisdom of this remark is not lost on experienced teachers of adults. Most adult learners are very much aware of the physical setting for learning, and they are accustomed to mention the physical setting when asked to complete evaluation forms. It should be noted that providing a conducive physical climate for learning does not motivate adults to learn. However, problems in the physical setting (poor lighting, too hot or too cold, uncomfortable furniture, etc.) can be *de*-motivators. That is, they can impede learning and become distractions. Removing these distractions do not motivate. They merely return the learner to a state of equilibrium.

Freedom of Expression

Adults should be made to feel that they may express themselves without fear of correction or rebuke by the teacher or by other adult learners. It is granted that some adults think of the instructional process only in terms of absorbing what is told to them by the teacher, and reject attempts on the part of the teacher to draw them into a discussion of issues. Even these adults, however, should feel free to express themselves, especially on the occasions they disagree with the teacher or other adult learners. Reticent adults may never take advantage of the freedom to speak, but the knowledge that such freedom is a normative condition of the instructional process tends to increase their positive feelings about the instructional situation.

Other adults are not reticent about expressing themselves. Indeed, in many places a goodly proportion of adults reject any instructional climate that appears to be repressive. These adults may not always openly critique such a climate; they tend ordinarily to remove or absent themselves from the instructional situation. Adults typically "vote with their feet." This is the most forceful way in their range of responses for evaluating instruction.

Freedom of expression implies that adults also feel free not to be called upon to recite or be "volunteered" by the teacher for an instructional task. This observation may seem needless, but it does happen sometimes that a teacher of adults reverts to tactics characteristic of childhood education. Children are usually not able to determine for themselves whether they will attend an educational activity. They have little power and are easily regimented. Because of the relative powerlessness of children, teachers develop instructional tactics that are sometimes repressive. Such tactics, in most situations, are indefensible even for the instruction of children, but children rarely have adequate recourse for the grievances they feel. Adults, on the other hand, are ordinarily self-determining people. Adults are generally less other-directed than children and refuse to be treated in ways that hearken back to the regimentalized classrooms of their youth.

Teachers of adults in church settings, it seems, have much to learn about encouraging freedom of expression in the instructional process. It has been previously noted that religious educators tend to stress the mastery of a given body of knowledge rather than critical, evaluative thinking about that body of knowledge; they tend to emphasize the formation of adults over their development as individuals.

Mutual Trust and Respect

The instructional climate should be shaped by the trust and respect that prevails between teacher and learner, and among learners. Communication can be complete and open only when learners feel free from psychological threat. When trust is present, communication is open, self-disclosure is possible, and the discussion of issues transcends small talk and word games. When trust is absent in the instructional situation, communication tends to take place only at superficial levels and learners do not become seriously engaged in the quest for knowledge and insight.

Richard Reichert points out that to trust others implies a degree of risk. Trust "is not based on any solid proof that the other person will not hurt you. If you have that kind of proof, you are dealing with a sure thing, and trust is always a gamble."[30] Reichert also avers that trust is related to respect, and that both are basic to human relationships. Respect for another person implies the belief that the person has worth and dignity. We see immediately how this element in the instructional climate is related to what Combs's research uncovered: The effective helper has positive regard for the worth of those who are being helped.

Respect for the worth of the individual leads ideally to what Peter Berger calls "cognitive respect."[31] Our respect for a person is evidenced specifically in our respect for his life experiences, and for the perspective from which he views reality; our respect for a person manifests itself concretely in our acceptance of his consciousness. That is, when another person's values conflict with ours, we do not infer that his consciousness is inferior and needs "raising" to the superior level of our consciousness. This does not mean that we must agree with everyone. Nor does it mean that everyone is equally informed and knowledgeable about each particular issue. Some adults are better informed than others; some adults speak out of a lack of knowledge; some adults do not perceive common mistakes in logic. Cognitive respect does suggest, however, that the values of any adult are partly a product of his previous life experiences and the perspectives he takes, and that we should attempt to understand empathetically the experiences and perspectives of others. Without such a respect, the thorough discussion of issues—made possible by mutual trust—leads to a debating game and gets in the way of a collaborative quest for truth.

The normative condition of mutual trust and respect supports the normative condition of free expression. The learner's sense of being free to express herself without fear of rebuke is based on the realization that she can trust the teacher and her fellow learners and that she will be respected regardless of the points of view she expresses. Vogel offers an apt illustration in recounting an experience. "Upon completing a Bible study session, the adult students were given an opportunity to reflect on the experience. One man said, 'She didn't really teach us. It was more like she invited us to reflect and share.'"[32] Such sharing and reflection take place only in a setting of mutual trust and respect.

Shared Responsibility

Adults typically exercise a great deal of responsibility for the conduct of their daily lives and the lives of children or dependents. In the work setting, men and women are held responsible for a host of complex activities. Adults are generally capable, resourceful, and practiced in problem solving. There is no reason why adults should abdicate responsibility in the instructional setting.

To the extent allowed by a particular set of circumstances, the responsibility for goal setting, instructional tasks, and instructional evaluation should be placed in the hands of the adult learners. The teacher can serve as an advisor and guide, and as a resource person. This is to say that the teacher should be able to help adults learn how to learn collaboratively. Adult learners can be gradually disabused of the notion that the teacher is solely responsible for learning outcomes; they can come to accept the idea that they and the teacher share the responsibility for learning outcomes. For more than twenty years the short-term Participation Training Institutes at Indiana University have helped adults learn how to formulate instructional objectives, organize learning activities, evaluate their progress, and share the responsibility for learning outcomes. Learning how to learn collaboratively and learning to take the responsibility for learning outcomes should be an integral part of most instructional situations for adults.

The acceptance of at least a partial responsibility for instructional processes and learning outcomes is tantamount to an investment of self in the instructional situation. Adults ordinarily strive to protect this self investment by participating more intently and enthusiastically in the instructional situation. The relative success or failure of instruction, and the attainment of the instructional objectives, becomes a matter of personal concern.

We come finally to a question of great practical import: How does the teacher go about installing the normative conditions of freedom of expression, mutual trust and respect, and shared responsibility? (The condition of physical comfort is made operative when the teacher attends to the physical surroundings and is sensitive to the reactions of adult learners to the physical environment.)

There are two fundamental approaches to the installation of normative conditions in any instructional situation. These approaches may be used conjunctively. First, the teacher reconciles expectations at the beginning of the instructional process and in so doing articulates the conditions of freedom, trust and respect, and shared responsibility as ideals. Second, during the course of instruction the teacher supports these norms by his behavior.

There is a sense in which the modeling of behavior can deprive learners of enriching experiences. When I tell someone, "Watch me and do what I do," I am assuming there is not a better way of doing whatever I am doing, and that if there is a better way the learners will not discover it. On the other hand, there is a sense in which the refusal to model behavior can deprive learners of the profitable and efficient use of time. Research in the area of group dynamics indicates that groups develop into productive working units by passing through relatively stormy periods during which group norms evolve.[33] It seems altogether unnecessary to allow adult learners to experience fully the vicissitudes associated with group formation unless, of course, the purpose of the instruction is to learn something about group development experientially. By his speech, demeanor, and style, therefore, the teacher can model normative conditions and set the tone or mood for the instructional process.

We have examined the management of instruction, instructional planning, the teacher-learner relationship, and the ideal conditions for adult learning. There are, no doubt, other cardinal concepts relating to teaching, but the four aspects of teaching treated above seem to be most salient for those who wish to become more effective teachers. A studious analysis of teaching in terms of the areas of concern identified in this chapter would go far to advance the quality of teaching. Indeed, what has been presented in this chapter can be employed by beginning and seasoned teachers as a framework for the ongoing critical evaluation of their performance.

Notes

[1] Michael Galbraith, *Facilitating Adult Learning: A Transactional Process* (Malabar FL: Krieger Publishing Co., 1991), 2.

[2] Paulo Friere, *Pedagogy of the Oppressed*, trans. Myra Bergman Ramos (New York: Herder and Herder, 1971).

[3] See, for example, the chapter by William Griffiths, "Paulo Friere: Utopian Perspectives on Literacy Education for Revolution," in *Paulo Friere: A Revolutionary Dilemma for the Adult Educator*, ed. Stanley Grabowski (Syracuse NY: Syracuse University Publications in Continuing Education, 1972), 67ff.

[4] Friere, *Pedagogy of the Oppressed*, 58.

[5] James Michael Lee, *The Flow of Religious Instruction* (Birmingham: Religious Education Press, 1973), 206.

[6] Daniel Pratt, "Conceptions of Teaching," in *Adult Education Quarterly* 42, no. 4 (summer 1992): 217.

[7] Steven Brookfield, *Becoming a Critically Reflective Teacher* (San Francisco: Jossey-Bass, 1995), 9.

[8] Daniel Soloman, William E. Bezdek, and Larry Rosenberg, *Teaching Styles and Learning* (Chicago: Center for the Study of Liberal Education for Adults, 1963), 58ff.

[9] Zvi Lamm, *Conflicting Theories of Instruction* (Berkeley CA: McCutchan, 1976), 49ff.

[10] Ibid., 59.

[11] Ibid., 70.

[12] James Michael Lee, *The Flow of Religious Instruction*, 240-41.

[13] Paul Bergevin and John McKinley, *Design for Adult Education in the Church* (New York: Seabury, 1965), 194ff.

[14] Malcolm Knowles, *The Modern Practice of Adult Education*, 2d ed. (Chicago: Association Press, 1980), 223-26.

[15] Leon McKenzie, *Adult Religious Education* (West Mystic CT: Twenty-Third Publications, 1975), 67-68.

[16] See, for example, Robert Mager's *Preparing Instructional Objectives* (Belmont CA: Fearon, 1962) and Caroline Dillman and Harold Rahmlow's *Writing Instructional Objectives* (Belmont CA: Fearon, 1972).

[17] Lee, *The Flow of Religious Instruction*, 215ff.

[18] Cf. Paul Bergevin, Dwight Morris, and Robert Smith, *Adult Education Procedures* (New York: Seabury, 1966).

[19] Bruce Joyce and Marsha Weil, *Models of Teaching* (Englewood Cliffs: Prentice-Hall, 1972), 8-26.

[20] Ibid., 9.

[21] Paul Bergevin, Dwight Morris, and Robert Smith, *Adult Education Procedures* (New York: Seabury, 1966).

[22] Jack Gibb, "Is Help Helpful?," in *Leadership and Social Change*, ed. W. Lassey (Iowa City: University Associates, 1971), 11ff.

[23] Allen Tough, *The Adult's Learning Projects* (Toronto: Ontario Institute for Studies in Education) 1971.

[24] Arthur Combs, Donald Avila, and William Purkey, *Helping Relationships: Basic Concepts for the Helping Professions* (Boston: Allyn and Bacon, 1974), 10-17.

[25] Ibid., 9.

[26] Parker Palmer, *The Courage to Teach* (San Francisco: Jossey-Bass, 1998), 2.

[27] Knowles, *Modern Practice,* 223.

[28] Bergevin and McKinley, *Design for Adult Education,* 13-60.

[29] For a good review of the aging process and its affect of learning ability, see Albert Tuijnman and M. Van de Kemp, eds., *Learning Across the Lifespan* (New York: Elsevier Science Publishers, 1992).

[30] Richard Reichert, *Self-Awareness Through Group Dynamics* (Dayton: Pflaum, 1970), 64.

[31] Peter Berger, *Pyramids of Sacrifice* (New York: Basic Books, 1974), 119ff.

[32] Linda Vogel, *Teaching and Learning in Communities of Faith* (San Francisco: Jossey-Bass, 1991), 64.

[33] For example, see Bruce Tuckman's "Developmental Sequence in Small Groups," in *Groups and Organizations,* ed. B. Hinton and J. Reitz (Belmont CA: Wadsworth, 1971), 74-78.

EVALUATION IN ADULT RELIGIOUS EDUCATION

The State of Evaluation in Religious Education

Any religious educator reading this book could probably give a five-minute extemporaneous talk on the importance of evaluation. Why then do we do so little serious examination of our work and the ministries we seek to lead for adults? Various reasons (or excuses) are given for why not much evaluation is done of church activities in general. Among the more honest ones is fear of the results! After all, we might discover things we do not want to know. Perhaps the real reason is that church leaders do not see the need. They just do not understand the value of evaluation.

Perhaps that is also the reason a survey of religious education literature reveals not only little treatment of the subject but very little mention at all. Peterson, in his well-used, conservative survey of adult religious education, lists evaluation of the outcomes of the educational process as a key issue in adult Christian education, yet largely ignores the subject in his broad treatment of church-based adult education.[1] A more recent and comprehensive volume, Gangel and Wilhoit's *The Christian Educator's Handbook on Adult Education*[2] only lightly treats the subject. A phone call to a friend, Daniel Aleshire, Executive Director of the Association of Theological Schools, revealed that to his knowledge not a single ATS-member seminary offers a course in evaluation. In general, evaluation seems simply to be ignored at worst, and not taken very seriously at best.

The simplest questions often go unasked:

- What are we doing?
- What are we trying to accomplish?
- Why do we do things the *way* we do them?
- Do we need to continue doing them?

Perhaps this last question is the most frightening of all, for it portends to entertain the possibility that we may discover we no longer need a program or activity. McLaughlin and Philips offer another explanation: lack of goals for educational offerings. They conjecture,

> Most religious education programs have no explicitly stated goals yet in most there *is* an implicit goal: expose adults to the content. That subtle goal is, of course, easy to evaluate. One merely needs to ask, "Was the content 'covered' by the teacher, or laid out in some form before the learner?" This is hardly education and hardly worth evaluating. Whatever the reason, religious educators, adult or otherwise, continue to plan training, enrichment, catechetical and special interest courses, programs, and activities with little more than an intuitive sense as to their effectiveness.[3]

For conference planners, denominational publishers, and local church educators, attendance figures, sales of literature, and educational materials are most often the criteria for judging an educational offering's worth. While these factors may help determine a program's operational worth, they give little indication of effectiveness from participants' perspectives. Lack of fortitude, stated goals, or adequate criteria forces overreliance on intuitive hunches about the effectiveness of efforts intended to be educational. Earlier, participation rates of adults in religious education were discussed and the conclusion drawn that many adults do not see churches as viable providers of quality educational opportunities. A contributing reason may be failure of religious educators to evaluate their program offerings and make needed improvements.

Evaluation in the Larger Field of Adult Education

Judging from the literature on educational evaluation, it is easy to conclude that evaluation is almost a science unto itself. It is used extensively in publicly funded education not only to demonstrate effectiveness but to justify the need for a program and its worth in meeting educational needs. More than a decade ago, Sanders, tracing the history of evaluation in education over a century and a half, concluded,

"Evaluation has played many roles in education over the years, and this varied use of evaluation in education has led to a large repertoire of evaluation approaches, techniques and principles."[4] According to Davis, current practice is broadly inclusive. She says, "The special features of evaluation, as a particular kind of investigation, include concerns with needs, descriptions, context, outcomes, comparisons, costs, audiences, utilization, and the supporting and making of sound value judgments."[5] Were Sanders's overview updated it would certainly contain one of the latest comprehensive treatments published to date, *Handbook of Practical Program Evaluation* (1994), which deals extensively with evaluation design, data collection procedures, data analysis, and management of evaluation processes. The use of such evaluations spans an array of applications from student achievement to curriculum and program effectiveness and ultimately seeks to inform decision-making and policy development. Evaluation provides the basis for the accreditation process and is usually of necessity tied to funding.

While there are volumes on evaluation in secondary and pre-secondary education, and somewhat less but still substantial literature focused on higher education, until the last decade there was precious little in the adult education literature that dealt comprehensively with evaluation. Various authors would acknowledge the need for evaluation, yet few gave it more than passing treatment. The paucity of literature betrays a prevalent attitude of indifference toward the subject by adult educators. Merriam and Caffarella offer a somewhat cynical assessment of this condition when they aver that any evaluation done "often focuses on institutional variables rather than the learning itself. . . . An example is the 'happiness indicators' administered at the end of many education and training events, which allow participants to evaluate such programs as to instructors' ability, the food, and the registration procedures. It is not that these aspects are unimportant; rather, that the participants learned anything is more often assumed than overtly measured."[6]

The growing sophistication of the field in general, along with increased need for justification and validation of programs (tied to funding in this case as well) has given rise to a gradual increase in interest and treatment of evaluation in the adult education literature. For example, Queeney's recent volume on needs assessment includes a valuable chapter on evaluating program effectiveness.[7] Caffarella not only includes formulating evaluation plans as a step in her "interactive model of program planning for adults," but devotes an excellent chapter to *how* to develop such an evaluation plan, including a description of various approaches and sample tools for use in data collection, data analysis, and reporting commensurate recommendations.[8] This work will provide the basis for much of the treatment in this chapter.

The Need for Evaluation

Perhaps the issue of evaluation is first and foremost one of accountability. Put another way, it may be a matter of stewardship. As educators, our sponsoring entities as well as our constituents have a right to hold us accountable for being good stewards of the resources entrusted to our use and the demands we make on people's time, money, and energy.

Second, evaluation is a matter of intelligent practice. It can be said that needs assessment is for all practical purposes useless without evaluation. Emphasizing its importance, Fitz-Gibbon and Morris explain that "One of the tasks of the evaluation is to enable us to constantly scrutinize and rethink assumptions and activities that underlay the program."[9] Evaluation helps us determine what might have happened had no intervention occurred, or how a different intervention might have affected an outcome. It helps us determine if we are "on target" with content and approach. Unfortunately, lack of evaluation often results in programs or approaches being repeated, often for years, until participation finally dwindles to a handful (or none) and the ultimate judgment is rendered: "This doesn't work anymore." At that point credibility may be lost, as well as opportunity to make improvements that help insure relevance, effectiveness, and thus participation.

Evaluation may be used for problem solving. For example, a small group of adults may be very unhappy with the progress and effectiveness of their weekday Bible study. The educator might jump to the premature conclusion that the leader of the group is ineffective. But what other factors may be involved? A thorough evaluation of the situation would take into consideration not only the leadership of the group (e.g., methods used, personality, grasp of the subject), but the curriculum materials being used (e.g., appropriateness in terms of content and developmental ability of the group), logistics (e.g., convenience of meeting place, time, and learning climate) and expectations and goals of participants.

Sometimes religious educators gather data (e.g., attendance records, written comments from participants at the end of a program) and compare the data with their expectations of the program. Such data collection does not constitute an evaluation, however. Fellenz, et.al., offer a helpful distinction between assessment and evaluation.[10] Assessment gathers facts, data, and perceptions that help determine if a program has accomplished its goal. Evaluation, on the other hand, renders judgments as to *value*. Whether a program was worthwhile cannot be determined from data alone. Rather, some judgments must be made on the basis of the assessed data. These judgments are the heart of evaluation. In the above example, a look at attendance records will provide information on participation trends, while observation of the leader will provide information on the way he or she conducts the session. An examination of the curriculum materials will provide data on intended audience, the author's treatment of content, and suggested learning approaches. Discussions with participants will reveal perceptions and expectations (as well as frustrations!). But this data and information alone are insufficient to determine the source of the perceived problem. *Judgments* must be made on the basis of the above gathered information. Does the leader use a sufficient variety of methods and approaches to meet the needs of the varied learning styles of participants? Does he or she have a sufficient grasp of the content under study? Is there a "personality clash" with members of the group? Are the study materials too elementary/too difficult for the group? Does the material effectively address the intended subject that the group wishes to examine? Are participant expectations realistic for this type of group? Are participants' perceptions limited to a few people, or widespread throughout the group? Answers to these questions require judgments, some admittedly subjective, which are required to adequately address a satisfactory solution.

Thus, evaluation helps us determine:

- If our program, activity, or course is effective. (Is it accomplishing what we intended?)
- If we are conducting the activity in the best possible way. (Is it accomplishing what we intended in the *way* we intended?)
- If participants have gained the knowledge and skills they expected. (Did they learn something not previously known, or can they do something new?)
- How the program, activity or course can be improved. (What changes need to be made if we offer this again?)
- What helpful feedback can be given to instructors/leaders. (What affirmation/encouragement, helpful criticism can be offered?)

Answers to these and more detailed evaluation questions provide important information to at least four audiences. *Program planners* use evaluation data for planning future programs, to determine the feasibility of repeating a given offering, to make improvements, and perhaps as a basis for advertising the benefits of participation. *The sponsoring organization* uses evaluation data to determine if its resources are being utilized efficiently and effectively. And a not-so-secondary concern is whether the sponsor is gaining "good will" with constituents as a result of the program. *Instructors* or *leaders* gain insight into their effectiveness in terms of instructional methods and relationships, as well as appropriateness and organization of content. And finally, *participants* gain information on the success of the program, the value to other participants, and how they may reinforce or enhance their learning.[11]

The Evaluation Process
The Focus of Evaluation Efforts

Practically any aspect of a religious education program or activity for adults can be evaluated. Planners, operators, and leaders are naturally interested in whether the intended purpose is met. More specifically, however, Caffarella suggests these major areas as objects for evaluation:

• Participant learning
• The educational program itself (format, content, staff)
• Outcomes of the program (such as changes in people or organizations)
• The policies, procedures, and practices of the educational unit/function (for example, the program planning process)
• The impact of a program on subunits or whole organizations
• The impact of a program on communities/society[12]

Galbraith includes course content as a subject for evaluation, but adds course methods, interpersonal processes, and the learning climate itself.[13] He relates course content evaluation to the matter of *meaningfulness*, recognizing that adults will consider meaningful that which they identify as meeting specific needs and problems. Content is therefore directly related to participant satisfaction. Course methods are also linked to an evaluation of meaningfulness, since the latter is really a measure of methods' effectiveness. Evaluating interpersonal processes takes into consideration the interactions among learners and is in some measure an indication of their freedom to bring their life experience and other personal resources to bear. In a similar vein, an evaluation of the total learning climate includes both emotional and physical factors. The learning climate may encourage or inhibit the level of trust which in turn enables or prevents personal sharing, challenging of ideas, and willingness to contribute to discussion and problem solving.

Caffarella reduces the evaluation process to five steps:

- Determine the approaches to be used in making the evaluation.
- Decide data collection techniques.
- Make preliminary decisions about how the data will be analyzed (including information gathered through informal as well as formal means).
- Describe how judgments about the program or activity will be made.
- Make recommendations based on these judgments.

While these steps seem simple enough on surface, implementing each step can become quite complex. In fact, Galbraith describes a similar process that, if followed to the degree he prescribes, would rival time spent in instruction. His procedures are complex enough to become a self-contained course on evaluation![14] Nonetheless, in order to conduct effective evaluation Caffarella suggests that we have a working knowledge of the five areas described in her model, and she will be the major source of the following description of these areas.[15]

Three approaches to evaluation are most likely to be of use to religious educators of adults. As described by Cafferella, they are objectives-based review, case study, and "levels of evaluation" which is broader in terms of the scope of factors evaluated.

Objectives-based review. This approach focuses on objectives of the program or activity related to what participants have learned and/or the way the program was conducted. For example, the evaluator may ask the following questions:

- Have the individual participants learned what they were supposed to learn?
- Did the program contribute to changes in the organization?
- Did the program contribute to changes related to social issues and concerns?
- Were specific changes made in the program operations?[16]

Data to answer these questions might be collected through observations, interviews, paper and pen questionnaires, tests, performance reviews, and/or case studies. It may be assumed, of course, that objectives (what exactly the program or activity is supposed to accomplish) have been set out beforehand!

Case Study Method. Case study is widely recognized as an effective instructional approach with adults. It involves learners in "real life" situations, but in a safe environment where alternatives can be tested and re-tested. In the same manner, adults may be asked to analyze case studies that apply the intended learnings of the program or activity. Caffarella suggests that this gives a "thick description" of outcomes from the perspective of interested parties (participants, staff, or the sponsoring organization). Questions appropriate to this approach might be:

- What are the prominent events/activities respondents would highlight?
- What value do participants, staff, and stakeholders place on the program?
- What are the program's strengths and weaknesses from the participants' perspective?[17]

When using the case study approach, data may be collected through observations, interviews, or a review of records from the organization or perhaps the community.

"Levels of Evaluation" review. As the most commonly used approach to evaluation, this method usually relies on a questionnaire of some sort on which participants are asked to indicate feelings, thoughts, an assessment of what they have learned, and perhaps what they consider to be strengths and weaknesses of the program. Thus, it measures participant reactions, perceived learning, changes in behavior, and perceived outcomes. This approach, therefore, focuses more on the adult learner than on the program itself. Questions may include:

- Did participants like the program?
- What knowledge or skills were learned?
- What changes in participant behavior have resulted that can be linked to the program?
- What overall impact has the program had on the organization?[18]

A sample questionnaire illustrating the "levels of evaluation" approach follows.[19]

Sample Participant Questionnaire

Title of Program:_____ Date: _____

Please assist us in evaluating the quality of the program by completing this questionnaire. For each question, circle the number that best represents your views: 1 ("No"), 2 ("Somewhat"), and 3 ("Yes, definitely"). Your specific comments and suggestions for improvement would be most appreciated, especially for those items you marked "No" or "Somewhat."

Have you had prior experience and/or training in this content area? If so, what?

_____

_____

Part 1: Session Content and Process

1. Were the program objectives clear and realistic?   1   2   3
Comments/suggestions: _____

_____

2. Did you learn what you expected to learn?   1   2   3
Comments/suggestions: _____

_____

3. Was the material presented relevant and valuable to you?   1   2   3
Comments/suggestions: _____

_____

4. Was the material presented at an appropriate rate?   1   2   3
Comments/suggestions: _____

_____

5. Was there an adequate amount of time allotted to each topic? 1   2   3
Comments/suggestions: _____

_____

6. Did the instructional and presentation techniques used adequately assist you in learning the material?   1   2   3
Comments/suggestions: _____

_____

7. If there were opportunities for you t o actively participate in
the various sessions, was this participation beneficial to you?   1   2   3
Comments/suggestions: _____

8. Could you relate the material to your particular life situation?   1   2   3
Comments/suggestions: _____

9. Did the instructional materials and aids used (transparencies,
manuals, videotapes, and the like)enhance the learning process?   1   2   3
Comments/suggestions: _____

10. Was the program well organized and effectively conducted?   1   2   3
Comments/suggestions: _____

Part 2: Presenter Skills

1. Were the presenters enthusiastic?   1   2   3
Comments/suggestions: _____

2. Were the presenters well prepared?   1   2   3
Comments/suggestions: _____

3. Did the presenters have expert knowledge of the content?   1   2   3
Comments/suggestions: _____

4. Did the presenters make an effort to help you feel comfortable?   1   2   3
Comments/suggestions: _____

5. Did the presenters provide you with adequate assistance
in learning the material?   1   2   3
Comments/suggestions: _____

6. Did the presenters communicate well with the participants (for example, use nonsexist language, attend to diversity of audience)? 1 2 3

Comments/suggestions: _____

7. Did the presenters hold your interest? 1 2 3

Comments/suggestions: _____

8. Did the presenters cover the content adequately in the allotted time? 1 2 3

Comments/suggestions: _____

Part 3: Logistical Arrangements

1. Were the registration procedures "participant-friendly"? 1 2 3

Comments/suggestions: _____

2. Was the program schedule well planned (allowing enough time between sessions and for lunch, for example)? 1 2 3

Comments/suggestions: _____

3. Would you recommend that these facilities be used again? 1 2 3

Comments/suggestions: _____

4 Would you want the same food menus again for breaks and meals? 1 2 3

Comments/suggestions: _____

Part 4: Overall Program

1. Will you be able to apply what you have learned in your work, at home, and/or in your personal life? _____ 1 2 3
Comments/suggestions: _____

_____

2. Were you challenged by the content and the way the material was taught?_____ 1 2 3
Comments/suggestions: _____

_____

3. How do you rate the program overall? _____ 1 2 3
Comments/suggestions: _____

_____

4. Please comment on the major strengths of the program and changes you would recommend.
Major Strengths: _____

_____

Suggestions for Improvement: _____

_____

Any other observations: _____

_____

Thank You for Your Help!

Part 2 could be modified to enable participants to give feedback on individual presenters/instructors; alternatively, separate evaluation forms could be used for each session.

Techniques for Collecting Data. Questionnaires such as the foregoing are but one of many approaches to collecting evaluation data. The *purpose* of the evaluation and the *kinds* of information sought from the evaluation will help determine the selection of data-gathering techniques. For example, if the religious educator wants to evaluate the knowledge his/her adult learners have gained, such a questionnaire may be appropriate. Or a rating scale, self-graded test, or interview may be used. On the other hand, if the point of the evaluation is to determine if behavioral change has occurred as a result of the learning experience, little useful information would be gained from these approaches. The evaluator would actually need to *observe* the learners in a setting where they have opportunity to apply what they have learned. (An exception might be interviews with other people who have had opportunity to observe learners). Several questions will help in the selection of appropriate tools.[20]

---

(1) What information is needed to evaluate the accomplishment of the program/seminar/class objective?

(2) Are there existing instruments available to conduct the evaluation or will they have to be constructed?

(3) What are the costs associated with alternative approaches (purchase costs, duplication, dissemination, etc.)?

(4) How much data are needed to conduct the evaluation effectively?

(5) Who will be the recipients of the data and analysis once completed?

Questionnaires and surveys may be the most commonly used tools in evaluation. It should be noted that while these are relatively easy to construct, the information gathered is not always useable or useful. A lot depends upon the careful wording of questions as well as instructions for completion of the instruments. Nonetheless, surveys may be the right choice to gain insight into participant perceptions, opinions, attitudes, and their perspectives on content, instructor, and logistics. There are a number of possible formats for questionnaires, such as forced-choice (e.g., yes/no, 1 or 2), checklists, ranking, or sentence completion (also called open-ended). The latter allows the one completing the questionnaire freedom of response in keeping with the guidance provided by the opening of the sentence. For example:

- What I liked most about this course was . . .
- The most important thing I learned was . . .
- Two things from this course I plan to use immediately are . . .
- Concerning the variety of instructional approaches used, the facilitator . . .
- In terms of convenience (date, time, place) the course . . .

Two general rules apply to using questionnaires and surveys with volunteer adult learners. With regard to length, generally the shorter the better (one page if possible). While more information may be gained by longer instruments, adults may be discouraged from completing them if the instrument is several pages long. This is particularly true of mailed instruments. Thus, the second rule—if possible, administer the questionnaire/survey on site before the adults leave to insure widest participation in the evaluation. Even this does not guarantee 100% participation (some adults may simply not want to complete the instrument, which is a freedom volunteer learners have). On the other hand, allowing them to take the instruments home to complete and return later almost guarantees a number will *not* be returned for one reason or another.

Interviews may be the second most commonly used tool by religious educators to gain data for evaluation. Interviews may seem easier to use than questionnaires, for they involve talking to adults about the program, course, or activity. However, this seeming ease may be deceptive in that *interviewer bias* is often difficult to avoid, and care must be used not to prejudice or lead the person being interviewed. In fact, for many years, especially when a premium was placed on quantitative research, this was the criticism of research conducted via interviews. The very use of the technique rendered results suspect because of the assumption that interviewer bias was almost impossible to avoid. Interviews are most often used to gather qualitative data, and even as qualitative approaches have gained favor and become more common, bias continues to be a major concern. Alreck and Settle offer this warning:

> The sources of interviewing *error* . . . affect survey results randomly. The effect of those sources of error is just as like to "push" the results in one direction as another. Random error reduces the reliability of the data, and it also reduces the validity of the data indirectly, by reducing the reliability. There are also several

sources of *systematic bias* associated with interviewing. Bias reduces the validity of the data directly, by consistently "pushing" the results in one particular direction. Because of this, bias is the more serious problem.[21]

As a simple example, assume the religious educator planned and conducted the program being evaluated. He or she is, in fact, also the evaluator, and is using interviews to gain information about adults' attitudes toward the course and about what they learned. The interviewer could ask the question, "What did you like about my teaching?" Unless those being interviewed have a particular dislike for the interviewer, they are likely to give "acceptable" responses, rather than offend the interviewer/teacher. This is an example of "pushing" the responses in one direction (in this case the obviously *desired* direction). A better approach would be to ask questions such as, "Did the class leader communicate clearly? Did the leader use a variety of teaching approaches? Which approaches were most helpful to you? What could the leader have done to enhance your learning?" Such questions may render useful information if they are part of a "levels of evaluation" approach described earlier. If, on the other hand, the primary purpose of the interview is to gain feedback about the effectiveness of the instructor (in this case the religious educator) it would be best to have someone else conduct the interview!

The above problems notwithstanding, interviews are still an effective way to gain rich perspectives and perceptions of learners not likely available otherwise. According to Caudle, "the ability to listen and explore actively frequently makes the difference between the success and failure of an interview."[22] This suggests that one advantage of interview as an evaluation technique is the ability to explore participant responses for more detail, as well as to detect emotion, body language, and other data that may enhance interpretation.

Interviews may be highly structured or rather informal. Either way, interviews need to be planned. Such planning usually includes gaining people's permission and agreement to participate, as through setting an appointment to conduct the interview. However, the interview may be spontaneous, as when conducted immediately following the conclusion of the program, course, or activity. Planning should always include preparation of the lead questions to be used, even though the interview may be informal or not highly structured, in which case other questions may be added to explore responses. (In highly structured interviews, there is rarely any deviation from planned or prescribed questions.)

Observation. One of New York Yankee catcher Yogi Berra's famous sayings was, "You can learn a lot just by watching." Yogi's wisdom applies to gathering data for evaluation as to many other things. Caffarella describes observation as "Watching participants at actual or simulated tasks and recording the knowledge, skills, and/or values/attitudes participants display."[23] Such "watching" should be done in a way that affects neither the behavior of those being observed, nor the data collection itself. For example, following a seminar on "A Moral Response to those in Need," the educator may wish to observe class members as they participate in a ministry to homeless people. Some things of which to make note might be how adults interact with homeless people, the attitude they exhibit toward them, whether they appear merely to fulfill their duty, or genuinely seek to discover and meet their needs for psychological well-being (such as respect) or physical care (such as hygiene, clothing, or minor medical attention). In a different situation, the educator may become a *participant observer*, actually taking part in an activity being led by a seminar or class member. In such situations notes are rarely made during the activity, but rather afterward in a mental "debriefing" of the activity.

With regard to the latter, observation might be combined with *performance review*, a technique that may seem strange in a volunteer learner situation. However, where the adult religious educator has provided a training course for lay Bible study teachers (other groups), such a review may be appropriate and can be done in a nonthreatening and unobtrusive fashion. Course participants may be observed in an actual teaching situation demonstrating their grasp of content from the training course, such as interpersonal skills, group leading techniques, or teaching methods. Where performance review is used, a carefully identified criteria for what will be observed should be set out beforehand. Information gathered in this fashion will not only be helpful to the educator in evaluating the effectiveness of the training course, but should be provided to the one being observed for feedback on his or her performance.

Buzz Groups. Use of buzz groups for evaluation has the advantage of informality and shared insight. The larger group may be divided into small groups of three or four with instructions to discuss a prescribed set of open-ended questions that relate to different aspects of the course or activity. Or they may simply be given categories to discuss, such as logistics (time, place, facilities), course organization, method of instruction, opportunities for student participation, and adequacy of content to meet student needs. A recorder in each group may jot down salient points from each discussion. Before concluding the evaluation session in small groups, recorders should read back what has been recorded in each category in order to assure that thoughts, feelings, and ideas of the group are fairly and accurately recorded. These recorded comments and observations are then given to the evaluator.

In-basket exercise. Most everyone is familiar with the standard "in-basket" and "out-basket" that sit on the front of the desk. Into the in-basket goes incoming mail, problems to be solved, and issues to be handled. As each piece in the in-basket is dealt with, it goes into the out-basket. In keeping with this "standard practice" an exercise can be devised to place in an actual or hypothetical inbox situations, issues, and problems that are related to the course content and that require the students to apply what they have learned to the contents of their inbox. This may be done individually (each student has an inbox and makes written responses that go into their outbox) or as a group. If done as a group, students may take turns removing pieces from the inbox and explaining how they would deal with the situation or problem. The larger group may contribute ideas and comments, often leading to a broader discussion of the application of course content to the situation. Thus, evaluation actually may contribute to further learning as students synthesize what they have gained. For example, in a course for lay teachers of adults, one item in the teachers' in-basket may be a note from a Bible study student who feels that there should be more application of the content under study. The discussion that follows may center on *ways* to encourage praxis, including structuring activities that permit deduction of content *from* an actual activity, or use of techniques that encourage trial and practice, such as case study or role-play.

Perhaps following a study of "Paths to Ethical Decision-making," various ethical dilemmas are presented in the in-basket. An interesting way to present them is as in contrived notes from a friend, family member, or colleague. In the latter case, a note may appear in the in-basket suggesting a profitable business opportunity proposed by a work associate that could come only at the expense of integrity, or at the expense of a colleague or competitor's welfare. The group members (or individual students) discuss how to apply the principles gained from the course to the situation in question. In-basket exercises may thus provide helpful evaluation feedback to the religious educator while providing an interesting and relevant learning activity for students.

Already mentioned as a broad category of evaluation approaches, *case studies* may be used as a data collection technique alone or in combination with other techniques as part of an evaluation approach such as the "levels of evaluation review" discussed above. Case studies may be complex, as in the Harvard Case Study Method where cases are often several pages long with multiple details requiring complex analysis. However, often they are brief (even one-half page) requiring straightforward if not simple analysis. A case study usually presents a situation or dilemma, includes sufficient detail to enable learners to grasp the setting and problem, may include decisions to be made or alternatives available, but never provides the solution. Even where cases are drawn directly from real life (cases may be real or contrived), what actually happened to resolve the situation is not disclosed until after the group has sufficiently discussed the case and offered their own ideas.

Perhaps, for example, a group of adults has been involved in a Bible study centered on forgiveness. Various Scripture passages have been studied, along with biblical stories where forgiveness was operative. At the conclusion of the study, the leader wants to evaluate students' learning and offer them an opportunity to apply what they have learned vicariously. So the following case study is offered:

> Tim is an equipment salesman for a large company and works on straight commission. He and his wife, Jill, have a son who is a freshman in college, and sixteen-year-old and ten-year-old daughters. Tim has been cultivating a prospective customer, Mr. Grey, who needs a particular piece of equipment, the commission on which will be significant in terms of paying college tuition and helping with the wardrobe expenses of a teenage daughter! Mr. Grey has been comparison shopping and has given Tim no indication as to when he may make a decision. One day, when Tim returns from an extended lunch break that included a visit to his dentist's office, he learns that Mr. Grey came in just after he had left, checkbook in hand. Furthermore, he learns that John, one of his associates, was the only salesman present when Mr. Grey came in. Although John knew that Tim had been dealing with Mr. Grey, instead of encouraging Mr. Grey to come back after Tim had returned from lunch and the dentist, John wrapped up the sale, scooped Tim on the commission and is "crowing" to colleagues about the significant sale he made during lunch!

How does Tim feel? How might you expect a person under such circumstances to react? How should Tim's faith help determine how he will respond to the situation? Is there "room" in this situation for forgiveness? Explain.

Case studies may be hypothetical or may be drawn from everyday life. The daily newspaper often offers stories and dilemmas that may be easily turned into cases for study.

Critical incident analysis. Similar to the case study approach, the critical incident technique asks participants to identify a situation where they have attempted to apply something learned in the course of activity. Participants are asked to be as specific as possible about the situation and information/skills applied. Thus a lay teacher may describe a class session where he or she used one or two new teaching methods learned in a training course on "Teaching Adults Effectively." Or a participant in a seminar on "Being my Brother's Keeper" may describe an incident in which he or she was confronted with a human need that required a decision about intervention, sorting out motives, and a choice of what action to take. Responses are evaluated on the basis of adults' ability to identify an incident where learning is applied, how well they are able to describe the incident, the specificity with which applied learnings are identified, as well as the accuracy, correctness and appropriateness of the application. Whether participants are asked to describe their critical incident orally or in writing may depend on the group's level of ability or comfort in writing activities.[24]

Discussed here are seven evaluation strategies deemed of practical use to the adult religious educator. They are certainly not exhaustive, as there are numerous other strategies that are useable with some modification. For a discussion of other approaches see chapter nine of Rosemary Caffarella, *Planning Programs for Adult Learners*. It should be noted that the strategies here discussed fall largely into the category of *qualitative* methods. Qualitative analysis provides richer data, often in the words of the participants themselves, and often enriched by further probing and questioning by the evaluator or fellow group members. *Quantitative* approaches are usually objective, require ratings or checking responses, and in short provide data that can be counted and reported in a form such as a frequency distribution. Sophisticated computer software programs are available to which evaluation data, like research data, may be subjected. However, such sophistication is usually beyond the needs and skills of the religious educator and under

most circumstances is unnecessary. In the opinion of these writers the
qualitative approaches described here provide the kind of rich, albeit
subjective, heuristic data most useful to the adult religious educator.

Analyzing Data and Making Evaluative Judgments

Two initial steps are necessary in order to make evaluation data man-
ageable and of maximum usefulness: *data reduction* and *coding.* Caudle
offers a helpful explanation of the purpose and process of data
reduction:

> Data reduction really starts in the actual data collection stage. Data reduction is
> the process of selecting, focusing, simplifying, abstracting, and transforming raw
> data from field notes and other sources. The reduction of data occurs from the
> very beginning of the evaluation as the evaluator decides on questions, selects
> sites to sample, firms up data collection approaches, decides on possible ways
> to code and categorize data, and works with what has been selected as the unit
> of analysis.[25]

Using the data collection techniques described above will net the evaluator a significant amount of accumulated information that must be
sorted and reduced. In reality, not all the comments, observations, and
notes recorded will ultimately be useful. Thus, the first task is to glean
from all the collected information that which is most useful in making
judgments related to the goals of the evaluation.

As data are sorted they may be categorized to fit the predetermined
evaluation criteria. Coding establishes categories for sorting evaluation
data and may be behaviors, attitudes, activities, relationships, reactions, events, settings, perspectives, processes, and social structures.[26]
A code is a symbol or notation attached to data segments in order to
classify the data for analysis. Codes are derived either from participants
themselves as they are involved in the evaluation or may be predetermined by the evaluator according to the evaluation criteria. Thus, an
evaluator-established category may be "Problem-solving Strategies"
under which observations and notations about participants'
approaches to, say, analysis of a case study, are recorded. Responses or
observations fitting this category are coded with a "PS" in the initial
sorting process. Or, the evaluator may become aware, as data are
sorted, that a particular word or phrase is used frequently by participants and this word or phrase is used as a category. Thus, noting that
participants often referred to principles gleaned from their study, a

category may be "Principles Applied" and the code for such responses, "PA."

When evaluation data have been sufficiently "cleaned" (all extraneous information deleted) and coded, the evaluator is ready to begin drawing conclusions of what the information says about the effectiveness and impact of the program or activity. In the jargon of the broader field of evaluation, this is called making *evaluation judgments*. All that has gone before in the evaluation process has been in preparation for this step. In this regard Boyle is adamant:

> Evaluation does not occur unless judgment occurs, no matter how detailed the description of the criteria or of the evidence. Some individuals feel that they have made an evaluation by just describing what happened during or as a result of a program. Descriptions become evaluation only if the programmer presents definite conclusions as to the value of the program.[27]

It is at this point that worth or value is assigned to the program or activity, based on analysis of the accumulated, coded, and categorized evaluation responses and measured by the evaluation criteria. Did the program or activity accomplish its intended end? Did participants gain what they and the educator expected from the endeavor? Was instruction effective? Did the logistical arrangements enhance or detract from participation and effectiveness? Should the program or activity be repeated? The evaluator should be able to answer these and other questions (whatever questions were specified), thereby rendering the needed evaluative judgments for use in planning future offerings, in justifying the program to sponsors, and/or providing helpful feedback to instructors and participants.

It is at this point that the evaluator must exercise the most care and self-criticism. Fellenz, Conti, and Seaman put it this way:

> Once assessment of what has occurred has finally been completed, the value judgments must be made. This is usually done by the individual most responsible for the program. This is the most sensitive aspect of the entire evaluation process because those who now must make the judgments are often the individuals who have invested the most time and effort in the program.[28]

It may be said that evaluation judgments are only as good as the objectivity and integrity of the person making them. This is usually the adult religious educator, the one responsible for planning and conducting the program or activity. Thus the educator must be sensitive to personal bias, and must avoid seeing only hoped-for results. Looking critically, in the best sense of the term, is essential.

Perhaps the most reliable basis for rendering effective and useful evaluation judgments is comparison of evaluation data to the predetermined criteria: in other words, compare what is (what happened) to what should be (what the program or activity was intended to do). Thus the case is made once more for setting out clear criteria in advance for what will be evaluated, and what will be acceptable results.

Following are some examples of such criterion-based evaluation approaches:[29]

Evaluation Questions	Criterion	Results of Data Analysis	Conclusion
Focusing on participants' learning. Did the participants following the three-month curriculum plan gain sufficient knowledge and skills in ethical decision-making?	In a case study analysis, 85% of participants will correctly identify and apply the principles for ethical decision-making.	38 of the 40 participants correctly identified and applied the principles.	The majority of the participants mastered the material; therefore, the curriculum plan was effective.

The above examples lend themselves fairly easily to quantification. Where criteria are not predetermined or not easily set beforehand, the evaluator may observe criteria as they emerge during the conduct of the program, in which case qualitative approaches are used for data gathering and analysis and for making evaluative judgments. In fact, it is now acceptable practice to draw the criteria from the contextualized themes that emerge during the evaluation process. Cafferalla acknowledges that for some programs criteria is highly personalized, and thus suggests that program planners must be prepared to find multiple ways to demonstrate a program's worth.[30]

Additional Considerations

The aforementioned approaches, and thus far most of the discussion, have centered on *summative evaluation*. In fact, most evaluations are summative, measuring the results or overall effectiveness of a program, activity, or event. Such evaluation takes place at the end of a course, program, or activity and usually focuses on the end product. Information thus gathered is useful for justifying the expenditure of resources or for repeating the program. Summative evaluation confirms the achievement of goals or identifies discrepancies between intended and actual outcomes.

Other questions implied by the evaluation criteria may focus on the process or development of the program and fall under the designation of *formative evaluation*. This term was introduced by William Scriven in 1967 primarily to describe the evaluation of new curricula in public schools as it was being implemented so that mid-stream adjustments and alternations could be made.[31] Scriven also referred to monitoring student progress as formative evaluation. While the latter purpose still applies, the term has subsequently been broadened to focus more on developmental aspects of programs and learning activities. Thus, in its current use, particularly in adult education, formative evaluation provides information to planners and conductors that enables improvements and refinements in programs and activities *while they are in operation*. Nearly all of us conduct informal formative evaluations as we monitor how things are going as a program is developing or as a session is conducted. One parish educator tells of putting a file folder in his desk as he begins working on any new program, conference, or course. It is labeled "Evaluation" with the name of the event attached. All through the planning process as well as during the operation of the event he jots notes on various aspects of the activity, which go into that desk folder. These notes are reviewed at the conclusion of the event. When the time to plan the event (or a similar one) comes the following year, this is the first folder he pulls out for review. This is, of course, an informal approach, but provides an example of a combination of formative and summative evaluation. In their summary of purposes for which evaluation is used, McLaughlin and Philips reveal that a combination of formative and summative evaluation enables the educator:

(1) to monitor present programs [formative].
(2) to select a better available program to replace one now in use that is deemed relatively ineffective [formative and summative].
(3) to assist in developing a new program [formative and summative].
(4) to identify the differential effects of the program with different populations of students or other clients [summative].
(5) to provide estimates of effects and costs in the catalogue of programs [formative and summative].
(6) to test the relevance and validity of the principles upon which the program is based [summative].[32]

It may be said that while summative evaluation determines *if* program objectives have been met, formative evaluation helps insure that such goals *will* be met. In that regard, Scriven referred to formative evaluation as "early warning summative."[33]

Questions asked and techniques used for formative evaluation are generally of a qualitative nature. Where student progress is being measured periodically, quantitative measures such as tests may be used. However, because of adults' general aversion to testing, even where their progress is being measured, qualitative approaches such as case studies or critical incident analysis are likely to be used. Information thus gathered may be used to identify where learners are confused or unclear about content or concepts and where instructional techniques or resources are ineffective, and may provide feedback on the pace of learning.

Questions related to program improvement might include:

• Are preliminary goals for the program still "on target"?
• Are there perceived or voiced needs, not initially recognized, that should be addressed?
• Do the chosen resources contribute to learning as anticipated? Are additional resources needed?
• Do student questions and discussion indicate needed adjustments to the course/program outline?
• Are there logistical matters that need to be adjusted (such as room comfort, lighting, seating, meeting time or place, refreshments)?
• Do attendance patterns indicate any problems that need attention?

Answers to such questions are of primary use to the person or people responsible for planning and conducting the activity and are usually of little interest to supervisors, sponsors, or policy makers. Formative evaluation may be conducted solely by those in charge, but the wise adult religious educator will recognize the advantage of involving participants rather than relying on intuitive hunches or unilateral observations and assumptions. And one further word should be offered: just as the evaluation plan should be an integral part of the larger program planning process, so intentional formative evaluation should find its place alongside summative evaluation in the plan.

An Illustration of Course Evaluation

The following illustration provides an example of a "levels of evaluation" approach, incorporating many of the strategies discussed above. The illustration used is an actual parish seminar for adults that, due to its popularity, has been offered several times. The leader is a layperson with experience in the subject who had done considerable study in preparation for leading the seminar.

Title of Seminar: Caring for Aging Parents

Goals

(1) To create an atmosphere conducive to free expression and exploration of ideas.
(2) To allow for and encourage sharing of personal stories and dilemmas.
(3) To provide helpful information on coping skills, available resources, and intervention strategies.
(4) To engage participants in mutual exploration of alternative problem solutions.
[Note: seminar goals provide the evaluation criteria]

Evaluation Strategies

Formative

(1) Monitoring group climate (openness, willingness to share)
(2) Questions raised in line with expectations/content outline
(3) Logistics are as planned, and conducive to effective physical climate
(4) Course sessions proceed as planned; sufficient time is reserved for adequate discussion and to cover needed content
(5) Attendance is consistent
(6) Methods, materials, and resources are effective
(7) Mid-course critical incident analysis

Summative

(1) Verbal discussion of seminar (buzz group or entire group)
  • feedback from participants on how comfortable they felt sharing
    their own situations
  • what information was most helpful to them
  • case study
(2) Paper and pen evaluation (in last session) including feedback on
    logistics (convenience of scheduling, facilities), course content
    (most helpful sessions and content), instructor competence (includ-
    ing group-leading skills), and remaining questions.
(3) One month delayed phone interview with selected participants
(4) Instructor's assessment:
  • the degree to which participants shared stories and dilemmas
  • participants' willingness to enter into content discussion
  • participants' perceived interest in topics explored
  • response to techniques and media employed
  • participant contribution to mutual problem solving
  • perceived success in reporting critical incidents and analysis of
    case study

An Illustration of Program Evaluation

The following illustrates an evaluation of an adjudicatory program that
is provided in some form every third year. Thus, information gained is
not only used to assess the effectiveness of the given program, but is
used in planning future events. While the subject of the program is
youth ministry, the target audience is professional and lay leadership
with youth in the local parish. The planning process included enlisting
a cross-section of professional and lay youth leaders as a steering committee for planning, implementation, and evaluation.

Program Title: Youth Ministry for a New Millenium

Goals

(1) To improve the staff relations skills of professional youth ministers.
(2) To assist youth ministers in developing and articulating a parish phi-
    losophy of youth ministry, including examination of the essential
    components of such a philosophy.
(3) To provide tools for pastors and staff ministers to use in identifying
    and enlisting gifted lay leaders for youth.

(4) To enhance the knowledge and skills of lay leaders related to under-standing and leading youth.

(5) To provide an exposure to a wide array of youth ministry resources for selection by professional and lay youth leaders for use in their parishes.

Evaluation Strategies

Formative

(1) Monitor understanding and effectiveness of steering committee in relation to the scope of their assigned tasks.

(2) Conduct ongoing assessment of the adequacy of resources (finan-cial, human, material).

(3) Assess effectiveness of publicity and make adjustments as necessary.

(4) Conduct informal interviews with participants at breaks relative to expectations and conduct of the program components (including individual seminars, plenary sessions, and resource area).

(5) Identify and deal with logistical problems as they arise.

(6) Check with conference leaders at each session to insure that they have needed materials and equipment; monitor sessions to see that they operate as planned.

Summative

(1) Conduct pre- and post-interviews with sample of professional youth ministers drawn from early registrants. Sample questions:

• How do you describe the state of staff relations in your parish?

• How do you describe the relationship between you and your supervisor?

• Describe the difficulty or ease of finding qualified lay leaders with youth.

• Do you have a stated philosophy of youth ministry for yourself or your church?

• What do you believe are the components of a sound philosophy of youth ministry?

• What are the three most pressing needs of your lay leaders in terms of effectiveness in leading youth? Are there specific skills that would enhance their effectiveness?

• Do you, and do you believe your leaders, have as broad a knowledge and awareness of resources for youth ministry as you would like? Is there an area of youth ministry where you have a particular need related to resources?

• What specific expectations do you have for your participation in Youth Ministry for a New Millenium?

(Post-interview will alter these questions slightly to determine the effect of conference participation.)

(2) One-page paper/pen open-ended questionnaire distributed in each conference during last session, to be completed before departing conference room.

(3) Informal, random exit interviews with participants including questions related to expectations met, satisfaction with content of conferences, logistics, and faculty effectiveness. Also, ask interviewees to name one thing from the overall conference they believe they will use "back home."

(4) Faculty appreciation dinner after which buzz groups will share evaluations around the tables with appointed recorder.

(5) Two-month follow-up interviews with original pre-interview sample to determine long-range effects attributed to conference participation. Sample questions:

• Are changes implemented in your youth ministry soon after the conference still in effect?

• Are the feelings/impact the participants experienced during the conference still felt?

• To what extent are participants still motivated about what they learned? To what extent has the impact diminished over the course of two months?

• Has the church's philosophy of youth ministry been developed/changed/been implemented since the conference?

• Have any changes occurred in staff relationships since the conference that may be attributed to conference participation?

• In what specific ways may the effectiveness of lay leaders be described since attending the conference?

• What generalizations can be drawn about the long-term effectiveness of this type of training event?

• How has the impact of the conference helped to shape or change the ministries of these youth leaders?

Notes

[1] Gilbert Peterson, ed.. *The Christian Education of Adults* (Chicago: Moody Press, 1984), 36.

[2] Kenneth Gangel and James Wilhoit, *The Christian Educator's Handbook on Adult Education* (Wheaton IL: Victor Books, 1993).

[3] Milbrey W. McLaughlin and D. C. Philips, *Evaluation and Education: At Quarter Century: Nineteenth Yearbook of the National Society for the Study of Education* (Chicago: University of Chicago Press, 1991), 1.

[4] J. Sanders, "The Teaching of Evaluation in Education," in Barbara Gross Davis, *The Teaching of Evaluation Across the Disciplines* (San Francisco: Jossey-Bass, 1986), 17.

[5] Barbara Gross Davis, "Demystifying Assessment: Learning From the Field of Evauation," in Peter J. Grey, *Achieving Assessment Goals Using Evaluation Techniques* (San Francisco: Jossey-Bass, 1989), 7.

[6] Sharon Merriam and Rosemary Caffarella, *Learning in Adulthood* (San Francisco: Jossey Bass, 1991), 24.

[7] Donna S. Queeney, *Assessing Needs in Continuing Education* (San Francisco: Jossey-Bass, 1995)

[8] Rosemary Caffarella, *Planning Programs for Adult Learners* (San Francisco: Jossey-Bass, 1994).

[9] Carl Taylor Fitz-Gibbon and Lynn Morris, *How to Present an Evaluation Report* (Beverly Hills: Sage Publications, 1978), 14.

[10] Robert A. Fellenz, Gary J. Conti, & Don F. Seaman, "Evaluate: Student, Staff, Program," Chester Klevins, ed., *Materials and Methods in Adult and Continuing Education* (Los Angeles: Klevins Publications, Inc., 1982), 342.

[11] Queeney, 227.

[12] Caffarella, 121.

[13] Michael Galbraith, *Adult Learning Methods* (Malabar FL: Krieger, 1990), 167-68.

[14] Michael Galbraith, ed., *Facilitating Adult Learning* (Malabar FL: Krieger Publishing Co., 1991), 163ff.

[15] For a complete treatment of Cafferella's evaluation process, see chapter 9, "Formulating Evaluation Plans," in *Planning Programs for Adult Learners*.

[16] Cafferella, 126.

[17] Ibid., 127.

[18] Ibid.

[19] Caffarella, 129-32.

[20] Adapted from Chester Klevens, ed., *Materials and Methods in Adult Education* (Los Angeles: Klevens Publications, 1982), 344.

[21] Pamela Alrech and Robert B. Settle, *The Survey Research Handbook* (Chicago: Irwin Professional Publishing, 1995), 225.

[22] Sharon Caudle, "Using Qualitative Approaches," Joseph S. Wholey, Harry P. Hatry, and Kathryn E. Newcomer, *Handbook of Practical Program Evaluation* (San Francisco: Jossey-Bass Publishers, 1994), 75.

[23] Caffarella, 133.

[24] Queeney, 236.

[25] Caudle, 76.

[26] Ibid., 79.

[27] Patrick Boyle, *Planning Better Programs* (New York: McGraw-Hill, 1981), 288.

[28] Fellenz, et al., "Evaluate: Student, Staff, Program," 345.

[29] Adapted from Caffarella, 139-40.

[30] Caffarella, 141.

[31] Michael Scriven, "The Methodology of Evaluation," in R. Taylor, R. Gagne, and M. Scriven, eds., *Perspectives on Curriculum Evaluation* (Chicago: Rand McNally, 1967).

[32] McLaughlin and Philips, *Evaluation and Education* (Chicago: University of Chicago Press, 1991), 4.

[33] *The Logic of Evaluation* (Inverness CA: Edge Press, 1980), 46.

THE INTERSECTION OF RELIGIOUS EDUCATION AND ADULT LIFE

A thorough knowledge of the adults whom we seek to serve and for whom we plan our educational offerings may be assumed as a first step in any process designed to use religious education as a successful intervention strategy. Stonehouse's admonition is certainly innocuous enough: "Understanding the process of development is important to Christian educators because persons relate to God with their developing selves. . . . Christian educators are most effective when they understand the process of development and what agendas are being worked on at each level."[1] Implicit within such pronouncements, however, is the subtle assumption that adult development, however we define it, is generally linear with easily identified "agendas" along the plane.

The value of relying on psychological models for designing interventions has been questioned by those seeking synthesis or integration (as opposed to compartmentalization) or at least a more workable model.[2] Such criticism is based on several issues including gender and culture bias of research samples, the invariable hierarchical and linear nature of such models, the difficulties of assessing the effectiveness of learning experiences in bringing about growth, and the general lack of criteria for evaluating movement from stage to stage, or level to level. Further complicating our efforts to understand adults are the seemingly disparate models of moral, intellectual, and faith development (though some do attempt generally to associate their stages with human development). For example, though not an explicitly faith-oriented model, T-Net's (Training Network International) four-stage model of discipleship used by a number of churches in several denominations makes no attempt to interface with human development. As might be expected, one is left to his or her own devices to determine the age-appropriateness (readiness, intellectual and emotional capabilities) of the listed criteria.

Merriam and Caffarella offer a succinct assessment of the current progress in understanding adulthood.

> . . . what is presently known about development in adulthood—especially how this knowledge is applied to learning—consists of fragmented facts, ideas, concepts, and theories from a variety of perspectives that have yet to be brought together into a holistic picture of adulthood. Perhaps when an integration of the physical, the psychological, and the social-cultural facets of adulthood is achieved, we will truly understand the adult life experience and its relationship to learning.[3]

Perhaps one of the most instructive inferences to be made from these various models is that adulthood is not a static "stage" or long "holding pattern" of stability following adolescence. Rather, there are periods of transition interlaced with periods of relative stability, "mountains and valleys," with general progress along a path of becoming that is influenced by a myriad of factors. As Merriam and Caffarella point out, "The learning that adults do arises from the context of their lives, which is in turn intimately tied to the sociocultural settings in which they live."[4]

None of the foregoing is intended, of course, to discourage religious educators from trying to understand the constituents they seek to serve. Rather, it is to suggest that the religious educator must have a gestalt, a broad view of adulthood that transcends any single model of adult development, one which benefits from all that the psychological literature offers but which takes into consideration culture, context, and life experience. Such a perspective will enable us to plan effectively and compassionately to meet, within the limitation of available resources and intended scope, the varied spiritual, intellectual, emotional, and educational needs of adults.

Transitions, Markers and "Triggers"

Though Daniel Levinson's early work on adult development was widely criticized for its narrow, all-male sampling base, at least one contribution of his research that has spawned considerable interest is the idea of transitions. Indeed, it seems that whether we characterize them as stages, seasons, eras, or passages, adults do seem to transition through different periods in their lives, and these transitions require to one degree or another some adjustment and reorientation. Young adults are making a transition from adolescence into a new realm of responsibility and opportunity. This transition brings new and more momentous choices related to relationships, work, and living arrangements. Midlife and older adults face transitions related to the same issues but often the conditions are more complex.

Such transitions often accompany certain generally (but not always) expected life events. These life events may be thought of as marker or "trigger" events that cause a certain sense of disequilibrium. The following list is certainly not exhaustive, but is representative of the life events faced by adults:

- graduation
- retirement
- marriage
- the empty nest
- divorce
- illness
- birth of a child
- death of a child, spouse, or parent
- loss of job
- menopause

A life event does not necessarily constitute for the individual adult a crisis, unless the event is "off-time" as culturally or physically defined. Bernice Neugarten is generally credited with bringing the importance of timing to the forefront of developmental thought.[5] For example, birth of a child to a couple in their twenties, thirties, or forties is considered quite normal in this country. On the other hand, a pregnancy in the fifties or sixties may be quite a different matter. Similarly, being fired from a job (or "downsized" to use the currently popular term), while not being a particularly happy experience for a younger adult, may be a traumatic crisis for a person in their forties, fifties, or sixties. Merriam points out that adults may seek to adapt to life events in several ways, including frantic activity, action, educative activity, desire for assistance, contemplation, and withdrawal.[6]

A life event may "trigger" a certain sense of readiness, or openness to the positive contribution educational activities may make to the process of adjustment. Tibbetts and Keeton report a California study related to the difficulty of unemployed persons to find work after they had been employed for even a short time. " For many reasons a person who has been unemployed for a number of months seems to project unemployability. What is fascinating is that individuals attending educational programs to develop new skills do not develop the self-image that they are unemployable. They find employment more quickly even if their classes were not for specific job skills."[7] A knowledge of the life course and its transitions, contextualized by the prevailing culture, may give the educator hints as to possible triggers that provide "teachable moments" for adults.

Education as Intervention

Whether anticipated or otherwise, adult education may be an invaluable resource to the adult in transition. Indeed, research indicates that "mediational factors" such as education may be more significant in predicting life adjustment than the occurrence of actual life events.[8] Champagne points out the supportive role of such intervention.

> Intervention, at the very least then, can be viewed as a potential support for the transitional adult and as an opportunity to minimize ambiguity by providing learning experiences which foster the adult's awareness of what might be expected before, during, and after the transitional event. It may further serve as a resource for expanding one's awareness of oneself, one's values, dreams, and choices. Depending on how one views transition and the adaptation process, it may also provide the opportunity for learning coping skills to deal with the transitional stress, or it may give the adult the chance to make anticipatory preparation for the transition so that stress may be reduced.[9]

Through appropriate educational interventions, such as using case studies and critical incident analysis enhanced with timely content, adults may have opportunities to anticipate a wide array of possible and probable life changes. Consideration of alternative responses and awareness of available resources may have an empowering effect for adults. Thus, educational interventions provide the practical balance to the theoretical purposes of adult education, fulfilling the grand ideal for adult education stated in McKenzie's definition, namely, that adult education should move adults toward their potentialities "to the end that the learners become more liberated as individuals, better capacitated to participate in the life of their communities and institutions, and empowered to create an authentically human future."[10]

In terms of adults' motivation to participate, the news is good. Often adults cite a past, present, or anticipated change in their lives as their motivation for seeking learning.[11] Further, the 1985 "American's Use of Time Project" found that among the 2,500 adult respondents, taking classes ranked sixth out of ten on the "enjoyment scale." As to the place of learning, "church" ranked 8.5 and was first in the Education/Organization category.[12]

Determining Appropriate Interventions

In discussing the integration of theory and practice, Merriam and Caffarella point out that "The learning that adults do arises from the context of their lives, which is in turn intimately tied to the sociocultural setting in which they live. . . . Thus learning in adulthood is characterized by its usefulness for immediate application to the duties and responsibilities inherent in the adult roles of worker, spouse, parent, citizen, and so on."[13] There are at least three implications here that are germane to the adult religious educator. First is the matter of relevance. It is clear that, except for those adults who engage in learning either for social reasons or for learning as an end in itself, adults expect to be able to use what they are learning. They are not particularly interested in the "faith" learning of children (who simply must have faith that one day they will need what the teacher says they must learn now). We must show as clearly as possible the connection between the content and their life situation, even when dealing with explicitly religious content. Second, recalling our claim that we may be involved in religious education either by virtue of content or intent, church-based adult education may legitimately address any and all issues emanating from adults' sociocultural setting. Third, although not the intended focus of their comments, the suggestion of adult roles offers an example of one organizing principle for determining appropriate educational interventions. That is, the various roles adults play in the their life course may provide hints as to content areas that may both interest them and provide resources for effective functioning in those roles. Thus, numerous courses, seminars, and activities may be planned around the adult role of parent, for example, or the role of spouse.

While roles are a feasible organizing principle, they will not be the primary focus here. Rather, roles will be integrated into a psycho-social framework that uses four categories with both distinct and overlapping issues to be addressed by our offerings in adult religious education. This is one among several possibilities, but seems more heuristic to the goals and purposes of church-based education.[14] Further, the framework suggested here reflects the realization that life issues, concerns, challenges, and potentials cut across roles and traditional age categories. For example, Search Institute discovered twelve "common stressful situations" experienced by adults that were largely unrelated to age, stage, or role.

Life Stresses and Changing Among Adults[15]

Listed here are common stressful situations experienced by adults in the past two or three years, according to their survey responses.

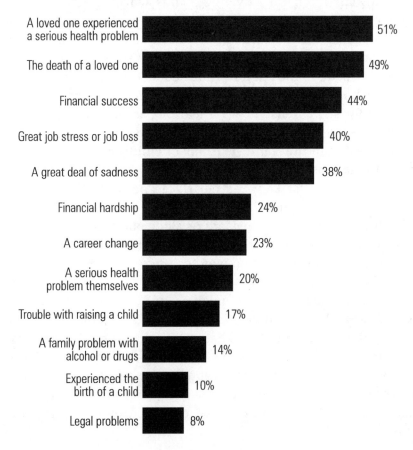

A loved one experienced a serious health problem	51%
The death of a loved one	49%
Financial success	44%
Great job stress or job loss	40%
A great deal of sadness	38%
Financial hardship	24%
A career change	23%
A serious health problem themselves	20%
Trouble with raising a child	17%
A family problem with alcohol or drugs	14%
Experienced the birth of a child	10%
Legal problems	8%

The content categories suggested here are self/personal development, family, work/vocation, and spiritual development. These will be discussed in narrative, along with salient issues and examples of educational offerings addressing the issues.

Content Category: Self/Personal Development

Issue: Making meaning. In his brief but rich monograph titled *Adult Education and Worldview Construction*, McKenzie posits the roots of constructing a personal view of the world in the inevitable human search for meaning. The eighty-page apologetic for this thesis suggests, in its own way, a provocative curriculum for helping adults bring coherence to their existence. We will briefly explore McKenzie's thesis as a basis for suggesting pathways to helping adults find meaning.

McKenzie uses the term meaning to indicate people's desire to "satisfy, in so far as possible, the yearning to understand, to find clarity, to locate a reason for the state of affairs, to come to grips with a problem."[16] He asserts, "The tendency to find coherence and intelligibility is one of the most powerful tendencies human beings can experience, even when they are not able to name the tendency."[17] Three categories of meaning are discussed: ultimate, penultimate, and those related to personal concerns. With regard to ultimate meaning, McKenzie explains:

> Ultimate concerns may be identified chiefly with questions that are, and have been for thousands of years, at the core of religious thinking. Is God real? What is God like? What does God want of us? What is our place and purpose in this immense cosmos? Why is there physical and moral evil in the world? Why suffering? What is the meaning of human history? What is the point of the "big bang" that birthed the universe? What is the significance of the evolutionary process?[18]

Perhaps it might be argued that the seed of such searching is found in the theological discussion of general and specific revelation, or in Augustine's observation regarding the restlessness of the human soul until it finds its rest in God.

Penultimate concerns relate more to the practical issues of life, including ethical and political issues, but also questions such as, "What constitutes a worthwhile education? To what extent has television influenced the learning habits of children? How can the economy be managed most effectively and fairly? What percentages of the gross national product should be spent on national defense?"[19] Thus, our worldviews in part consist of the interpretative formulations we construct regarding political, ethical, legal, economic, educational, and social realms.

Closer at hand still are immediate personal concerns of work and leisure, family and community, relationships, and self. Thus, McKenzie suggests these questions as examples of such personal concerns: "What are the patterns of my leisure-time activities? What do these patterns tell me about myself? Should my free time be spent totally in play or should I dedicate some of my time to the service of others? Have I fallen into a rut regarding the things I do? What new activities belong in my life? What is the meaning of my relationship with my parents? What is the truth of my relationship with my spouse? How should I define my relationships with my children? What relationships, if any, are poisoning my life? What can I do to strengthen and renew relationships with friends? What is the meaning of my life in terms of the entire constellation of relationships in my life?"[20]

Meaning cannot be taught, nor can it be imposed by any other means than mutually critical reflection. It is mutual because such reflection is both an individual and corporate experience. It is, as well, the process through which Mezirow's transformational learning takes place. As Foster observes in relation to what he calls "event-full" education:

> Mutually critical reflection requires sharing our experience of the events in which we participate; that is, to tell our own story as a part of the greater story we engaged. It necessitates assessing meanings we draw from that engagement from the perspective of our faith traditions, the biblical witness, and the experience of people who draw different meanings from their won engagement in the event. Mutually critical reflection becomes transformational when we begin to live out of our commitment to the meanings we have discovered.[21]

The search for meaning is universal among humans, and grappling with ultimate, penultimate, and personal concerns is not only where we find such meaning, but is the stuff of which personal worldviews are constructed. If we want adults to develop a God-like view of the world, we must address such concerns.

Issue: Aging. Regarding the church as a context for ministry with older adults, too many of our good intentioned efforts have fit the stereotypic activities assumed to interest "senior citizens," e.g., shuffleboard, board games, card parties, and trivial entertainment and occasional sightseeing trips. Perhaps unwitting contributors to such a view were two of the sages to whom adult educators turned for decades for wisdom, Robert Havighurst and Erik Erikson. Not at all intending to suggest either had a dim view of older adulthood, both nonetheless lumped the last quarter of life into one "stage," giving little attention to the continuing developmental potential of adults past, say, expected retirement age. Perhaps, as well, adults were not comfortable dealing with issues of old age for fear the experience would prove too painful.

Betty Friedman confronted us all with our reluctance to face creatively our own aging in an interview for *Time* magazine in 1993. Her challenge was provocative:

> Obsessed with stopping age, passing as young, we do not seek new functions in the years of life now open to us beyond the sexual, child rearing, power-seeking female and male roles of our youth. . . . Seeing age only as decline from youth, we make age itself the problem—and never face the real problems that keep us from evolving and leading continually useful, vital and productive lives. . . . How do we help each other finally affirm the integrity of full personhood at last—that radiant inner self that seems to carry the mystery and meaning of our life—and break through the barriers that keep us from really using what we dimly recognize as our own unique late style? How do we find ways to use the wisdom we have derived from the painful, joyful experience of our lives as we have lived them in society, so that we may live out our generativity? . . . Acceptance, however, must first come from ourselves. How do we create new roles for older people in society? That will take a lot of us saying no to the age mystique and demanding a continuation of our human birthright—to move in the new years of life as full persons in society, using our unique human capabilities as they have evolved through years of work and love and our capacities for wisdom, helping society transcend decline and move in new life-affirming directions."[22]

Now that the scales have tipped in terms of shear numbers toward the older end of the spectrum (there are now more adults over age sixty-five than under age twenty-five in America), it is time to look closely and creatively at the potential, the problems, and the possibilities of later life. To do so adequately and accurately, we must be more descriptive in terms of the segments of older adults we seek to serve, no longer accepting the antiquated and simplistic designations of young, middle, and older adulthood. Fisher, for example, uses a grounded theory approach to propose five age-independent periods of older adulthood: (a) continuity with middle age, (b) an early transition,

(c) a revised lifestyle, (d) a later transition, and (e) a final period.[23] Such new schemes offer helpful guides to more adequately address the needs and interests of the fastest growing segment of our population.

It is not sufficient to focus our educational resources solely on older adults in dealing with issues of aging. Rather, helping younger and middle-aged adults anticipate and plan for their own aging is not only an opportunity but a responsibility of adult religious education. The challenge may be in making discussion of the personal issue of their own aging attractive and nonthreatening to adults who often choose to defer thinking about such issues. Thus, anticipating life after retirement, compensating for declining strength and health, transitions in living arrangements, etc., are legitimately within the scope of church-based adult education.

Issue: Personal health. When we move beyond the sense of "invincible-ness" assumed by adolescence and even young adulthood, we become more concerned about health issues. We begin to carefully monitor our own bodies and the signals they send us about our well-being. While we may learn to live with a certain level of disfunction (joint stiffness, for example) and even pain (as in chronic back ailments) without alarm, we nonetheless pay more attention to "normal" and abnormal functioning of our bodies. Such awareness is not confined to the physical, as we are aware of bouts of depression and anxiety, memory difficulties, stress, or other issues related to our mental well-being.

Adults are increasingly becoming aware of the need not only to be more responsible for their own health and welfare, but that of family and neighbors. Welton observes,

> Many clients of medical bureaucracies . . . believe that they have been forced into unwanted dependency (i.e., disempowered by the expert culture). The emergence of a vast network of self-help, social support groups, and health coalitions, where individuals learn about their well-being through interaction with peers, contests the dominance of the medical model. Men and women are struggling within self-help sites to learn how to take responsibility for their own physical and mental health.[24]

Support groups for adults may be found throughout the community, many sponsored by local churches, dealing with a wide-range of health related issues from "Stop Smoking Clinics" to cancer support and AIDS support groups. Adults gather in such groups to share feelings, learn about their disease or health challenge, and find personal and spiritual support in their struggles. Memberships in local health and athletic clubs have soared in recent years. Whereas the motivation for belonging to such clubs in the past was often muscle-building (often for cosmetic reasons), more adults now frequent these facilities for aerobic, cardiovascular health enhancement as well has for building bone mass, with "body-building" often a secondary concern. Nor are these facilities limited to physical workouts, as many offer educational opportunities on a wide range of subjects from stress management to nutrition and yoga.

Church-based adult education need not duplicate the offerings of other community agencies related to health and well-being. Careful needs assessment can, however, identify the gaps in addressing the concerns, interests, and needs. Further, there is undoubtedly a spiritual dimension to these issues that can be uniquely addressed by the adult religious educator.

Issue: Citizenship. A popular bumper sticker admonishes, "Think Globally, Act Locally." Indeed, we are realizing more and more that we are world citizens, not just citizens of Hometown, USA. Our actions often have consequences that reach far beyond ourselves and our immediate context. If we accept Erikson's master task of adulthood, what we want is to be intentional about the extent and quality of our generativity. We want to have a positive effect on world, beginning in our neighborhoods. To be effective, however, we must be informed, we must understand our responsibilities as citizens, and we must have a perspective on issues. Therefore, politics, ethics, social issues, and concerns of the broader community are the purview of our interest and potential involvement. Adults as citizens are concerned about crime, ecology, schools, the cultural diversity of their community, the social well-being of fellow citizens, and the quality of elected leadership as well as many other issues confronting us and our neighbors. National Issues Forums are springing up in many churches to bring a Christian perspective to such issues. While not intended to be confined to the context of church, NIF nonetheless encourages churches to start such forums and gladly supplies discussion materials and resources to anyone interested in beginning such groups. NIF is just one of numerous resources available to churches wishing to include citizenship as a category for its adult religious education offerings.

Content Category: Work and Vocation

Work is necessary for most of us, for by our labors we "learn" a wage that pays for the material necessities of life. However, is work only a means to the end of collecting a wage, or could it perhaps be an avenue through which we find fulfillment and meaning? McKenzie observes, "Once embarked in a line of work it is not unusual to seek meaning in that work, a meaning that transcends the paycheck. Serious reflection leads to serious questions: What is the significance of my work for personal growth? What goals am I accomplishing? What is it that I want out of work? What challenges have I set for myself? Career changes frequently are made in the wake of these questions."[25] Resolving such issues is complicated by our tendency to compartmentalize our lives, so that we fail to understand the intersection of work, family, faith, a sense of purpose in life, and relationships.

Merriam and associates did extensive research into adults' interpretation of the interplay of work, love, and learning.[26] What they discovered is that adults seek a balance between the two major arenas of love and work, tending toward a dominate pattern favoring one or the other that affects their perspectives, their life orientation, and ultimately how they deal with life issues. Since these life patterns were found to be stable across time, Merriam suggests that if adults' patterns can be identified it may be possible to predict how they might respond to future normative events (e.g., the empty nest or retirement). This is fledgling research, however, and we can only speculate on the implications for intervention. As the researchers conclude, "Finally, we want to find a healthy balance between work and love in our lives, yet both our experience and the extensive literature on this issue indicate the difficulty in achieving this. How do we effectively integrate both domains on a day-to-day basis? Are there ways to balance the two and thereby increase our sense of well-being? The fact that these questions of balance continue to confront us is proof enough that the answers still elude us."[27]

In order to deal satisfactorily with the issues of finding meaning in work and of successfully striking a balance in love and work, we must consider the issue of vocation. Many adults either consider work and vocation as synonymous, or they have no notion of vocation. In order to help adults confront the compartmentalization of work and other areas of life, they must understand the significance of vocation, or the sense of "this is my place in the world; this is why I am here." This is a spiritual issue. And if we accept Erikson's idea of generativity as being the overarching task of adulthood, we must believe that there is an inner desire to achieve such understanding that is divinely placed. Yet, Wilhoit observes, "In our professionally oriented society many Christians fall into the spiritual trap of confusing their professional identity and success with their identity as a person. The latter looms so large it becomes the most important standard for judging life. The notion of cultivating a rich spiritual life almost seems unnecessary to those who succeed well as attorneys, accountants, or physicians."[28] A sense of vocation is a matter of spiritual identity. The church can help adults consider the interface of vocation, work, and relationships.

Content Category: Family

Changes in the American family have become one of the most talked about and written about subjects both in the popular and professional literature. The chart on page 256 indicates the statistical changes that give rise to a myriad of issues to be addressed by church educators and ministerial staffs. The following discussion of some of these issues is certainly not exhaustive.

Issue: Marriage. While the number of adults choosing to remain single continues to increase, marriage is still the norm at this turning point of a new century. At least two things are different, however. Whereas around the turn of the twentieth century it was not uncommon for people to marry in their late teens, the average age for marriage has steadily climbed, so that the average age for first marriage is now 26 for men and 24 for women, with the number of Americans 35+ who have never married increasing rapidly. Second, about half of all marriages end in divorce. In fact, the rate of divorce has climbed alarmingly to the point that the United States has the highest number of divorces of all developed nations. For the record, in 2001 there were 2,344,000 marriages. Annually, 957,200 marriages end in divorce.[30]

There are several opportunities for intervention that churches can take to help adults strengthen the marriage bond and anticipate challenges to the relationship. Stevens-Long points out that "When marriage is seen as a context in which personal growth and self-fulfillment occur (rather than a context for economic production) people want more satisfying emotional relationships within marriage."[31] A beginning point is to become aware of the critical points at which marriages may become "stressed," such as the first two years, rearing young children (and the accompanying physical and emotional stress), when children reach

U.S. Households 1970 and 1995 [29]

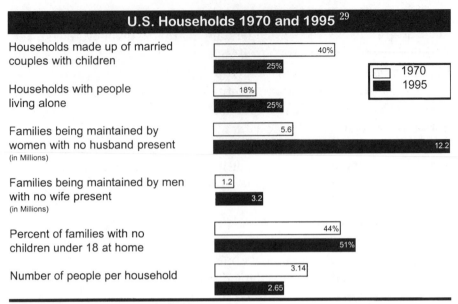

Households made up of married couples with children
- 1970: 40%
- 1995: 25%

Households with people living alone
- 1970: 18%
- 1995: 25%

Families being maintained by women with no husband present (in Millions)
- 1970: 5.6
- 1995: 12.2

Families being maintained by men with no wife present (in Millions)
- 1970: 1.2
- 1995: 3.2

Percent of families with no children under 18 at home
- 1970: 44%
- 1995: 51%

Number of people per household
- 1970: 3.14
- 1995: 2.65

An Eye Towards The Year 2010

According to U.S. Census Bureau projections, the fastest growing households from 1995 to 2010 will be nonfamily households--people living alone or with a nonrelative--and single parent families. Married-couple households and two-parent families are projected to continue to decline as a percent of total households. Indicated below is the percent chage projected for 2010 by category.

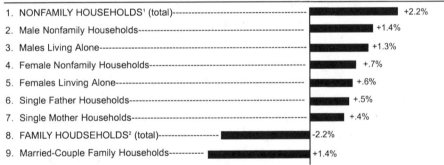

1. NONFAMILY HOUSEHOLDS[1] (total)--- +2.2%
2. Male Nonfamily Households--- +1.4%
3. Males Living Alone-- +1.3%
4. Female Nonfamily Households--- +.7%
5. Females Linving Alone--- +.6%
6. Single Father Households-- +.5%
7. Single Mother Households-- +.4%
8. FAMILY HOUDSEHOLDS[2] (total)--------------------- -2.2%
9. Married-Couple Family Households------------ +1.4%

[1] A **nonfamily household** consists of a person living alone or a householder who shares the home with nonrelatives only, for example, boarders or roommates.

[2] A **family household** is a group of two or more people, one of whom is the householder, living together, who are related by birth, marriage, or adoption.

high school and seek growing independence, and the empty nest. Another helpful intervention is helping couples understand the developmental differences between men and women. Stonehouse observes, "Some of the turmoil in marriages is rooted in developmental changes taking place or needed in the life of husband or wife. If these developmental transitions are understood, couples can deal with them and both partners grow through the experience."[32] The popularity of a best-selling book as of this writing exemplifies both the need and the desire of people of opposite gender to understand each other. *Men Are from Mars, Women Are from Venus* by John Gray has even found its way into the church classroom as subject of study by coeducational groups of adults.

Issue: Blended families. This issue is closely related to marriage and parenting, but it is such a common phenomenon today that the challenges and opportunities for ministry necessitate separate treatment of the blended family issue. "Blended" is the term used to describe families consisting of children from previous marriages, and extends to the wider circle of grandparents. This seemed to have been a favorite subject of television sitcoms in the late nineties. The challenges are so great that some estimates set the rate of divorce for second marriages involving children at sixty percent. Some of the strains of blended families have been identified by Barron:[33]

• No grace period—newlyweds return from the honeymoon to resume parenting, having to develop relationships with not only a new spouse, but new children.
• Bonding disorder—confusion and strain created by relationships with natural parents and stepparents.
• Discipline patterns—Parents must work to reconcile their discipline patterns so as to avoid confusion and conflict. Children must often adjust to different patterns than those to which they were accustomed.
• Displacement—This may include children now having to share the attention of one parent, the change in birth order, and disruption of what was previously considered private space.
• Uncertainty about the future—This includes a variety of challenges, including reestablishing trust, reinvesting emotionally in relationships, as well as finding a satisfactory and fulfilling "sense of place" in the new family.

Intervention naturally begins in premarital counseling. Such counseling should include not only the couple to be wed, however, but should involve the children as well. Churches are increasingly providing support groups for blended families. Seminars and workshops on discipline, building trust, investing in relationships, learning to have fun together, and establishing new family rituals are among many possibilities.

Issue: Parenting. This issue could find numerous subdivisions, as there are both common challenges of general parenting and unique challenges of parenting preschoolers, school-aged children, and teenagers. There are issues of nurture, discipline, growth, and development that emanate from this broad topic. Education and support are often cited needs of adults who parent. This writer and his wife once started a support and discussion group at our church for parents of middle schoolers (when our middle son reached age thirteen). At first we did not advertise widely, but rather let the idea spread word-of-mouth. The first evening we met, nine parents were present. When given the choice of a regularly planned program or simply discussing whatever present problem someone might bring to the group, they chose the latter! In subsequent weeks and months, discussion topics ranged from homework to telephone, dating, and sibling rivalries.

Occasionally a guest speaker was invited or a video provided stimulus for discussion. When the group adjourned for the summer, over thirty parents were involved! All through the summer, various ones asked, "When are we going to begin meeting again? I need the group!" Sometimes there were no solutions to problems posed, only mutual understanding and support. At other times, practical tips were passed along for all to benefit. For example, in one discussion about telephone habits (one in which my wife and I had particular interest), one of our fathers shared that this was no longer a problem at his house. He gave his daughter a twenty-minute maximum on the phone, then said to her, "In three minutes I am going to pick up the extension." Not once had he had to do so. We tried his solution, and after picking up the extension once, we never had a problem again! Such support and discussion groups are now popular among parents of various ages of children and youth.

Parents often cite the need for appropriately and effectively offering spiritual guidance to their children. However, they continue to look to the clergy for counseling on spiritual matters with their children. Is this because they erroneously believe that is the purview of the clergy, or because they do not know how? We believe the latter to be the case.

How important is this issue? When Search Institute set about to discover the factors that contribute most to faith development, interviews with adults revealed that conversations with their parents (mother first, father second) were the most influential factors. Yet only one in ten of the larger sample ever remembered hearing parents talk about their faith! Ironically, it seems that traditionally there have been two subjects that parents have been reluctant to address with their children: sex and faith! On both counts, the primary reason, we believe, has been discomfort with the subjects born of not knowing how to approach such discussions.

In 1978, Princeton Religious Research Center published a survey by George Gallup titled, "The Unchurched American." Then the survey was replicated and published again under the title, "The Unchurched American—10 Years Later."[34] In both previous studies Gallup found that parents were willing to provide religious education in the home if they only knew how. If we are to rediscover the Old Testament concept of the home as the primary place of religious instruction, if we accept the Search Institute findings concerning the importance of parents in the faith development of their children, and if Gallup is correct that parents are interested and willing to teach their children, the implications are clear. We must help parents learn to talk about their own faith, the struggles as well as the victories, and we must give them the tools to nurture their children's developing faith, appropriately stimulating and responding to questions, and counseling their own children in matters of faith instead of depending upon their clergy to experience the joys that rightfully belong to parents.

Issue: Aging parents. People who are blessed to enjoy their parents after they themselves have become adults, perhaps even parents themselves, find that just as with friends, spouse, and children, relationships with parents change over time. Wise adults (both the aging parents and their adult children) are aware of the dynamic nature of such relationships and adjust appropriately, sometimes even engaging in occasional dialogue with one another about such changes. Often, however, adults are caught off-guard, even when they think they are being sensitive and understanding. Andy and Judy Lester make an astute observation: "As parents grow older, they may become less concerned with the social pressures that dictated their lives during the middle years. They may begin to live in ways that are disturbing and upsetting to you. They may get involved in offbeat religion, join radical political causes, dye their hair, or spend money on seemingly foolish activities. Any of these choices may lead you to feel angry, embarrassed, or worried about what other people will say aboutyour parents!"[35] Guilt, grief, gratitude, affection, and reflection on past experiences are part of the emotional milieu surrounding adult children of aging parents. There is much to be "unpacked" and dealt with creatively in order to enhance such relationships and prepare for joys and difficulties ahead.

Role changes are among the most difficult challenges for both aging parents and their adult children. If parents live long enough, we and they may experience a complete reversal in roles, so that whereas we were once totally dependent on our parents, they may become totally dependent on us. This often includes not only providing shelter and food (or overseeing their provision) but assisting with decision-making regarding the whole array of life choices. The challenge is to accept and accommodate this transition with grace and respect, enabling parents to maintain a sense of autonomy as long as possible.

Adult religious education can assist adult children of aging parents as they anticipate the challenges and opportunities of their changing relationships and roles relative to their parents. Understanding the aging process, anticipating the death of one parent, loss of health, and eventual changes in living arrangements all are meat for educational intervention.

Issue: Finances. One source of marital difficulty is discord over family finances. One popular seminar offered by a church is titled "Money: His, Hers, and Theirs." This seminar recognizes that there are often disagreements about ownership and sharing of resources. Such problems are often exacerbated by poor stewardship or unexpected financial drains such as illness or catastrophe. The news frequently carries reports of record credit debt (often related to credit cards), and personal bankruptcies are at an all time high. Worries about money hang like a dark cloud over many families, heightening tensions and provoking heated arguments. Both print and human resources are available in most every community within easy reach. Most churches have people within the congregation qualified to lead seminars or courses on responsible money management. Solving problems related to too little money is, of course, only one dimension of the issue. Teaching stewardship involves effectively and responsibly sharing monetary resources and may also include intelligent investing.

Issue: Single adults. As noted earlier, not only are more adults delaying marriage, but increasing numbers of adults are choosing to remain unmarried, so that some estimates set the number of single adults in the United States at seventy million. Reporting on the increasing numbers of adults who choose to delay marriage or remain single, The U. S. Census Bureau notes that

> Since 1970, the proportions of men and women who had never married have at least doubled and in some cases tripled for the age groups between 25 and 44 years. For example, the proportion of persons 30 to 34 years old who had never married tripled from 6 to 20 percent for women and from 9 to 30 percent for men between 1970 and 1994. Among persons 35 to 39 years old, the proportions never married doubled from 5 to 13 percent for women and tripled from to 19 percent for men, during this period.[36]

Several factors help explain these statistics. In part they are due to increased social support for those who are single. Such support may be found in housing, magazines, newspapers, social groups, health clubs, and even packaging of food products targeted to the single person. Even so, American society struggles to recognize satisfactorily singleness as a legitimate life choice, and many single adults complain that they are often treated as immature or somehow less than whole. Pressure from parents or married friends who try to play matchmaker adds to their woes. It is a misnomer to accept the stereotype that single adults are "swingers" and that they are usually affluent (after all, they don't have all the expenses marriage entails). Single adults will be quick to point out that they do not have "help mates," usually have no help with household chores, and have the same (sometimes more) difficulties stretching their income to cover expenses.

A church blessed with single adults in the congregation must first come to terms with attitudes about singleness. Thus, not only are educational offerings that address the needs of singles appropriate, but so also are interventions that assist the congregation in accepting and effectively relating to single adults. Single adults generally face the same challenges of the broader adult population and should be included in educational offerings that address those needs. They may have special challenges, however, in terms of relationships and moral issues. Including single adults in the planning process will help insure that their needs are effectively addressed in the adult religious education offerings of a congregation.

Issue: Older adults. No satisfactory term has yet been coined to refer to adults past midlife. Senior adult or senior citizen are now considered pejorative terms by many of the people to whom they are meant to refer. Mature or older adult is acceptable but often not preferred. Perhaps the dissatisfaction with terminology has to do with the categorization that usually accompanies it, and is reflective of a growing aging population who do not fit the stereotypes of the past. Statistics debunk common myths about older adults, such as dependency and institutionalization. For example, the U. S. Census Bureau reports that fifty-two percent of the aged seventy-five and over live independently and alone.[37] As babyboomers age into later life, we can expect an increasing discontent with such stereotypes of mature adults, and a new model of an active, multi-careered, multi-talented older adult population. Tom Brokaw's human interest segment on the NBC Nightly News recently featured a basketball team consisting of women in their seventies, energetically working plays and shooting layups!

Not content to be merely entertained, older adults are increasingly active learners. They will benefit from educational interventions that offer variety in subject matter and approaches. Chautuaquas have expanded to hundreds of college campuses with thousands of older adults involved in classes and seminars on a variety of subjects. However, popular as they are, these tend to attract the more affluent segment of the older adult population. Church-based education may offer not only affordable but convenient opportunities for learning and need not be of lesser quality or variety. Thus discussion groups, formal classes, participatory learning, and informal approaches such as activities that encourage learning through observation and reflection will be as appropriate for older adults as for younger adults. One manual for church leaders of older adults lists subjects that would seem to be attractive to adults of all ages, suggesting that older adults continue to have wide interests and needs. Thus, we should not be surprised at older adults' interest in spiritual and personal enrichment, nutrition, world affairs, budgeting, finances, politics, legal matters, home safety, world religions, current events, history, defensive driving, and car care. "Hands-on" learning experiences such as gardening, learning new hobbies, developing manual skills, physical fitness, creative writing, and oral history of advocacy are among the many choices that may be of interest to older adults.[38]

Content Category: Spiritual Development

For religious educators there is a spiritual dimension to each of the above named issues, making them the purview of church-based adult education. But there are explicitly religious issues that adults both want and expect to be addressed through their involvement in church. While only two issues are addressed under this content category, the reader will find an array of subject areas addressed in the curricular model to be discussed later in this chapter.

Issue: The Bible. While the Bible continues to be listed near the top of best-selling book lists, studies show that it is not well read. Perhaps one reason is people's difficulty in understanding the Scriptures. The variety of translations available, some of which seek to put the message of Scripture in contemporary English, still do not enlighten perplexities related to context, construction, seeming internal contradictions, and interpretation. Relevance is often an issue to adults seeking to understand the Bible, and while many appreciate and enjoy the beautiful poetry of the Psalms, for example, or the fascinating human interest stories found within the Bible's pages, they still want to know how it applies to daily life. Painful as it may be, adults seriously seeking to lead a life of meaningful discipleship are willing to confront the perplexities and complexities of Scripture as it relates to their culture and lifestyle. Peter Gomez asserts that

> The Bible must be understood not as a thing in and of itself but as a part of the whole teaching and practice of the Christian faith. The confrontation between our social and moral presuppositions is what we bring to the text, and what we find in the text and in its context is something we will have to face. That conflict, if it is to be resolved, must be done not on the basis of expedience but on the basis of the Christian principles with which we interpret biblical practice.[39]

Neither inspirational devotionalizing on Scripture nor simplistic and uncritical treatment of texts will satisfy the hunger truly to know and understand Holy Scripture, nor will it be helpful to adults searching for a word from God.

Meaningful spirituality demands an understanding of the Bible, and classes, seminars, and discussion groups focusing on the content of the Scriptures are certainly needed. In order to apply the message of Scripture to the complexities of daily life, adults want to explore and grapple with the practical application of the Bible. A balance needs to be struck between dealing with the content of Scripture within the context of life, and life as the content informed by Scripture.

CONTENT   CONTENT

	Understanding	Implications	
Scripture			Life
	Study Skills	Application	

⌐→ Scripture ————————————— Life ←————————⌐
│   │
└─ The context of the study is life ————— Life issues informed by Scripture ─┘

*Balancing Scripture as the content of study, in the context of life,
with life as the content of study as it is informed by Scripture.*

Most churches, both Catholic and Protestant, offer Bible study classes for adults in some setting, whether in the traditional Sunday school on Sunday morning or at other times. Many adults will point to participation in such groups over the years as the source of their Bible knowledge, and yet Bible literacy remains low even among people who have spent most of their lives attending Bible study groups. Today the Sunday school is struggling with an identity crisis. Is it primarily a Bible study program? Or is it primarily a way to reach new people for the church while offering a weekly devotional on the Scripture? In some churches Sunday school is seen as a social group intended to assimilate new people into the fellowship of the congregation, again while devotionalizing on the Scriptures. Even where churches attempt to keep a focus on Bible study in such groups, it is often unclear whether the purpose is to provide an exegetical study of the Scriptures or to provide a setting where adults may find one kernel of truth to help them in their daily life this week. A number of models are extant that attempt to address the issue of how the Bible is treated in adult Bihle study groups. One model is shown in the figure below. In this model, Bible studies are selected that address biblical perspectives on subjects of concern to adults, while spin-off groups explore in more detail specific issues related to these subjects.

Issue: Discipleship. Discipleship is here defined as people's attempt to follow the teachings of Scripture, particularly the commands of Jesus and his example, as they proceed along a personal and corporate spiritual journey. Churches and denominations that have held closely to a programmatic approach to religious education have seen participation in programs focused on discipleship decline markedly over the past

Balancing Content Studies

The following diagram demonstrated an example of adult Bible study groups who study a theme found in scripture, then determine for themselves breakout groups to pursue specific issues relate to the theme.

Bible Study	Bible Study	Bible Study	Bible Study	Bible Study
The Church	God's Ideal for families	Christian Conduct	Uniqueness of Christianity	God's Sovereignty
		Salt and Light	Teachings of Jesus	
Breakout	**Breakout**	**Breakout**	**Breakout**	**Breakout**
Church History	Parenting	Ethical issues	World Religions	Christian Doctrine
Baptist History	Finances	Christianity and policies	Pursue subjects of Sermon on the Mount	Theology
	Aging Parents	Sanctity of life		

twenty years. Attempts to include discipleship as a task of Bible study groups have largely resulted in diluting Bible study (in part, again, due to the aforementioned identity crisis). Yet, adults voice a strong interest in dealing with issues of discipleship. Rhoehlkepartain, summarizing the Search Institute study, reports the following subjects as being important to adults:[40]

- Developing a personal relationship with Jesus, 74%
- Improving and sharing love and concern, 74%
- Applying my faith to daily living, 73%
- Learning how Christians make moral decisions, 68%
- Getting help with my spiritual journey, 62%

Linda Vogel offers a model of discipleship that is rich in possibilities for adult religious education. Vogel suggests that

People who are contented with their lives are not very hungry. Those who want and need feeding generally have:

(1) A disruption in their lives: there are questions and perplexities that need attention. Raw experience is becoming lived experience, and there is a present situation that they are ready to address.

(2) A need to reflect on their own experience: there are stories to be told (and retold) and new questions to be pursued. This is the time of exploration.

(3) New ears for hearing the scriptures: these people are ready to look to the past with a readiness to hear old words in new ways to help in the present.

(4) New eyes for seeing connections between personal stories and the faith story: these are connections that compel individuals to move beyond seeing to acting. This is revelation (a new way of seeing) that leads to a reflective-active dialogue that leaves little room for those who would observe from the sidelines.

(5) A desire to celebrate through remembering and ritualizing: one the Story is owned, it must be celebrated. Passover and Eucharist demonstrate this truth in profound ways. But celebrating can never stand alone; otherwise, it is empty and lifeless. If it is to be authentic, celebrating must be preceded by owning the Story and followed by acting on it.

(6) A commitment to serve: having received insight, grace, understanding, and hope, persons must act. Authentic celebration and service are inseparable. This way of understanding teaching and learning can provide a model for discipleship that can be visualized as an interactive process that includes the six aspects listed above. It is a process that is in constant motion.[41]

The astute adult religious educator will recognize immediately that the kind of approach Vogel here advocates cannot be confined to the classroom nor be accomplished by traditional teacher-controlled learning environments. Rather, only dialogical interchange centered in adults' social context (the "stuff" of Mezirow's transformational learning) and tested in praxis will accomplish such growth in discipleship. In terms of content, the spiritual disciplines may provide a point of departure.

The chart on the following pages is an attempt merely to offer examples of the kinds of learning activities church-based education may include in their repertoire of adult religious education. These are drawn both from the authors' imagination and from actual activities observed by the authors. While it is hoped these may be useful illustrations, the caution is once more offered that planning for adults is best done cooperatively with those involved in the activities, and is based on the perceived needs of constituents rather than their assumed needs as ascribed by some church agency or officials.

In planning interventions with adults, the religious educator must consider frequently the motivation and overarching goals toward which he or she, and the ministry, lead. Adhering to a broad view of what constitutes religious education both in terms of subject matter and approach, the adult religious educator will do well to keep in mind the positive stance of McKenzie, who reminds us, "Adults can be helped to liberate themselves for clear and creative thinking, for relating well with others, for valuing the feelings that contribute to the shaping of a human community, and for searching out ways of solving economic, social, and political problems."[42]

Some Interventions of Adult Life and Adult Religious Education

Content Category: Self/Personal Development
Issue: Making meaning
Sample studies:
The Nature of God: Is God Real?
Why Do Bad Things Happen to Good People?
Finding a Purpose to Our Existence
What Is the Place of Education in Our Culture?
Finding My Role in Local/Global Affairs
Finding Meaning in the Everyday Activities of Life
Setting New Goals, Reaching New Heights

Issue: Aging
Sample studies:
Effectively Negotiating Life's Transitions
Facing Losses Gracefully: Physical and Social
Taking Stock: Finding Meaning in Later Life
Battles Won and Lost: A Reflective Journey
Choosing Lifestyle Changes in Later Life
Planning to Age Gracefully (and Have Fun in the Process)
Life after Retirement: Writing the Next Chapter
Long-term Health Care: What Is It?

Issue: Personal Health
Sample Studies:
Body-monitoring
Maximizing Functionality in the Face of Declining Strength
Learning to be Heart-Healthy
Cold Turkey: Leaving Unhealthy Habits Behind
Mind and Body: Maximizing the Connection

Good Nutrition and Good Health
Making the Most of the "Temple" God Gave Us
Identifying and Handling the Stresses That Kill Us
The "Sexual Diamond": What Does It Mean for Relationships?
Developing a Personal Wellness Model

Issue: Citizenship
Sample studies:
National Issues Forum Groups
Making a Difference in My Community
Becoming an Effective Advocate: What's Your Cause?
What Does It Mean to Be a Global Citizen?
An Update on Local Community Issues and Where You Can Help
Being the Church in the World: Implications for Community Involvement

Content Category: Family
Issue: Marriage
Sample studies:
Communication in Marriage: He Said/She Said
Ways to Keep the Big "D" Off Your Doorstep
Building a Nurturing Relationship in Marriage
The Sexual Diamond and Spousal Relationships
Keeping Love in the Relationship
When Both Spouses Work: Maintaining Healthy Perspectives

Issue: Parenting
Sample studies:
Effective Discipline in the Home
Help for Parents of . . . (Preschoolers, Children, Teenagers)
Parent Support Group
Storytelling for Parents
Talking to Your Child about God
Nurturing Faith in Your Child
Becoming a Partner with Your Child's Teacher
Identifying Risk Factors with Teens
How to Talk Successfully to Your Teenager
Passing on Your Faith Story to the Next Generation

Issue: Aging Parents
Sample Studies:
Helping Adult Parents Maintain Their Independence
Extended Families: Issues and Challenges
Support Group for Adult Children of Aging Parents
Helping Adult Parents Choose Appropriate Living Arrangements
As Roles Change: Understanding Aging Parents
Helping Parents Deal with Life's Losses
Learning to Celebrate and Remember: Enhancing Relationships with Aging Parents

Issue: Finances
Sample Studies:
Money: His, Hers, and Ours
Planning and Living by a Family Budget
Family Stewardship: Finding a Balance
Planning for a Child's Education
Making Wise Decisions about Money

Issue: Single Adults
Sample Studies:
Setting Goals and Reaching Them
Finding, Building, Maintaining Healthy Relationships
Single and Loving It: Opportunities and Challenges
Cooking for One: Buying and Cooking for Good Health
Home Maintenance for Singles
Keeping Your Car Healthy: Checkpoints and Simple Maintenance
Discovering and Pursuing God's Will for My Life

Issue: Older Adults
Sample Studies:
(Note: most of the offerings under "Aging" as well as "Citizenship" are appropriate here)
Keeping Your Will Current: Power of Attorney and Other Legal Matters
Keeping Your Driving Skills Sharp
Setting and Achieving Goals in Later Life
Maximizing Your Social Support Systems
Being the Storybearer: Sharing Your Story
Effective Grandparenting
Relating Effectively to Your Adult Children

Content Category: Work/Vocation
<u>Sample Studies:</u>
Evaluating Career Options: Making Choices
Balancing Love, Work, and Life
Biblical Perspectives on Work
Relating Work and Vocation: A Perspective on "Calling"
Work, Love, and Learning: Finding My Dominant Pattern
From Success to Significance

Content Category: Spiritual Development
Issue: The Bible
<u>Sample Studies:</u>
Where Did We Get Our Bible?
Great Themes in the Bible
Translations of the Bible: Which One Is Best?
Harmonizing the Gospels
Must I Take the Bible Literally?
Using the Bible as Life's Map
Biblical Perspectives on Contemporary Issues

Issue: Discipleship
<u>Sample Studies:</u>
The Meaning of Reconciliation for Salvation and Relationships
Transformation: The Renewing of Our Minds
Responding to Jesus' Call to "Follow Me"
Living in the World but Not of the World
The Stewardship of Life
Growing a Vital Life of Prayer
Finding and Developing My Spiritual Gifts
Growing a Dynamic Faith
Understanding and Practicing Spiritual Disciplines
Learning to Share My Faith

More Sample Studies for Adults

The following list of studies, retreats and activities are drawn from churches the authors have observed as well as from their own experience. Sources are footnoted where possible. The listings are not intended to be exhaustive, but rather illustrative.

For All Adults[43]

• A Bible study on hope based on an examination of the musical *Carousel*.

Carousel offers several thematic learning opportunities: spousal abuse, neurotic relationships, and social class issues. But one overriding theme, the theme that perhaps keeps this fifty-year-old musical alive, is hope. This study will examine the issue of hope through the characters of *Carousel*.

• An Introduction to Bowen's Family Systems Theory
Topics covered include:
Family of Origin, Birth Order, and Genograms
Differentiation of Self
Overfunctioning and Underfunctioning
Triangles and Relationships

• Creativity and the Christian Journey
A retreat, led by a working artist, exploring creation and personal creativity as a gift.

• Meeting God in Community: A Retreat for Women
A special time for getting away from the routines and chores of daily living to focus on the self in a context of friendships, learning, fun, and relaxation.

• A Retreat for Men Exploring the Contemplative Lifestyle
A retreat focusing on the yearning for a more contemplative and balanced approach to life by making time to experience prayer, study of Scripture that addresses those concerns, silence, and reflection.

• A Journal-writing Retreat
For those who want to learn how to keep a journal for personal and spiritual growth, and for those who want an extended time for reflection and journaling.

• Juggling the Rhythms of Family: A Family Retreat
A chance to get away for a time of family recreation, relaxation, fun, fellowship, and spiritual renewal.

• Covenant, Communication, and Calling: Marriage Enrichment Retreat
Examine how God has chosen to relate to God's creation through a
covenant relationship, which becomes a model for our relationships as
marriage partners.

• Spiritual Growth Small Groups for Women[44]
Designed to connect women in small group settings that emphasize
learning and applying biblical truths, and sharing friendships. Topics
include "Becoming a Mom of Influence," "The Ups and Downs of Life,"
and "Becoming a Contagious Christian." (Willow Creek)

• Women's "Drop-in Bible Studies"
Groups to chose from:
The Joy of Homemaking
Becoming the Wife God Intended You to Be
We Are What We Think
Shaping Your Child's Future
Drowning in Loneliness
Blended Families

• The Christian and Citizenship
Explores the questions:
What should be the Christian's attitude toward civil authority?
Can the Christian participate actively in political activity?
Should the Christian church seek special advantages, such as tax
exemptions?
Should the Christian participate in war?

Sample Studies for the Adult Lifespan
Young Adults
• Work, Calling, and Vocation . . . What's the Connection?
A retreat for young adults exploring God's will for our lives.

• Sibling Rivalry: Techniques for Domestic Tranquillity
Subjects parents will explore:
Why can't siblings get along?
The Problem with Comparisons
How to Handle Fighting
How to Handle Yourself

• Giving God a Prominent Place in Our New Home
Learn the importance of establishing Godly values to guide relationships, family dynamics, choices, and management of financial resources.

• Building and Sticking to a Budget for Family Money Management

• Parents as Spiritual Mentors: The Basics of Religious Education in the Home

• Especially for Singles: Establishing and Managing My Own Home

Median Adults
• Now That the Nest Is Empty
• Effectively Parenting Teenagers
• Finding Renewal at Midlife
• A Different Kind of Investment: Exploring Ways to Give Yourself Away
• Relating to and Helping Aging Parents

Older Adults
• Charting a New Course: Life after Retirement
• Developing Mentoring Relationships
• Wisdom, the Gift of Age: Now What Do I Do With It?
• Successful Grandparenting
• Redefining Family Relationships
• Passing On Our Faith Stories
• Expanding Faith in the Later Years
• Living Independently in Later Life

Notes

[1] Catherine M. Stonehouse, "Learning from Gender Differences," in Kenneth Gangel and James Wilhoit, *The Christian Educator's Handbook on Adult Education* (Wheaton IL: Victor Books, 1993), 112-13.

[2] See, for example, Bradley C. Courtenay, "Are Psychological Models of Adult Development Still Important for the Practice of Adult Education?," Adult Education Quarterly 44/3 (Spring 1994).

[3] Sharan Merriam and Rosemary Caffarella, *Learning in Adulthood* (San Francisco: Jossey Bass), 58-59.

[4] Ibid., 303.

[5] See for example Bernice Neugarten, "Adaptation and the Life Cycle," *Counseling Psychologist*, no. 6 (1976): 16-20.

[6] Sharan Merriam, *Adult Development: Implications for Adult Education* (Columbus OH: ERIC Clearinghouse on Adult, Career, and Vocational Education, 1984), 22.

[7] J. Tibbetts and P. Keeton, "Transitions Are Here. Is Adult Education Ready?" *Adult Learning* 4/5 (May-June 1993): 7.

[8] E. Christopher Payne, et al., "Goal Directedness and Older-Adult Adjustment," *Journal of Counseling Psychology* 38/3 (1991): 302.

[9] Delight E. Champagne, "Planning Developmental Interventions for Adult Students," paper presented to the Annual Meeting of the American College Personnel Association/National Association of Student Personnel Administrators (Chicago: 16 March 1987).

[10] Leon McKenzie, *Adult Education and the Burden of the Future* (Washington, D.C.: University Press of America, 1978), iii.

[11] See for example Carol Aslanian and Henry Brickell's oft-cited research published in *Americans in Transition: Life Changes as Reasons for Adult Learning* (New York: College Entrance Examination Board, 1980).

[12] Reported in "As We Life It," by J. Robinson, *American Demographics* 2/93: 44-48.

[13] Merriam and Caffarella, 303-304.

[14] For example, Merriam cites the "Holistic Life Cycle Curriculum Model," which uses four content areas (careers, relationships, health, and a miscellaneous category) that cut across young, middle, and late adulthood. To these writers, however, this model is too general to be useful to the adult religious educator. See S. Merriam, *Adult Development: Implications for Adult Education*.

[15] Eugene Roehlkepartain, *The Teaching Church: Moving Christian Education to Center Stage* (Nashville: Abingdon Press, 1993), 132.

[16] Leon McKenzie, *Adult Education and Worldview Construction* (Marabar FL: Krieger Publishing Co., 1991), 8.

[17] Ibid., 9.

[18] Ibid., 8.

[19] Ibid., 12.

[20] Ibid., 14.

[21] Charles R. Foster, *Educating Congregations* (Nashville: Abingdon Press, 1994), 48.

[22] *Time* (6 September 1993): 61-64.

[23] James C. Fisher, "A Framework for Describing Developmental Change Among Older Adults," *Adult Education Quarterly* 43/2 (Winter 1993): 76.

[24] Michael Welton, "The New Social Movements as Learning Sites," *Adult Education Quarterly* 43/3 (Spring 1993): 160.

[25] McKenzie, 13.

[26] Sharan Merriam and M. Carolyn Clark, *Lifelines: Patterns of Work, Love, and Learning in Adult Life* (San Francisco: Jossey-Bass), 231.

[27] Ibid., 219.

[28] James Wilhoit, "Christian Adults and Spiritual Formation," in Gangel and Wilhoit, *Christian Educator's Handbook*, 60.

[29] SAM Journal 14/5, issue no. 124 (Colorado Springs: Cook Communications Ministries, September/October 1997): 4.

[30] National Center for Health Statistics website, 1; American for Divorce Reform website, 1.

[31] Judith Stevens-Long, *Adult Life: Developmental Processes* (Palo Alto CA: Mayfield Publishing Co., 1984), 172.

[32] Stonehouse, "Gender Differences," in Gangel and Wilhoit, *Christian Educator's Handbook,* 113.

[33] B. Barron, "The Blended Bunch," *Homelife Magazine* (Nashville: LifeWay Press, November 1997), 14.

[34] An excellent analysis of Gallup's research, along with comparisons with more recent similar research, may be found in "From Church Traditions to Consumer Choice: The Gallup's Surveys of the Unchurched American" in David A. Roozen and C. Kirk Hadaway, *Church and Denominational Growth* (Nashville: Abingdon Press, 1993).

[35] Andrew Lester and Judy Lester, *Understanding Aging Parents* (Philadelphia: Westminister Press, 1980), 10.

[36] Arlene F. Saluter, "Marital Status and Living Arrangements," *Current Population Reports*, November 1986, U. S. Census Bureau, I.

[37] Ibid.

[38] Horace Kerr, *How to Minister to Senior Adults in Your Church* (Nashville: Broadman Press, 1980), 93.

[39] Peter Gomes, *The Good Book* (New York: William Morrow and Company, 1996), 82.

[40] Eugene Rhoehlkepartain, *The Teaching Church: Moving Christian Education to Center Stage* (Nashville: Abingdon Press, 1993), 130.

[41] Linda Vogel, *Teaching and Learning in Communities of Faith* (San Francisco: Jossey-Bass, 1991), 15-16.

[42] McKenzie, 133.

[43] The following activities represent a sampling of adult education offerings of Vienna Baptist Church in Vienna, VA.

[44] The following three seminars and retreats are representative of adult activities provided by Willow Creek Community Church, South Barrington, IL.